PHOTOGRAPHY TERRY JONES. MARC JACOBS AUTUMN/WINTER 2009.

Edited by Terry Jones

L-Z

100
CONTEMPORARY
FASHION
DESIGNERS

TASCHEN

100 zeitgenössische Modedesigner
100 créateurs de mode contemporains

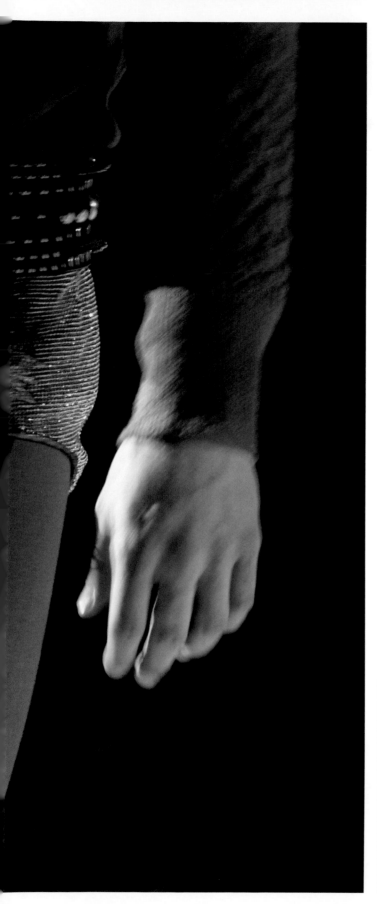

PHOTOGRAPHY TERRY JONES. VIVIENNE WESTWOOD, MAN.

Volume I
A - K

PHOTOGRAPHY TERRY JONES. MAISON MARTIN MARGIELA.

Volume II
L - Z

"My fashion is more a way of living life with your roots, and finding your own true self, than having a logo to put on your back"
CHRISTIAN LACROIX

Christian Lacroix made fashion history with his July 1987 debut couture collection backed by LVMH. His was the first Paris haute couture house to open since Courrèges in 1965. Lacroix took the bustles, bows, corsets and crinolines painted by 18th-century artists Boucher, Fragonard and Nattier and mixed them up with ruffles, feathers and fringes of Toulouse-Lautrec's cancan dancers and the gypsies in his hometown Trinquetoulle, Provence. Lacroix's puffball skirt – a taffeta or satin balloon of fabric that gathered a crinoline at the hem – reinvented the ball gown for the late 20th century. "Personally I've always hovered between the purity of structures and the ecstasy of ornament," says the designer who brought Rococo back to couture. Born on 16 May 1956, Lacroix moved to Paris in 1971, where he studied at the Sorbonne and the Ecole du Louvre, where he planned a career as a museum curator. Instead, he began designing, first for Hermès (1978), then Guy Paulin (1980) and Patou (1981), before being offered the keys to his own couture house by Bernard Arnault of LVMH in 1987. Lacroix's inspiration was as broad as Arnault's plans for the label: Cecil Beaton's Ascot Scene in 'My Fair Lady'; Oliver Messel's neo-Rococo interiors; Velázquez's Infantas; Lautrec soubrettes; Provençal gypsies and his dynamic wife Françoise. Christian Lacroix ready-to-wear followed the couture in 1998 and diffusion line Bazar arrived in 1994. Lacroix's sensibility translates superbly to theatre, opera and ballet. He designed landmark productions of 'Les Enfants du paradis', 'La Gaîté parisienne' and 'Sheherazade' as well as the jewelled corsets worn by Madonna for her 2004 Reinvention Tour. In 2002, Lacroix was appointed creative director of Florentine print house Pucci, and in 2005, a new chapter began for the designer when his fashion house was sold by LVMH to an American company, the Falic Group. Lacroix has since launched the perfumes Tumulte and C'est la fête, worked with Madonna and various opera/theatre companies.

Christian Lacroix schrieb im Juli 1987 mit seiner Couture-Debüt-Kollektion, unterstützt von LVMH, Modegeschichte. Seit der Eröffnung von Courrèges 1965 war dies das erste neue Pariser Haute-Couture-Haus. Lacroix übernahm die Tournüren, Schleifen, Korsetts und Krinolinen aus den Gemälden von Künstlern des 18. Jahrhunderts wie Boucher, Fragonard und Nattier und kombinierte sie mit den Rüschen, Federn und Fransen von Toulouse-Lautrecs Cancan-Tänzerinnen sowie den traditionellen Kleidern der Zigeunerinnen in seiner provençalischen Heimatstadt Trinquetoulle. Sein Ballonrock – aus Taft oder Seide, am Saum von einer Krinoline zusammengehalten – war die neue Ballrobe für das ausgehende 20. Jahrhundert. „Ich habe immer zwischen klaren Strukturen und ekstatischen Ornamenten geschwankt", sagt der Designer, der das Rokoko in die Couture zurückbrachte, über sich selbst. Geboren wurde er am 16. Mai 1956. 1971 zog Lacroix nach Paris, um an der Sorbonne und der Ecole du Louvre zu studieren. Er hatte damals den festen Vorsatz, Museumskurator zu werden. Stattdessen begann er jedoch Mode zu entwerfen. Zunächst für Hermès (1978), dann für Guy Paulin (1980) und schließlich für Patou (1981). Im Jahr 1987 übergab ihm Bernard Arnault von LVMH die Schlüssel für sein eigenes Couture-Haus. Die Inspirationen des Designers waren so weit gefasst wie Arnaults Pläne mit dem Label:

von Cecil Beatons Ascot-Szene in „My Fair Lady" über Olivier Messels Einrichtungen im Neo-Rokoko-Stil, die Infantinnen von Velázquez, Lautrecs Soubretten, provençalische Zigeunerinnen bis hin zu seiner dynamischen Ehefrau Françoise. Seit 1998 entwirft Lacroix auch Prêt-à-porter. 1994 kam die Nebenlinie Bazaar hinzu. Die Empfindsamkeit und das Gespür des Designers passen perfekt zu Theater, Oper und Ballett, sodass er herausragende Produktionen wie „Les Enfants du paradis", „La Gaîté parisienne" und „Sheherazade" ausstattete, aber auch Madonna für ihre Reinvention Tour 2004 mit juwelenverzierten Corsagen belieferte. 2002 wurde Lacroix Creative Director des für seine grafischen Muster berühmten florentinischen Modehauses Pucci. Ein neues Kapitel begann 2005 für den Designer, als LVMH sein Modehaus an die Falic Group aus den USA verkaufte. Seither brachte Lacroix die Düfte Tumulte und C'est la fête auf den Markt und arbeitete mit Madonna sowie diversen Opern- und Theaterbühnen.

Christian Lacroix est entré dans l'histoire de la mode avec sa première collection de haute couture présentée en juillet 1987 grâce au soutien financier de LVMH. Depuis Courrèges en 1965, personne n'avait ouvert de maison de haute couture à Paris. Lacroix emprunte les tournures, les nœuds, les corsets et les crinolines présentés dans les tableaux de peintres du XVIII siècle, tels que Boucher, Fragonard et Nattier, et les mélange avec les volants, les plumes et les franges des danseuses de cancan de Toulouse-Lautrec et des gitans de sa ville natale de Trinquetoulle en Provence. La jupe « boule » de Lacroix, sorte de ballon en taffetas ou en satin froncé en crinoline à l'ourlet, réinvente la robe de bal de la fin du XX siècle. « Personnellement, j'ai toujours oscillé entre la pureté structurale et l'extase ornementale », déclare ce créateur qui a remis le rococo au goût du jour. Né le 16 mai 1956, Lacroix s'installe à Paris en 1971 pour étudier à la Sorbonne et à l'Ecole du Louvre, envisageant alors de devenir conservateur de musée. Il se lance finalement dans la mode, d'abord chez Hermès (1978), puis pour Guy Paulin (1980) et Jean Patou (1981), avant de se voir remettre les clés de sa propre maison de haute couture en 1987 par Bernard Arnault, PDG de LVMH. Les inspirations de Lacroix sont aussi diverses que les projets d'Arnault pour la griffe : le décor créé par Cecil Beaton pour la scène d'Ascot dans « My Fair Lady », les intérieurs néo-rococo d'Oliver Messel, les Infantes de Vélasquez, les soubrettes de Lautrec, les gitans de Provence, ou encore sa dynamique épouse Françoise. Une collection de prêt-à-porter Christian Lacroix est lancée en 1998, après la ligne secondaire Bazar en 1994. La sensibilité de Lacroix s'applique magnifiquement bien au théâtre, à l'opéra et au ballet : il a réalisé les costumes de grosses productions telles que « Les Enfants du paradis », « La Gaîté parisienne » et « Shéhérazade », ainsi que les corsets ornés de bijoux portés par Madonna lors de sa tournée Reinvention Tour de 2004. En 2002, Lacroix est nommé directeur de la création de la maison florentine Pucci, connue pour ses imprimés. En 2005, un nouveau chapitre de l'histoire du créateur s'est ouvert quand LVMH a vendu sa griffe à une entreprise américaine, le Falic Group. Depuis, Lacroix a lancé les parfums Tumulte et C'est la fête. Il a aussi travaillé avec Madonna et plusieurs compagnies d'opéra et de théâtre. JAMES SHERWOOD

PHOTOGRAPHY KARL LAGERFELD. STYLING CHRISTOPHER NIQUET. MODEL GEORGIA FROST. SEPTEMBER 2007.

PHOTOGRAPHY SEAN ELLIS. STYLING NEIL STUART. MARCH 2002.

PHOTOGRAPHY KAYT JONES. STYLING GERIADA KEFFORD. MODEL LIBERTY ROSS. NOVEMBER 2002.

PHOTOGRAPHY KAYT JONES. STYLING GERIADA KEFFORD. MODEL LAETITIA CASTA. JUNE 2001.

What are your signature designs? Let's say – red. Something crazy! **How would you describe your work?** It's based on individuality and self-expression. It's not exactly anti-fashion, but it's contrary to the way that fashion is. My fashion is much more a way of living life with your roots, and finding your own true self, than having a logo put on your back **Can fashion still have a political ambition?** I would like to express much more violence in my work. I'm very, very angry when I see all this globalisation. If we want the most sensual things in life, we have to fight for them. My house is based on an ethnic art and on gypsies, and I hope that through it I will succeed in expressing their heritage, something that is stronger than the poor everyday life that globalisation would like us to have **Who do you have in mind when you design?** A kind of gypsy. Everybody who is free enough to express this way of life **Who has been the greatest influence on your career?** My wife: if I had not met her, I would be in the south of France, eating goat's cheese. I was lazy, I was shy and she gave me a spine **What's your definition of beauty?** Beauty is not a very well-balanced thing; it has to be disturbing and uncomfortable. It's about the period and art rather than anything physical **What's your philosophy?** I'm totally despairing and totally joyful at the same time.

"I love fashion and the evolution of time"
KARL LAGERFELD + CHANEL

Karl Lagerfeld is perhaps the ultimate fashion designer. Lagerfeld's ever-present pony-tail, fan and sunglasses are iconic; his personal preference for bespoke white shirts by Hilditch & Key, Chrome Hearts jewellery and Dior Homme suits is well documented. In addition to his work for both Chanel and Fendi, since 1998, Lagerfeld has designed his own label, Lagerfeld Gallery. Born in Hamburg in 1938, Lagerfeld moved to Paris at the age of 14. At just 17, he landed his first job, at Pierre Balmain, moving to Jean Patou three years later. Despite this traditional start, Lagerfeld chose not to establish his own house but instead to pursue a career as a freelance designer. From 1963 to 1983 and 1992 to 1997 Lagerfeld designed Chloé. In 1965, he also began to design for Fendi, a role that he retains to this day; in 1983, he was appointed artistic director of Chanel. 1984 saw the first incarnation of his own label, Karl Lagerfeld, which was later superseded by Lagerfeld Gallery, an art/retail venture. It is the latter that expresses the remarkable range of this genuine polymath. In addition to ready-to-wear collections, Lagerfeld Gallery is a platform for his myriad passions, including photography (he often shoots his own ad campaigns, along with editorial for numerous magazines), books (he has his own imprint, 7L, and a personal library of 230,000 volumes), perfume, art and magazines. In December 2004, it was announced that Tommy Hilfiger had purchased Lagerfeld Gallery. This followed a phenomenally successful link-up with mass-market retailer H&M in autumn 2004, when shoppers clamoured for a garment designed by an acknowledged maestro of fashion. Lagerfeld's artistic direction continues to build on Chanel's empire in the 21st century: epic commercials for Chanel No.5 starring Nicole Kidman (2005) and a Mobile Art project designed by Zaha Hadid that travelled from Tokyo to New York (2008).

Man könnte Karl Lagerfeld als den Inbegriff des Modedesigners bezeichnen. Sein Pferdeschwanz, sein Fächer und seine Sonnenbrille sind legendär, seine persönlichen Vorlieben für weiße Maßhemden von Hilditch & Key, Schmuck von Chrome Hearts und Anzüge von Dior Homme bestens dokumentiert. Neben seiner Tätigkeit für Chanel und Fendi entwirft Lagerfeld seit 1988 auch für sein eigenes Label Lagerfeld Gallery. Geboren wurde der Modeschöpfer 1938 in Hamburg. Mit 14 Jahren kam er nach Paris, und mit 17 Jahren hatte er bereits seinen ersten Job, und zwar bei Pierre Balmain. Drei Jahre später wechselte er zu Jean Patou. Trotz dieses traditionellen Karrierestarts entschied Lagerfeld sich gegen die Gründung eines eigenen Modehauses und schlug stattdessen die Laufbahn eines unabhängigen Designers ein. Von 1963 bis 1983 sowie von 1992 bis 1997 entwarf er für Chloé. 1965 begann er außerdem mit seiner Tätigkeit für Fendi, die bis heute andauert. 1983 berief man ihn schließlich zum künstlerischen Leiter von Chanel. 1984 machte er dann erstmals mit einem eigenen Label, Karl Lagerfeld, von sich reden, das später von dem Kunst- und Einzelhandelsprojekt Lagerfeld Gallery abgelöst wurde. Dieses Unternehmen wird der bemerkenswerten Bandbreite des Universalgenies am besten gerecht. Neben den Prêt-à-porter-Kollektionen ist Lagerfeld Gallery auch Bühne für die unzähligen

Passionen des Designers, darunter Fotografie (oft fotografiert er außer Fotostrecken für zahlreiche Magazine auch seine Kampagnen selbst), Bücher (sein eigenes Imprint heißt 7L, die Privatbibliothek umfasst 230.000 Bände), Parfüm, Kunst und Zeitschriften. Im Dezember 2004 wurde bekannt, dass Tommy Hilfiger Lagerfeld Gallery gekauft hatte. Dem war eine ungeheuer erfolgreiche Kooperation mit der Kette H&M im Herbst desselben Jahres vorausgegangen. Damals rissen sich die Kunden um die Entwürfe des berühmten Modezaren. Lagerfelds künstlerische Ziele liegen nach wie vor in der Weiterentwicklung des Chanel-Imperiums im 21. Jahrhundert: etwa durch epische Spots für Chanel No.5 mit dem Star Nicole Kidman (2005) oder mittels eines von Zaha Hadid kreierten Kunstprojekts namens Mobile Art, das von Tokio bis nach New York tourte (2008).

Karl Lagerfeld est peut-être l'incarnation même du créateur de mode. La queue de cheval, l'éventail et les lunettes noires qu'il porte en permanence sont devenus cultes ; son goût personnel pour les chemises blanches taillées sur mesure par Hilditch & Key, les bijoux Chrome Hearts et les costumes Dior Homme a été largement commenté. Outre son travail chez Chanel et Fendi, Lagerfeld dessine sa propre griffe depuis 1998 sous le nom de Lagerfeld Gallery. Né en 1938 à Hambourg, Lagerfeld s'installe à Paris dès l'âge de 14 ans. A 17 ans seulement, il décroche son premier emploi chez Pierre Balmain, puis part chez Jean Patou trois ans plus tard. En dépit de ces débuts très classiques, Lagerfeld décide toutefois de ne pas ouvrir sa propre maison, préférant poursuivre sa carrière en tant que créateur free-lance. De 1963 à 1983 et de 1992 à 1997, il dessine les collections de Chloé. En 1965, il commence également à travailler pour Fendi, poste qu'il occupe encore aujourd'hui ; en 1983, il est nommé directeur artistique de Chanel. 1984 voit la naissance de sa propre griffe, Karl Lagerfeld, plus tard remplacée par Lagerfeld Gallery, un projet mêlant art et mode. Lagerfeld Gallery, avec sa boutique rue de Seine à Paris et une autre à Monaco, exprime toute la palette des talents de ce grand érudit. Outre les collections de prêt-à-porter, Lagerfeld Gallery représente une belle plate-forme d'expression pour sa myriade de passions, notamment la photographie (il réalise souvent ses propres campagnes publicitaires ainsi que des shootings photo pour de nombreux magazines), les livres (il possède sa propre maison d'édition, 7L, ainsi qu'une bibliothèque personnelle de 230 000 volumes), le parfum, l'art et les magazines. En décembre 2004, Tommy Hilfiger annonce le rachat de Lagerfeld Gallery, peu de temps après une collaboration couronnée de succès avec la chaîne de boutiques H&M à l'automne 2004 : la mise en vente de la petite collection dessinée par Lagerfeld a provoqué de véritables scènes d'empoigne, avec des clients tous impatients de s'offrir des vêtements signés par un maestro reconnu de la mode. Au XXIᵉ siècle, la direction artistique de Lagerfeld continue à développer l'empire Chanel, des films publicitaires épiques pour Chanel N° 5 avec Nicole Kidman (2005) au pavillon d'exposition itinérant conçu avec l'architecte Zaha Hadid, un projet qui a voyagé de Tokyo à New York (2008).

SUSIE RUSHTON

PORTRAIT COURTESY KARL LAGERFELD. PHOTOGRAPHY MAX VADUKUL. STYLING JOHN HULJUM. MODEL NATASA VOJNOVIC. FEBRUARY 2004.

PHOTOGRAPHY DAVID BENGREEN REBODY 1981

PHOTOGRAPHY KARL LAGERFELD. STYLING CHRISTOPHER NIQUET. MODEL CHAN MARSHALL. MAY 2007.

PHOTOGRAPHY ALASDAIR MCLELLAN, STYLING JANE HOW. MODEL LARA STONE. NOVEMBER 2008

PHOTOGRAPHY PIERRE BAILLY. STYLING CATHY KASTERINE. MODEL CONSTANCE JABLONSKI. APRIL 2009.

PHOTOGRAPHY JAMES COCHRANE AND KIM WESTON-ARNOLD, OCTOBER 2001

PHOTOGRAPHY RICHARD BUSH STYLING SARAH RICHARDSON MODEL ISELIN STEIRO SEPTEMBER 2007

PHOTOGRAPHY MANUELA PAVESI. STYLING ANNA DELLO RUSSO. MODEL FRANCESCA CASELLA. SEPTEMBER 2008.

PHOTOGRAPHY KAYT JONES. DECEMBER 2007.

TO BLACK
PROMOTERS!!!

RIGHT
LANE
MUST
TURN
RIGHT

TOTALLY
GHETTO

Brothers
Look
Ahead
Chase
Knowledge

Let
Our
Violence
End
(Let Love Begin)

Million

CAA,
YOU ARE GUILTY

PHOTOGRAPHY ROBERT WYATT. STYLING LUCY EWING. MODEL BRIDGET HALL. MARCH 2001.

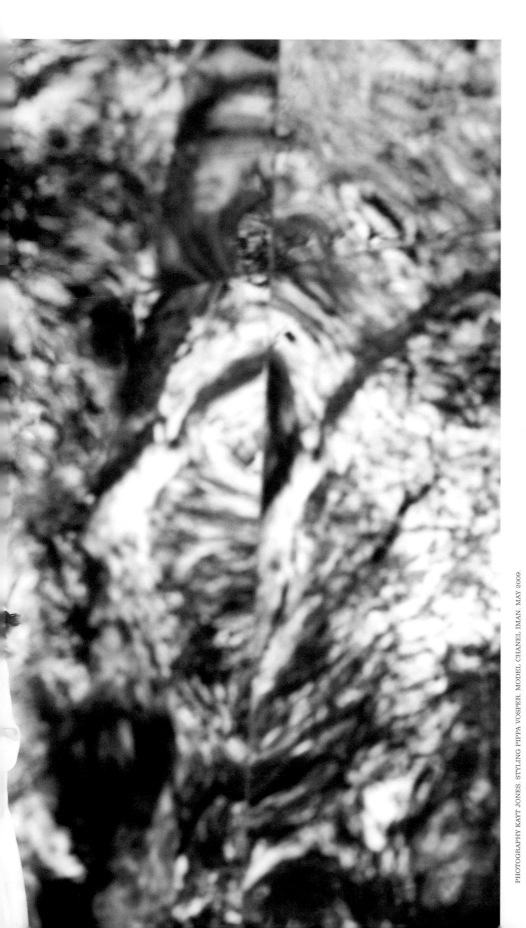

PHOTOGRAPHY KAYT JONES. STYLING PIPPA VOSPER. MODEL CHANEL IMAN. MAY 2009.

What are your signature designs? Every detail and look that makes identification instantly possible **What is your favourite piece from any of your collections?** Pieces from the next collection **How would you describe your work?** I remember Voltaire's line: Everything that needs an explanation or description is not worth it **What's your ultimate goal?** The next collections **What inspires you?** Everything – there should be only one rule: eyes open!! **Can fashion still have a political ambition?** Should it? It should reflect it… **Who do you have in mind when you design?** Several women, never and always the same, women who change with the times and are interested in what is going on – not only in fashion **Is the idea of creative collaboration important to you?** Difficult to do without **Who has been the greatest influence on your career?** The events we have all gone through, changes in the times **How have your own experiences affected your work as a designer?** Difficult to analyse – and I am not sure one should think about what makes the past what it became… **Which is more important in your work: the process or the product?** Both are very important **Is designing difficult for you? If so, what drives you to continue?** No. I love fashion, the evolution of time, and fashion is the reflection of it **Have you ever been influenced or moved by the reaction to your designs?** You have to fight that…! **What's your definition of beauty?** Marlow said: there is no beauty without some strangeness in the proportions **What's your philosophy?** Every decision (also in fashion) is a refusal (Spinoza) **What is the most important lesson you've learned?** You can only learn what not to do – there are no lessons what to do…

"I believe in style, not fashion"
RALPH LAUREN

Ralph Lauren (born 1939) is a household name. Jamaica has even issued a commemorative stamp (in 2004) featuring Lauren. The man and his brand's logo of a polo player riding a horse is recognised by all. From a $50,000 loan in 1968, Polo Ralph Lauren's humble beginnings grew into the internationally famous lifestyle brand that everyone knows today. Lauren was one of the first designers to extend his production of clothing lines to houseware and furniture. He was also the first of the megabrand American designers to set up shop in Europe, in 1981; the Polo Ralph Lauren Corporation now has 280 stores in operation globally and its collections are divided into myriad different labels. In October 2004 in Boston the company opened its first Rugby store, a lifestyle collection for 18-to-25-year-old men and women. The Rugby line joins Lauren's other collections, Purple Label (1994), Blue Label (2002) and Black Label (2005). Underpinning Lauren's designs is an unmistakable preference for old-world gentility. In fact, he has made the Ivy League, preppy style his own. "I don't want to be in fashion – I want to be a fashion," he once told 'Vogue' magazine. And indeed, the Ralph Lauren look is distinctive, nowhere more purely expressed than in his advertising campaigns that always feature a cast of thoroughbred models, often posed as if holidaying in the Hamptons. Lauren's entrance into fashion can be traced back to 1964 with Brooks Brothers, and then Beau Brummell Neckwear in 1967, where he designed wide ties. In the following year, the beginnings of what was to become a billion-dollar brand took root. The Polo menswear line was launched and in 1970 he won the Coty Menswear Award; Lauren added womenswear to the brand in 1971. He has been awarded the CFDA's Lifetime Achievement Award (1992) along with its Menswear designer (1995) and Womenswear designer (1996) prizes. Lauren is also involved in philanthropic activities. The Polo Ralph Foundation organises campaigns such as Pink Pony (2000), which supports cancer care and medically underserved communities. In 2006, Lauren became the official outfitter of Wimbledon and in 2008 an official outfitter of the 2008 US Olympic and Paralympic teams.

Ralph Lauren (Jahrgang 1939) ist ein allgemein bekannter Name. Jamaika brachte 2004 sogar eine Lauren-Gedenkbriefmarke heraus. Polo Ralph Laurens bescheidene Anfänge mit einem Kredit über 50.000 Dollar im Jahr 1968 haben sich zu einem international berühmten Lifestylelabel, das heute jeder kennt, entwickelt. Lauren dehnte als einer der ersten Modedesigner seine Produktpalette auf Wohnaccessoires und Möbel aus. Er war auch einer der ersten Designer amerikanischer Megamarken, die Läden in Europa eröffneten (1981). Heute betreibt die Polo Ralph Lauren Corporation 280 Läden rund um den Globus und hat ihre Kollektionen auf unzählige verschiedene Labels verteilt. Im Oktober 2004 eröffnete das Unternehmen in Boston den ersten Laden namens Rugby, der eine Lifestylekollektion für 18- bis 25-jährige Männer und Frauen führt. Rugby ergänzt die Linien Purple Label (1994), Blue Label (2002) und Black Label (2005). Allen Entwürfen Laurens liegt eine unzweifelhafte Vorliebe für das Elitedenken der Alten Welt zugrunde. Genau genommen hat sich der Designer den Ivy-League- und Preppy-Stil zu eigen gemacht. „Ich möchte nicht in Mode sein – ich möchte eine Mode sein", hat er der Vogue einmal gesagt. Und tatsächlich ist sein Look unverwechselbar und springt nirgendwo klarer ins Auge als in seinen Werbekampagnen,

die immer eine rassige Schar von Models zeigen, die wirken, als machten sie gerade Ferien in den Hamptons. Laurens Anfänge in der Modebranche lassen sich bis ins Jahr 1964 und zu Brooks Brothers zurückverfolgen. 1967 entwarf er bei Beau Brummell Neckwear breite Krawatten, und bereits im folgenden Jahr nahm das, was einmal eine Milliarden-Dollar-Marke werden sollte, seinen Anfang. Alles begann mit der Herrenlinie Polo, für die Lauren 1970 den Coty Menswear Award erhielt. 1971 kam Damenmode ins Sortiment des Labels. Von der CFDA wurde er mit dem Lifetime Achievement Award (1992) ausgezeichnet, bevor er den Designerpreis sowohl für Menswear (1995) als auch für Womenswear (1996) erhielt. Lauren ist aber auch gemeinnützig tätig. Die Polo Ralph Lauren Foundation organisiert Kampagnen wie Pink Pony (2000), die Krebspatienten und medizinisch unterversorgten Gemeinden in den USA zugute kommen. 2006 wurde Lauren offizieller Ausstatter von Wimbledon, und 2008 wurde er offizieller Ausstatter der amerikanischen Olympia- und Paralympics-Mannschaft 2008.

Ralph Lauren (né en 1939) est connu dans le monde entier. En 2004, la Jamaïque a même édité un timbre commémoratif à son effigie. Tout le monde connaît l'homme, comme son logo de joueur de polo. A partir d'un prêt de 50 000 dollars obtenu en 1968, les débuts modestes de Polo Ralph Lauren se sont transformés en une marque de lifestyle incontournable et mondialement connue. Ralph Lauren est l'un des premiers créateurs de mode à s'être diversifié dans le meuble et les articles pour la maison. Sa mégamarque américaine est également la première à ouvrir une boutique en Europe dès 1981; Polo Ralph Lauren Corporation possède aujourd'hui 280 boutiques à travers le monde et ses collections sont divisées en une myriade de griffes différentes. En octobre 2004, l'entreprise ouvre sa première boutique Rugby à Boston, une collection complète destinée aux 18–25 ans, hommes et femmes. La ligne Rugby vient s'ajouter à Purple Label (1994), Blue Label (2002) et Black Label (2005). Une indubitable prédilection pour la distinction à l'ancienne étaye les créations de Lauren, qui s'est en fait approprié le chic BCBG de l'Ivy League. «Je ne veux pas être à la mode: je veux être une mode», déclare-t-il un jour au magazine Vogue. En effet, le look distingué de Ralph Lauren s'exprime de façon plus qu'évidente dans ses campagnes publicitaires qui présentent toujours un casting de mannequins racés, souvent mis en situation dans un décor de vacances rappelant les Hamptons. Les débuts de Lauren dans la mode remontent à 1964 chez Brooks Brothers, puis chez Beau Brummell Neckwear en 1967, où il commence à dessiner des cravates larges. L'année suivante voit la naissance de ce qui devait devenir un énorme groupe évalué à un milliard de dollars. Après avoir lancé la ligne masculine Polo, Ralph Lauren remporte le Coty Menswear Award en 1970, puis crée une collection pour femme en 1971. Le créateur a été couronné du Lifetime Achievement Award du CFDA (1992), avant d'obtenir des prix dans les catégories masculines (1995) et féminines (1996). Ralph Lauren s'implique également dans des activités caritatives: la fondation Polo Ralph organise des campagnes telles que Pink Pony (2000) en faveur du traitement contre le cancer et des communautés mal desservies sur le plan médical. En 2006, il devient le styliste officiel de Wimbledon et en 2008 de les équipes olympiques et paralympiques américaines.

KAREN LEONG

PORTRAIT BRUCE WEBER. PHOTOGRAPHY TERRY RICHARDSON. STYLING ANDRE AUSTIN. MODEL JAY-Z. AUGUST 2005.

PHOTOGRAPHY TESH. FASHION DIRECTOR EDWARD ENNINFUL. MODEL JULIE. OCTOBER 2004.

RALPH LAUREN

PHOTOGRAPHY WILLY VANDERPERRE. STYLING OLIVIER RIZZO. AUGUST 2002.

PHOTOGRAPHY TAKAY. STYLING MARK ANTHONY. MODEL JOANNA PREISS. OCTOBER 2002.

PHOTOGRAPHY MITCHELL SAMS. AUTUMN/WINTER 2009.

What is your favorite piece or pieces from any of your collections? I don't really think in terms of pieces... Each piece is a complement to the bigger picture **What is your ultimate goal?** I am satisfied with my life and feel fortunate to be doing what I love **What inspires you?** I'm constantly drawing inspiration from everything I see – places I travel to, people I know, films, photographs, classic cars... I'm always inspired by authenticity **Is the idea of creative collaboration important to you?** It's very stimulating to go from designing menswear to womenswear to a home collection; to meet about a new store concept or ad campaign. I enjoy being connected with all that I do **Who or what has been the greatest influence on your career?** My family – everything I do is a reflection of my life **Which is more important to you in your work: the process or the product?** For me, designing is not merely about an idea for a suit or a dress. I also see each detail as a complement to the bigger picture – whether the collar is turned, the proportions of a jacket, the colour and size of the buttons. For me, it's about building a concept and nurturing an idea. I'm not just creating products; I'm creating a whole world **Is designing difficult for you? If so, what drives you to continue?** I like the excitement of the challenge. The question I ask myself is: What can we do next? How much further can we go? **What's your philosophy?** Fashion is transient, trends come and go. I believe in style, not fashion **What is the most important lesson you've learned?** Business is about taking risks, but it's also about being consistent with your vision.

"I find designing actually quite natural and exciting"
CHRISTOPHE LEMAIRE • LACOSTE

Recognised for his fresh, flawless cuts and elegant tailoring, Christophe Lemaire of Lacoste is concerned more with the quality of his lines than with slavishly following trends. With a style he describes as "graphic, pure, relaxed and precise", he captures the balance between fashion and function, creating classic, wearable clothing season after season. Born in Besançon, France, in April 1965, Lemaire initially assisted at the Yves Saint Laurent design studio before going on to work for Thierry Mugler and Jean Patou. Through the Jean Patou house, he met Christian Lacroix, who was so impressed with the young designer that he appointed him head of his own women's ready-to-wear line in 1987. Lemaire went solo with his eponymous womenswear label in 1990. His functional designs, with their understated elegance, ensured the label's success and a menswear label followed in 1994. In May 2001, Lemaire became creative director of heritage sportswear brand Lacoste, where he has re-established the company's position on the fashion map. Infusing his own contemporary, sharp style into classics such as the tennis skirt, polo shirt or preppy college jumper, he has attracted new customers while retaining enough of the brand's 70-year-old tradition so as not to lose the old. In June 2001, under his direction, Lacoste staged its first catwalk show. A true fashion DJ, for his own collections Lemaire mixes Western classics with one-of-a-kind ethnic pieces. The result is resolutely modern yet always wearable. "I don't create in a rush," he explains. "I always take time so I can distance myself from things that are too fashionable. As a designer, I aim for an accessible balance between beauty and function to create a vision of contemporary 'easy wearing'." The synergy between Lemaire and Lacoste has been a classic win-win that has allowed Lemaire to retail his own label while reinventing Lacoste as a cool, savvy brand for a global market. For his autumn/winter 2009 collection, Lemaire introduced a more upmarket tailoring and streamlined silhouettes with the crocodile subtlety camouflaged tone on tone.

Der für seine frischen, tadellosen Schnitte und die elegante Verarbeitung bekannte Christophe Lemaire kümmert sich mehr um die Qualität seiner Linien als um die sklavische Befolgung von Trends. Sein Stil, den er selbst „grafisch, puristisch, entspannt und präzise" nennt, trifft exakt den richtigen Ton zwischen Fashion und Function und bringt Saison für Saison klassische, tragbare Kreationen hervor. Lemaire wurde im April 1965 im französischen Besançon geboren. Bevor er für Thierry Mugler und Jean Patou arbeitete, war er zunächst Assistent im Atelier von Yves Saint Laurent. Über Jean Patou lernte er Christian Lacroix kennen, der von dem jungen Designer so begeistert war, dass er ihn 1987 zum Chef seiner Prêt-à-porter-Linie für Damen machte. Sein eigenes, nach ihm benanntes Damenmode-Label brachte Lemaire 1990 auf den Markt. Die funktionalen Entwürfe mit ihrer zurückhaltenden Eleganz sorgten für unmittelbaren Erfolg. Ein entsprechendes Männerlabel folgte 1994. Im Mai 2001 wurde Lemaire Creative Director der traditionellen Sportswear-Marke Lacoste und brachte das Unternehmen zurück in die Erste Liga der Mode. Er ließ seinen eigenen zeitgemäß klaren Stil in Klassiker wie Tennisröcke, Polohemden und Collegepullover einfließen und sprach damit eine neue Klientel an. Zugleich bewahrte er aber auch genug von der 70-jährigen Tradition der Marke, um die Stammkundschaft nicht zu verprellen. Im Juni 2001 veranstaltete Lacoste unter Lemaires Leitung seine erste Catwalk-Show. Als wahrer Fashion-DJ mixt Lemaire für seine eigenen Kollektionen abendländische Klassiker mit Ethno-Unikaten. Das Ergebnis ist entschieden modern, aber immer tragbar. „Meine Entwürfe folgen nie einem spontanen Impuls", erläutert er seine Arbeitsweise. „Ich lasse mir immer Zeit, um Abstand zu Dingen zu gewinnen, die mir zu modisch sind. Als Designer suche ich einen gangbaren Weg zwischen Schönheit und Funktionalität, um eine Vision von zeitgemäßem ‚Easy Wearing' zu kreieren." Die Synergie von Lemaire und Lacoste ist eine klassische Win-win-Situation, die Lemaire erlaubte, sein eigenes Label zu vertreiben, während er Lacoste als eine coole, abgeklärte Marke für den Weltmarkt neu erfand. Für seine Kollektion Herbst/Winter 2009 setzte Lemaire auf exklusivere Schnitte, stromlinienförmige Silhouetten und tarnte das Krokodil dezent Ton in Ton.

Reconnaissable à ses coupes inédites et parfaites comme à ses tailleurs élégants, Christophe Lemaire s'intéresse plus à la qualité de ses lignes qu'aux tendances servilement suivies. Dans un style qu'il décrit comme « graphique, pur, décontracté et précis », il saisit l'équilibre entre mode et fonction en créant saison après saison des classiques faciles à porter. Né en avril 1965 à Besançon, Lemaire commence sa carrière comme assistant dans l'atelier d'Yves Saint Laurent avant de travailler pour Thierry Mugler et Jean Patou. Par l'intermédiaire de la maison Jean Patou, il rencontre Christian Lacroix, qu'il impressionne à tel point que ce dernier le nomme directeur de sa propre ligne de prêt-à-porter en 1987. Lemaire lance sa griffe éponyme pour femme en 1990. Ses créations fonctionnelles douées d'une élégance discrète assurent le succès de la griffe et une collection pour homme suit en 1994. En mai 2001, Lemaire devient directeur de la création de la respectable marque de sportswear Lacoste, où il redore le blason de l'entreprise. Insufflant son style contemporain et précis à des classiques tels que la jupe tennis, le polo ou le pull BCBG à l'américaine, il attire une nouvelle clientèle tout en respectant suffisamment les 70 ans d'histoire de Lacoste pour ne pas perdre ses clients d'origine. Sous son impulsion, Lacoste donne son tout premier défilé en juin 2001. Véritable DJ de la mode, pour ses propres collections, Lemaire mélange les classiques occidentaux à des pièces ethniques absolument uniques en leur genre. Le résultat est résolument moderne mais toujours portable. « Je n'aime pas créer dans l'urgence », explique-t-il. « J'ai toujours pris mon temps afin d'avoir suffisamment de recul par rapport aux choses trop à la mode. En tant que créateur de mode, je cherche à trouver un équilibre accessible entre beauté et fonction pour proposer une vision contemporaine de ‹ l'easy wearing ›». La synergie mutuellement profitable entre Lemaire et Lacoste a permis au créateur de commercialiser sa propre griffe tout en imposant Lacoste comme une marque cool et branchée sur le marché mondial. Dans sa collection automne/hiver 2009, Christophe Lemaire a introduit des coupes plus haut de gamme et des silhouettes épurées où le crocodile apparaît subtilement camouflé en ton sur ton.

HOLLY SHACKLETON

PHOTOGRAPHY KENNETH CAPPELLO. STYLING FRANCESCA BURNS. MODEL JESSICA STAM. AUGUST 2006.

PHOTOGRAPHY SEBASTIAN KIM. STYLING MICHELLE CAMERON. MODEL MEY BUN. MAY 2007.

PHOTOGRAPHY DAVID DORCICH SEPTEMBER 2002

What are your signature designs? The essential wardrobe, mixing modern classics with pop elements in subtle, twisted ways **How would you describe your work?** I always look for 'good sense' in style, a certain 'evidence', simplicity and function with allure, taste and precision **What inspires you?** Everything... life... **Can fashion still have a political ambition?** Fashion really is about aesthetics... Of course, if we think about fashion as an expression of individuality, as style, as attitude towards others, then, yes, style can have a political meaning. I would rather say that fashion must have a cultural meaning **Who do you have in mind when you design?** I am generally inspired by people from the

music scene, like Nick Cave, Serge Gainsbourg, PJ Harvey, Deborah Harry... I have always found that people connected to music are more stylish, free-minded and expressive than the majority of the fashion crowd **Is the idea of creative collaboration important to you?** Fundamental. That's what everyday life should be about – sharing ideas. My work as a designer would mean nothing without the team around me **Who has been the greatest influence of your career?** Japanese culture, rock 'n' roll (Stooges, The Who, Bo Diddley), my training with Christian Lacroix, Yves Saint Laurent and Street 'Free-Style' (the second-hand culture) **How have your own experiences affected your work as a designer?** Too

complex, unconscious, to answer precisely! **Which is more important in your work: the process or the product?** As a designer, what really matters at the end of the day is the product: is it good or is it bad? But through the years, I have also learned how essential the process was. A better process – creative, focused, positive – makes a better product **Is designing difficult for you? If so, what drives you to continue?** I find designing actually quite natural and exciting. What's more difficult for me and demands more discipline and concentration (I am rather impulsive and impatient) is all the process to make the design happen, become real and faithful to my first intuition. That's why the process is as important as

the product **Have you ever been influenced or moved by the reaction to your designs?** I am probably too sensitive to the opinions of others and I try to free myself from that dependence. I can easily lose my confidence if I don't feel good reactions to my work **What's your definition of beauty?** Grace **What's you philosophy?** Stay faithful to my dreams. Listen to my heart as much as my brain, fight against laziness, conformism, mediocrity (starting with my own) and look for quality in everything. Show respect to others **What is the most important lesson you've learned?** Patience.

"Ultra-sexy, ultra-glamourous, sparkly and short: that sums up what I do"
JULIEN MACDONALD

"I don't want to be avant-garde," says Julien Macdonald of his upfront brand of showgirl glamour: "I like beautiful clothes. I don't care what people think about me." Macdonald's love for fashion was inspired by the knitting circles his mother held at home in the Welsh village of Merthyr Tydfil. Studying fashion textiles at Brighton University, his sophisticated knitwear went on to win him a scholarship at London's Royal College of Art. By the time he graduated in 1996, with a spectacular collection styled by Isabella Blow, he had already designed for Koji Tatsuno, Alexander McQueen and Karl Lagerfeld. Lagerfeld spotted Macdonald's knits in the pages of i-D and appointed him head knitwear designer for Chanel collections in 1997. Utterly devoted to the female form, Macdonald reinvigorated knitwear with his glitzy red-carpet creations. His barely-there crochet slips of cobwebs and crystals, shocking frocks and furs guarantee headlines for a devoted throng of starlets and celebrities. Macdonald's catwalk antics – including appearances from the Spice Girls and a Michael Jackson lookalike, plus an autumn/winter 2001 presentation held at the Millennium Dome and directed by hip-hop video supremo Hype Williams – have earned him a reputation as a showmaster. After being crowned the British Glamour Designer of the Year for the first time in 2001 (an award he picked up again in 2003), Macdonald went on to take his high-octane street-style to couture house Givenchy, where he succeeded Alexander McQueen as creative director. Under his direction, sales for the luxury label increased despite some mixed reviews from fashion critics, and with three years under his belt, he produced an acclaimed farewell show for autumn/winter 2004. For now, Macdonald continues to present his flamboyant collections in London, where he also oversees his homeware, fragrance and high-street lines. In 2006, he was awarded an OBE for services to fashion.

„Ich möchte nicht Avantgarde sein", sagt Julien Macdonald über seine freizügige Revuegirl-Mode. „Ich mag schöne Kleider. Und es ist mir egal, was die Leute von mir denken." Macdonalds Interesse an Mode wurde von den Strickkränzchen seiner Mutter zu Hause in dem walisischen Dorf Merthyr Tydfil geweckt. Nach dem Modestudium an der Universität Brighton brachten ihm seine raffinierten Stricksachen ein Stipendium am Londoner Royal College of Art ein. Als er 1996 mit einer spektakulären, von Isabella Blow gestylten Kollektion seinen Abschluss machte, hatte er bereits für Koji Tatsuno, Alexander McQueen und Karl Lagerfeld entworfen. Lagerfeld entdeckte Macdonalds Strickkreationen in i-D und machte ihn 1997 zum Chefdesigner der Strickwaren für die Chanel-Kollektion. Als absolutem Verehrer weiblicher Formen gelang es Macdonald mit seinen schillernden Kreationen, die für den roten Teppich prädestiniert sind, die Strickmode neu zu beleben. Seine klitzekleinen Häkelslips aus Spinnwebmustern und Kristallen, die schockierenden Kleider und Pelze garantieren der treuen Anhängerschaft aus Starlets und Prominenten Schlagzeilen. Macdonalds Mätzchen auf dem Laufsteg, wie Auftritte der Spice Girls und eines Michael-Jackson-Doubles oder die Präsentation der Kollektion Herbst/Winter 2001 im Millennium Dome

unter der Regie des Hip-Hop-Videostars Hype Williams, haben ihm den Ruf eines Showmasters eingebracht und seinen Status als König der Londoner Glitzerwelt gefestigt. Nach der ersten Auszeichnung als British Glamour Designer of the Year 2001 (ein Preis, der ihm erneut 2003 verliehen wurde) machte Macdonald sich daran, seinen hochklassigen Street Style auf die Couture bei Givenchy zu übertragen, wo er als Creative Director die Nachfolge von Alexander McQueen antrat. Unter seiner Leitung stiegen die Verkaufszahlen des Luxuslabels, auch wenn einige Journalisten ihn kritisierten. Nach drei Jahren lieferte er mit der Kollektion für Herbst/Winter 2004 eine hochgelobte Abschiedsshow. Gegenwärtig präsentiert Macdonald seine extravaganten Kollektionen weiterhin in London, wo er auch über seine Wohnkollektion, seine Düfte und hochwertigen Street-Labels wacht. 2006 wurde er für seine Verdienste um die Mode als Officer of the British Empire ausgezeichnet.

« Je ne cherche pas à être d'avant-garde », dit Julien Macdonald de son glamour sans détour digne des showgirls de Las Vegas : « J'aime les beaux vêtements. Je me fiche pas mal de ce que les gens pensent de moi ». La passion de Macdonald pour la mode est née dans les cercles de tricot que sa mère organisait chez eux dans le village gallois de Merthyr Tydfil. Après avoir étudié le textile à l'Université de Brighton, sa maille sophistiquée lui vaut une bourse d'études pour le Royal College of Art de Londres. Lorsqu'il en sort diplômé en 1996 avec une collection spectaculaire mise en style par Isabella Blow, il a déjà collaboré avec Koji Tatsuno, Alexander McQueen et Karl Lagerfeld. Ce dernier, qui avait repéré les créations de Macdonald dans les pages du magazine i-D, l'embauche comme responsable de la maille des collections Chanel en 1997. Entièrement dévoué aux formes du corps féminin, Macdonald a ressuscité la maille à travers ses créations brillantes et ultra-glamour. Ses combinaisons très osées réalisées au crochet en toile d'araignée et ornées de cristaux, ses robes choquantes et ses fourrures garantissent la une des journaux à une foule dévouée de starlettes et autres célébrités. Grâce à l'extravagance de ses défilés, avec des apparitions des Spice Girls et d'un sosie de Michael Jackson, sans oublier la présentation de sa collection automne/hiver 2001 au Millennium Dome sous la direction du parrain de la vidéo hip-hop Hype Williams, Macdonald s'est forgé une réputation de maître du spectacle. Couronné British Glamour Designer of the Year pour la première fois en 2001 (un prix qu'il raflera de nouveau en 2003), Macdonald traduit son streetwear explosif pour la maison Givenchy, où il succède à Alexander McQueen en tant que directeur de la création. Sous son impulsion, la griffe de luxe voit ses ventes décoller en dépit de critiques mitigées, mais après trois années à ce poste, Macdonald fait ses adieux à Givenchy avec une collection automne/hiver 2004 cette fois largement plébiscitée. Aujourd'hui, il continue de présenter ses flamboyantes collections à Londres, d'où il supervise également ses lignes de mobilier, de parfums et de grande diffusion. En 2006, il a été fait membre de l'Ordre de l'Empire Britannique pour services rendus à la mode.

JAMIE HUCKBODY

PHOTOGRAPHY YELENA YEMCHUK. STYLING SORAYA DAYANI. MODEL PHOEBE JAMES. JANUARY 2004.

What are your signature designs? Ultra-sexy, ultra-glamorous, sparkly and short: that sums up what I do **What's your favourite piece from any of your collections?** The hand crocheted or cobweb knits are my favourites. There's nothing of them, so they look best on people with gorgeous bodies who just want to squeeze into something small **How would you describe your work?** It's dangerous, exciting, high-octane glamour but, most of all, it's fun. I create clothes people would notice when you walk into a room **What's your ultimate goal?** To build up both my brand name and my label – I've got a goal in both fashion and power **What inspires you?** Life itself **Can fashion still have a political ambition?** I think fashion is basically a service provider, it's as simple as that **Who do you have in mind when you design?** I suppose I design for a kind of Amazonian woman; someone who's not afraid of her body and wants to go out and show it **Is the idea of creative collaboration important to you?** As a designer, you basically work on your own. You have an idea for a collection and then you just bring in different people to help you achieve it. The designer is the person it stems from – without them, there's nothing **Who has been the greatest influence on your career?** I spent two years working with Karl Lagerfeld at Chanel and he educated me in the way a woman with culture and status dresses **How have your own experiences affected your work as a designer?** I think that the older you get, the more interesting you become as a person and the more interesting you become as a designer **Which is more important in your work: the process or the product?** People don't pay attention to the process – they just want the product **Is designing difficult for you? If so, what drives you to continue?** I don't think designing is difficult. What is difficult is managing and running a business **Have you ever been influenced or moved by the reaction to your designs?** There's nothing more satisfying than seeing a woman looking fantastic in one of your outfits. My aim is to make women feel comfortable, happy and glamorous **What's your definition of beauty?** Beauty is in the eye of the beholder, as they say. Beauty can be very cruel or very pretty. It's a difficult one **What's your philosophy?** I don't really have one. I just want to design clothes and be happy and enjoy what I do – if you don't enjoy it, give up **What is the most important lesson you've learned?** Always be nice.

"I find the women around me always a great inspiration"
HANNAH MACGIBBON · CHLOÉ

Born in 1970 in Camden Town, London, Hannah MacGibbon is raising the heat at the house of Chloé. Since Phoebe Philo's departure in 2005, the company lost its magic touch in igniting the flames of desire amongst fashion critics and Chloé fans. All that is set to change with MacGibbon at its helm. Her autumn/winter 2009 collection of luxurious blanket coats and relaxed evening glamour showed that MacGibbon had her finger firmly on the pulse of Chloé. After graduating from Central Saint Martins, MacGibbon cut her teeth at Valentino (she was Mr Valentino's first assistant) before joining Chloé in 2001. Working closely with Philo, MacGibbon was integral to the ascendancy of Chloé in the early noughties. When Philo left Chloé, MacGibbon was offered the top job but she turned it down – she went on to art direct special projects including the Eau de Parfum launch. On 10 March 2008, MacGibbon was named creative director, taking over from Paolo Melim Andersson.

Die 1970 im Londoner Viertel Camden Town geborene Hannah MacGibbon sorgt gegenwärtig im Hause Chloé für steigende Temperaturen. Seit dem Weggang von Phoebe Philo 2005 hatte das Unternehmen seine zauberische Gabe verloren, flammende Begierde bei Modekritikern und Chloé-Fans zu entzünden. Mit MacGibbon an der Spitze wird sich das alles ändern. Ihre Kollektion für Herbst/Winter 2009 mit luxuriösen Blanket Coats und lässig glamouröser Abendmode bewies, dass MacGibbon den Finger exakt am Puls von Chloé hat. Nach ihrem Abschluss an der Central Saint Martins sammelte MacGibbon ihre ersten eigenen Erfahrungen bei Valentino (als Signor Valentinos erste Assis-

tentin), bevor sie 2001 bei Chloé anfing. Als enge Mitarbeiterin von Phoebe Philo war sie wesentlich am Aufstieg Chloés zu Beginn des 21. Jahrhunderts beteiligt. Als Philo Chloé verließ, bot man MacGibbon den Job an der Spitze an, doch sie lehnte ab – und blieb zunächst als Art Director für Spezialprojekte wie die Markteinführung des Eau de Parfum zuständig. Am 10. März 2008 wurde Hannah MacGibbon schließlich als Nachfolgerin von Paolo Melim Andersson zum Creative Director ernannt.

Née en 1970 dans le quartier londonien de Camden Town, Hannah MacGibbon fait monter la température chez Chloé. Depuis le départ de Phoebe Philo en 2005, la maison avait perdu cette magie qui attisait le désir des critiques de mode et des fans de Chloé, mais tout va changer avec l'arrivée d'Hannah MacGibbon à la direction. Entre de luxueux manteaux-capes et des tenues de soirée aussi glamour que décontractées, sa collection automne/hiver 2009 a démontré qu'elle avait vraiment le doigt sur le pouls de Chloé. Après l'obtention de son diplôme à Central Saint Martins, la créatrice s'est fait les dents chez Valentino (elle était la première assistante de M. Valentino) avant de rejoindre Chloé en 2001. Travaillant en étroite collaboration avec Phoebe Philo, elle a joué un rôle essentiel dans l'ascension de la maison au début des années 2000. Après le départ de Phoebe Philo, son poste a été proposé à Hannah MacGibbon, qui a préféré décliner l'offre pour s'occuper de la direction artistique de projets spéciaux comme le lancement de l'Eau de Parfum. Le 10 mars 2008, elle a repris la direction de la création à la suite de Paolo Melim Andersson. KAREN LEONG

PORTRAIT COURTESY HANNAH MACGIBBON. PHOTOGRAPHY PAUL WETHERELL. STYLING MICHAEL PHILOUZE. MODEL MARINA PEREZ. MAY 2009.

What are your signature designs? Collections that are just effortless, desirable. Clothes that you want to wear **How would you describe your work?** For a design to go through, I really have to question myself. I have to love every piece **What inspires you?** I find the women around me always a great inspiration **Who do you have in mind when you design?** It's not starting from references. I think that keeps it fresh. There's a sentiment at Chloé that I love. It's the house, rather than any particular period **How have your own experiences affected your work as designer?** My years at Valentino, I learnt so much – the process, the sense of respect, the feel for fabric and colour **Which is more important in your work: the process or the product?** I would like to concentrate more on the product, and raising the level of the product. Fashion is just so much more demanding, there's been a lot of work on cut. I wanted to not just embellish so much and concentrate on some light structure and cut. It's simplicity I love. That's something quite personal **Is designing difficult for you? If so, what drives you to continue?** The fact that I don't think there's any house that provides clothes for the girls we design for **Have you ever been influenced or moved by the reaction to your designs?** There was one moment backstage (spring/summer 2009) when all the girls were lined up: That so excited and pretty, that was beautiful **Whats your philosophy?** To maintain a naïve, fresh approach that's so important **What is the most important lesson you've learned?** You must stay true to your vision.

"At the end of every cycle there is a desire to move on"
TOMAS MAIER · BOTTEGA VENETA

Bottega Veneta's pedigree in fine leather goods makes it a world leader in its field. Founded in Vicenza, Italy, in 1966, the house quickly became the choice of the Studio 54 crowd; Andy Warhol bought his Christmas presents at the New York store. At that time, Bottega was a family company designed and run by husband and wife team Vittorio and Laura Moltedo, and it was famed for its hand-made, super-soft bags created from signature 'intrecciato' woven leather. Following this heyday, Bottega looked like being consigned to fashion history until the intervention of two forces: one, the Gucci Group, which in 2001 spent $60 million on acquiring two thirds of the company, giving it the financial clout to undergo an extensive relaunch. The other was the appointment of Tomas Maier as creative director; previously in the company's recent history, British designer Giles Deacon had been head designer. Maier's revamp has included BV's Milan headquarters, its stationery, staff and uniforms. Collections, too, have returned to a more sophisticated aesthetic and have been extended to cover laptop cases, shoes in exotic leathers, cashmere knits and homeware ranges. The focus, Maier has stated, is to stick with accessories and niche products. Miami-based, German-born (1958) Maier trained at the Chambre Syndicale de la Haute Couture in Paris and has a long history as a luxury-goods designer – including nine years as designer of womenswear for Hermès and, in 1998, the launch of his own collection – and is now being tipped as a man to watch.

Bottega Venetas langjähriger Ruf als Hersteller feinster Lederwaren machte die 1966 im italienischen Vicenza gegründete Firma zu einer der internationalen Marktführerinnen. Bald kauften die Leute vom Studio 54 dort. Andy Warhol erledigte seine Weihnachtseinkäufe im New Yorker Laden. Das vom Ehepaar Vittorio und Laura Moltedo erdachte und geführte Familienunternehmen war berühmt für seine handgefertigten, superweichen Taschen aus dem typisch eingeflochtenen (intrecciato) Leder. Nach dieser Blütezeit schien es zunächst, als wäre Bottega bald nur noch Modegeschichte, doch dann traten zwei Kräfte auf den Plan: zum einen die Gucci-Gruppe, die 2001 für 60 Millionen Dollar zwei Drittel des Unternehmens erwarb und diesem damit einen umfassenden Relaunch ermöglichte; zum anderen die Ernennung von Tomas Maier zum Creative Director. Maiers Großreinemachen umfasste einfach alles – auch den Firmensitz in Mailand, Briefpapier, Personal und dessen Outfits. Bei den Kollek-

tionen kehrte man zu einer edleren Ästhetik zurück und erweiterte die Produktpalette um Laptophüllen, Schuhe aus exotischen Ledersorten, Kaschmirschals und Heimtextilien. Dabei ist es allerdings Maiers erklärtes Ziel, bei Accessoires und Nischenprodukten zu bleiben. Der in Miami lebende, 1958 in Deutschland geborene Maier hat an der Chambre Syndicale de la Haute Couture in Paris gelernt und besitzt langjährige Erfahrung als Designer von Luxusartikeln. Dazu gehören u. a. neun Jahre als Designer für Damenmode bei Hermès und die erste eigene Kollektion 1998. Heute gilt er in der Branche als ein Mann, den man unbedingt im Auge behalten sollte.

Grâce à son immense savoir-faire, le maroquinier de luxe Bottega Veneta est devenu l'un des leaders mondiaux dans son domaine. Fondée en 1966 à Vicence en Italie, la maison s'impose rapidement comme le choix de prédilection des habitués du Studio 54 : Andy Warhol avait l'habitude d'acheter ses cadeaux de Noël dans la boutique de New York. L'entreprise est alors une affaire familiale créée et dirigée par les époux, Vittorio et Laura Moltedo, qui proposent des sacs ultra-souples faits à la main et coupés dans le cuir tressé « intrecciato » qui a fait la gloire de la maison. Aprés de cet âge d'or, Bottega Veneta semble voué à sombrer dans les oubliettes de la mode jusqu'à l'intervention de deux puissantes forces : d'abord le groupe Gucci, qui en 2001 investit 60 millions de dollars pour acquérir les deux tiers de l'entreprise et lui offrir ainsi le poids financier nécessaire pour être relancée sur le marché, et ensuite le recrutement de Tomas Maier à la direction de la création, en remplacement du styliste anglais Giles Deacon. Maier ira même jusqu'à transformer le siège milanais de l'entreprise, son papier à lettres et l'uniforme de ses employés. Les collections reviennent alors à une esthétique plus sophistiquée et s'enrichissent de housses d'ordinateurs portables, de chaussures taillées dans des cuirs exotiques, de pulls en cachemire et de gammes d'articles pour la maison, l'intention déclarée de Maier consistant à rester spécialisé sur les accessoires et les produits de niche. Né en 1958, le styliste allemand Tomas Maier vit aujourd'hui à Miami. Il a suivi une formation à la Chambre Syndicale de la Haute Couture de Paris et revendique une longue expérience de création dans l'industrie du luxe : il a notamment travaillé pendant neuf ans comme styliste pour femme chez Hermès, et lancé sa propre collection en 1998. On le considère aujourd'hui comme un talent à suivre de très près. JOSH SIMS

PORTRAIT COURTESY BOTTEGA VENETA. PHOTOGRAPHY REBECCA PIERCE. STYLING MARCUS ROSS. MODEL IRINA. OCTOBER 2004.

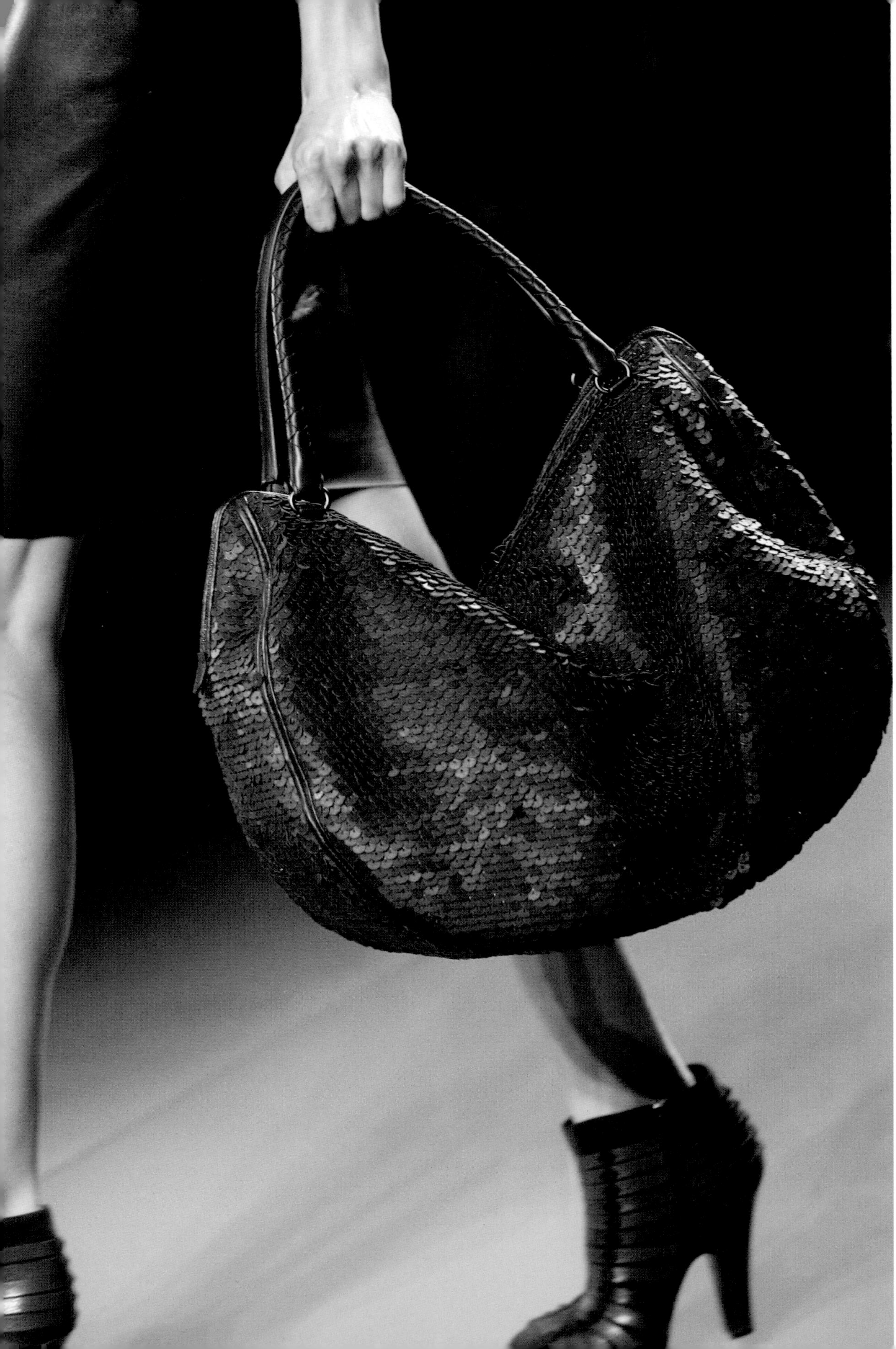

PHOTOGRAPHY MITCHELL SAMS. AUTUMN/WINTER 2009.

PHOTOGRAPHY BEN DUNBAR-BRUNTON. STYLING SIMON FOXTON. MODEL DOMINIQUE HOLLINGTON. FEBRUARY 2009.

What are your signature designs? Casual, low-key luxury **What is your favourite piece from any of your collections?** My surf shorts, my Bottega Cabat **How would you describe your work?** A combination of design, material and colour research, to fulfil a desire for beauty and function **What's your ultimate goal?** Underlining personality rather than the opposite **What inspires you?** Anything around me and everything that I have stored in my brain **Can fashion still have a political ambition?** Fashion is a reflection of our time and many times an indicator of human sensibility **Who do you have in mind when you design?** Nobody in particular because my motto is everybody different – please! **Is the idea of creative collaboration important to you?** Absolutely and everyday of my life **Who has been the greatest influence on your career?** A group of people I encountered in my life as well as my family and upbringing **How have your own experiences affected your work as a designer?** Very much for having worked in so many different categories, areas and countries **Is designing difficult for you? If so, what drives you to continue?** It is not because at the end of every cycle there is a desire to move on **Have you ever been influenced or moved by the reaction to your designs?** I am interested in reactions but I can judge the result by myself **What's your definition of beauty?** It's when everything comes together – harmony **What's your philosophy?** There is always room for improvement **What is the most important lesson you've learned?** Passion and patience go together.

"To evolve is to continue to breathe creatively"
MARTIN MARGIELA · MAISON MARTIN MARGIELA

Martin Margiela is the fashion designer's fashion designer. Normally this comment could be read as a casual cliché, but in the case of Margiela, it is justified. For unlike any other designer, he produces work that could be seen as a distinct form of 'metafashion': his clothes are essentially about clothes. With his own peculiar yet precise vision, he is one of the most influential and iconoclastic designers to have emerged over the past 15 years. Born in 1959 in Limbourg, Belgium, he studied at Antwerp's Royal Academy and was part of the first wave of talent that would emerge from the city. Between 1984 and 1987, he assisted Jean Paul Gaultier; in 1988, Maison Martin Margiela was founded in Paris and his first womenswear collection, for spring/summer 1989, was shown the same year. Struggling to come to terms with a definition of Margiela's fashion, with its exposure of and mania for the process and craft of making clothes, the press labelled this new mood 'deconstruction'. Eschewing the cult of personality that attends many designers, Martin Margiela has instead fostered a cult of impersonality. Never photographed, never interviewed in person or as an individual ('Maison Margiela' answers faxed questions), even the label in his clothing remains blank (as in the main womenswear line) or simply has a number circled ('6' for women's basics and '10' for menswear). In 2000, the first Margiela shop opened, in Tokyo, followed by stores in Brussels, Paris and London, and three further shops in Japan. From 1997 to 2003, in addition to his own collections, Margiela designed womenswear for Hermès, and in July 2002, Renzo Rosso, owner and president of the Diesel Group, became the major shareholder in Margiela's operating group, Neuf SA, allowing the company further expansion. Margiela has also participated in numerous exhibitions and in 2004 curated 'A' Magazine.

Martin Margiela ist der Modedesigner der Modedesigner. Diese Aussage könnte wie ein unbedachtes Klischee klingen, doch im Fall von Margiela hat sie tatsächlich ihre Berechtigung. Im Unterschied zu allen anderen Modeschöpfern erschafft er etwas, das man als besondere Form von „Meta-Mode" bezeichnen könnte: Seine Kleider sind die Quintessenz ihrer selbst. Dank seiner eigenwilligen, aber präzisen Vorstellungen ist er einer der einflussreichsten und umstürzlerischsten Designer, die in den vergangenen 15 Jahren von sich reden gemacht haben. Geboren wurde Margiela 1959 im belgischen Limbourg. Nach seinem Studium an der Königlichen Akademie in Antwerpen gehörte er zur ersten Welle neuer Talente aus dieser Stadt. Von 1984 bis 1987 arbeitete Margiela als Assistent für Jean Paul Gaultier; 1988 gründete er dann in Paris sein Label Maison Martin Margiela und präsentierte noch im selben Jahr seine erste Damenkollektion für Frühjahr/Sommer 1989. Die Presse taufte diese neue Strömung „Dekonstruktion", weil es ihr schwer fiel, den Stil des Designers mit seiner Passion für die Entstehung von Mode und die Offenlegung dieses Prozesses genau zu umrei-

ßen. Margiela lehnte den Personenkult ab, den so viele Designer pflegen, und machte stattdessen eher Unpersönlichkeit zum Kult. Der Designer lässt sich weder fotografieren noch als Person oder als Individuum interviewen – Maison Margiela beantwortet lediglich gefaxte Anfragen. Und selbst die Etiketten in den Kleidern bleiben leer (wie in der Hauptkollektion für Damen) oder tragen nur einen Kreis mit einer Ziffer darin (eine 6 für Damen-Basics, eine 10 für Herrenmode). Im Jahr 2000 wurde der erste Margiela-Laden in Tokio eröffnet, gefolgt von Filialen in Brüssel, Paris und London sowie drei weiteren Dependancen in Japan. Zwischen 1997 und 2003 entwarf Margiela zusätzlich zu seinen eigenen Kollektionen auch Damenmode für Hermès. Im Juli 2002 wurde der Eigentümer und Präsident der Diesel-Gruppe, Renzo Rosso, Mehrheitsaktionär von Margielas Betreibergesellschaft Neuf SA, was dem Unternehmen die weitere Expansion ermöglichte. Margiela hat bereits an zahlreichen Ausstellungen teilgenommen und kuratierte 2004 eine Ausgabe des A-Magazins.

Martin Margiela est le créateur de mode des créateurs de mode et en l'occurrence, ce banal cliché est tout à fait justifié. Contrairement à tout autre créateur, il produit un travail qui s'apparente à une forme distincte de « métamode » : en effet, ses vêtements parlent avant tout de vêtements. Sa vision particulière et bien définie l'a imposé comme l'un des stylistes les plus influents et les plus iconoclastes qui ont émergé ces 15 dernières années. Né en 1959 à Limbourg en Belgique, Martin Margiela étudie à l'Académie Royale d'Anvers et fait partie de la première vague de nouveaux talents de la ville. Entre 1984 et 1987, il est assistant de Jean Paul Gaultier ; en 1988, il fonde Maison Martin Margiela à Paris et présente sa première collection pour femme printemps/été 1989 la même année. Cherchant désespérément à définir la mode de Margiela, avec sa franchise et sa manie du procédé artisanal, la presse baptise ce nouveau style « déconstruction ». Evitant le culte de la personnalité qui guette de nombreux designers, Martin Margiela cherche au contraire à développer un culte de l'impersonnalité. Jamais pris en photo, jamais interviewé en personne (c'est Maison Margiela qui répond aux questions envoyées par fax), même la griffe de ses vêtements reste vierge (comme c'est le cas de la ligne principale pour femme) ou comporte simplement un numéro dans un cercle (« 6 » pour les basiques féminins et « 10 » pour les hommes). En l'an 2000, la première boutique Margiela ouvre ses portes à Tokyo, suivie par Bruxelles, Paris et Londres, puis par trois autres boutiques au Japon. Entre 1997 et 2003, outre ses propres collections, Margiela travaille comme styliste des lignes pour femme chez Hermès. En juillet 2002, Renzo Rosso, propriétaire et président du groupe Diesel, devient actionnaire majoritaire de Neuf SA, le groupe d'exploitation de Margiela, ce qui permet à l'entreprise de poursuivre son expansion. Margiela a également participé à de nombreuses expositions et présidé le comité de rédaction du magazine « A » en 2004. JO-ANN FURNISS

PORTRAIT MAISON MARTIN MARGIELA. PHOTOGRAPHY KAYT JONES. STYLING KANAKO B KOGA. MODEL ANNE SOPHIE ARPE 2009

PHOTOGRAPHY CHAD PITMAN. STYLING HAVANA LAFFITTE. MODEL RACHEL CLARK. SEPTEMBER 2007.

PHOTOGRAPHY NICK HAYMES. STYLING HAVANA LAFFITTE. MODEL NATALIA CHABANENKO. APRIL 2009.

PHOTOGRAPHY DAVID BENJAMIN SHERRY. STYLING DAVID VANDEWAL. MODEL ABBEY LEE. JANUARY 2009.

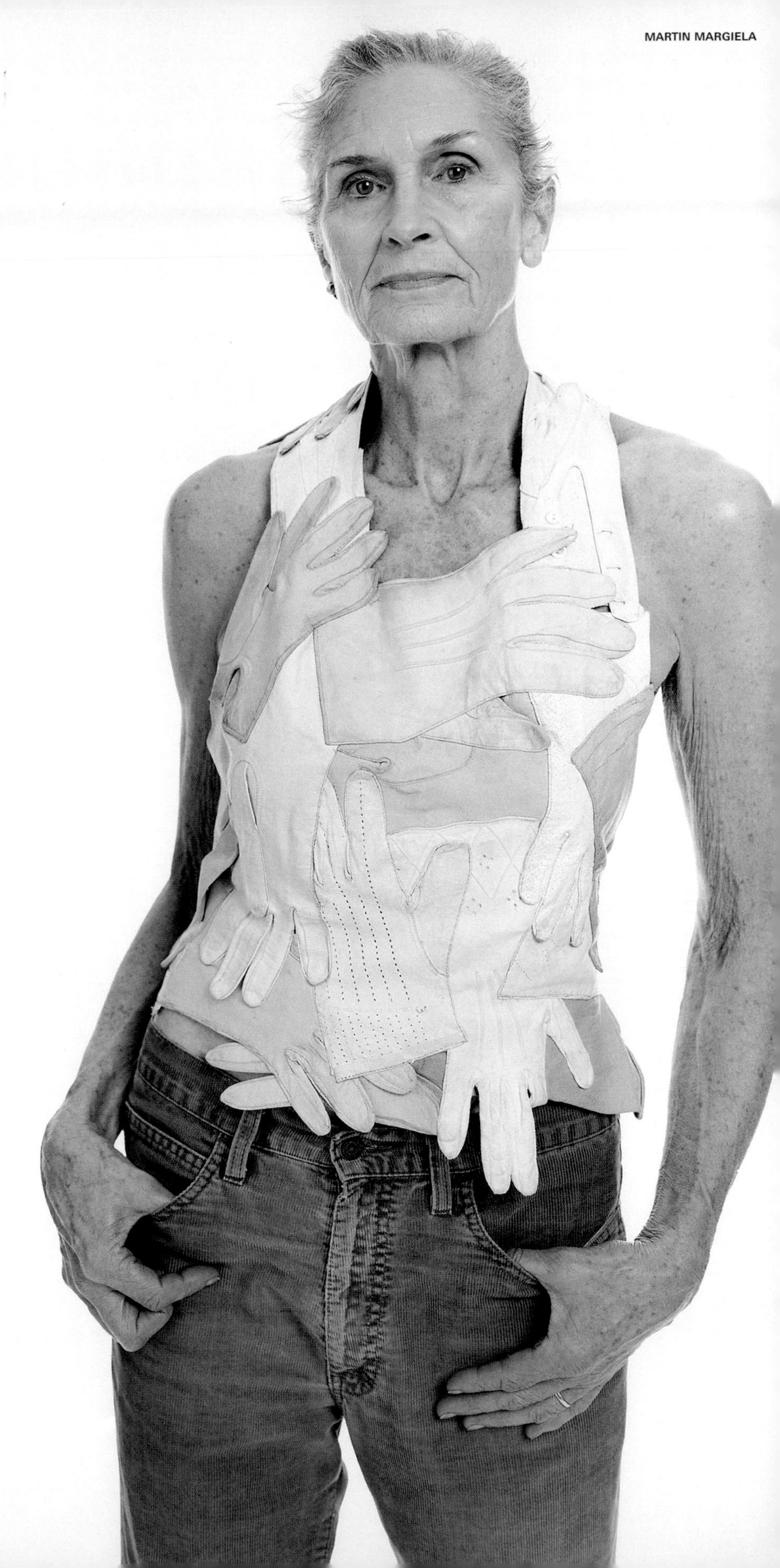

PHOTOGRAPHY RICHARD BUSH. STYLING JANE HOW. MARCH 2001.

PHOTOGRAPHY WALTER PFEIFFER. STYLING ERIKA KURIHARA. MODELS CHRISTIAN AND ALBAN. AUGUST 2007

PHOTOGRAPHY SIMON THISELTON. STYLING SIMON FOXTON. MODEL KUPAI. AUGUST 2008.

PHOTOGRAPHY BENJAMIN ALEXANDER HUSEBY STYLING JANE HOW MODEL ANJA RUBIK OCTOBER 2005

PHOTOGRAPHY SHIRO. STYLING ERIKA KURIHARA. SEPTEMBER 2004.

What are your signature designs? This is always a very tricky thing for a team in our position to answer. Others – especially those who follow our work and wear our clothes – will always have a totally different view on this. We will however venture to suggest some individual garments, as well as a few overriding themes of our collections, that might be worthy of being remembered after we are long gone! Among these might be… Our work for every collection since our first on what we refer to as our 'Artisanal Production' – the reworking of men's and women's vintage garments, fabrics and accessories. The silhouette that dominated our first ten collections – the 'cigarette' shoulder for which a roll of fabric was placed above the shoulder, leaving the wearer's natural shoulder line to define the garment. These were usually worn with long apron skirts in washed men's suiting fabric or men's jeans and suit trousers that were opened and reworked as skirts. The Martin Margiela 'Tabi' boot 6 spring/summer 1989 to the present day – based on a Japanese 'Tabi' sock, these have been present in all of our collections and first commercialised in 1995. They were made up in leather, suede and canvas and mounted on a wooden heel of the diameter of the average human heel. Since 1991 – vintage jeans and jeans jackets painted by hand. Winter 1991 – a sweater made entirely from opened and assembled military socks. The heels of the original socks helped form the shoulders, elbows and bust of the sweater. Autumn/winter 1994 – Elements of a doll's wardrobe were enlarged 5.2 times to a human scale. The disproportions and structures of the dolls pieces were maintained in the upscaled reproductions – often rendering oversized, knit, collars, buttons and zips etc. Summer 1996 – A wardrobe for summer of photographed elements of a man's and woman's winter wardrobe. The photographs were printed on light fluid summer fabrics. Summer 1997 and winter 1997 – garments evoking the trial and development of prototype garments as worked on with a 'Tailor's Dummy'. A jacket of each of these seasons was in the shape of a 'Tailor's Dummy'. Spring/summer 2000 autumn/winter 2001: A work on scale. The creation of a fictive Italian size 78. Elements of a man's and woman's wardrobe – dress jackets, suit jackets, bombers, pants and jeans are proposed in this one size and over the seasons the ways of treating these up-scaled garments varied. Trousers are fitted to size by folding them over and stitching them. The final version was for spring/ spring 2002, when these garments were raw cut to the waistline of the wearer. Spring/summer 2002 – garments constructed entirely as circles. When laid flat, they seem like an object and when worn they take the form of the body, creating a draping effect. Vintage men's perfecto leather flight jackets are reworked into a circular shape making them seem cropped when worn. Autumn/ winter 2003 – the gesture of lifting the hem of a garment incorporated into their structure. Hemlines of shirts and dress are lifted and attached onto the garment – at the waistline or even the shoulder – creating a draping effect and often making their lining visible. Spring/summer 2005 – garments inspired by vintage dresses, skirts, men shirts etc. constructed to be worn shifted horizontally on the body. Evening dresses in bright colours look like short skirts with necklines and arms draped to one side of the skirt and the original skirt hanging to the opposite side. The neckline of a man's shirt becomes an armhole with the line of central buttons worn horizontally across the chest **What is your favourite piece from any of your collections?** Impossible to say – so many have their own place, importance and significance for us in our memory of our work and development **How would you describe your work?** A continuation and deepening of our creativity, technical experience, collaboration and craft **What's your ultimate goal?** Evolving while seeking out those new challenges that continue to stimulate us **What inspires you?** Integrity, attentiveness, conviction, individuality, patience, respect and courage **Can fashion still have a political ambition?** Garments, creativity, tradition and style, rather than fashion, will always touch on the human politic **Who do you have in mind when you design?** Not one person, male or female, in particular and more an overall, yet sometimes, specific attitude **Is the idea of creative collaboration important to you?** Yes, it is a lifeblood albeit not often easy! An individual creative point of view has often little to do with the democracy of a group in its collective expression! It is for this reason that individual conviction within a team often demands extra effort and the unremitting respect of which it is so, so worthy **Who has been the greatest influence on your career?** Those who support us and above all those who encourage us by taking what we produce into their lives, wardrobes and style **How have your own experiences affected your work as a designer?** We all here have another approach to this – yet, in the main – a constant questioning of our 'purpose' and our creative point of view. Our recognition that we have a constant responsibility to reassess and challenge ourselves in our work and lives together. That to evolve is to continue to breathe creatively **Which is more important in your work: the process or the product?** The process of course and the result! – As it hangs on the hanger and more so, on the body **Is designing difficult for you? If so, what drives you to continue?** Yes! The great liberty and stimulation which the expression of our creativity brings us. The fact that our creative expression touches and encourages others **Have you ever been influenced or moved by the reaction to your designs?** Constantly, thankfully **What's your definition of beauty?** The courage of honesty. Subjectivity. Integrity. Reality. Nature **What's your philosophy?** That the heart should and can always rule the head **What is the most important lesson you've learned?** That talent, in others and oneself, is to be cherished and nurtured. That a team is only as fast as its slowest member.

"Every single piece is a piece of my heart"
ANTONIO MARRAS + KENZO

Since 2003, Antonio Marras has been in the limelight as artistic director of womenswear for Kenzo – an appointment, perhaps, that reflects the sense of tradition that was so important to Kenzo Takada when he was designing his eponymous line. Although Marras' first collection under his own name was launched as recently as 1999, with 2002 seeing his first men's ready-to-wear collection, he is already established as an international designer in his own right. With his first collection under his own name launched in 1999 and his first menswear ready-to-wear collection in 2002, Marras was already established as an international designer in his own right. He remains firmly based in his native Sardinia, working with his extended family in Alghero, where the locality and culture have a strong influence on his design. It is here that Marras (born 1961) pulls together his cut-and-paste aesthetic. This is characterised by his high standard of craftsmanship (laborious and highly detailed embroidery), random destruction (holes burned in fine fabrics), extravagant brocades sitting cheek-by-jowl with an unfinished hem, deconstructed shapes with vintage fabrics and a wide repertoire of what Marras calls "mistreatments": tearing, matting, staining, encrusting with salt and so on. Marras takes this approach to its logical conclusion, creating a range of off-the-peg one-offs made from the material scraps saved in making his main line, the kind of scraps he grew up surrounded by in his father's fabrics shop. Lacking any formal training, it took a Rome-based entrepreneur to spot Marras' potential, allowing him to launch a career as a designer in 1988. That same year, he won the Contemporary Linen Prize for a wedding dress. In 2006, the Fondazione Pitti Discovery published the monograph 'Antonio Marras' and, to mark the decade, anniversary of the brand, the Fondazione Sandretto Re Rebaudengo of Turin hosted the photography exhibit 'Antonio Marras. Dieci anni dopo' (Antonio Marras. Ten Years Later). In May 2007, Marras was once again owner of the brand that bears his name and at the same time, he signed an agreement with Interfashion for the licensed production and marketing of a second line beginning with the autumn/winter 2008–2009 season. In September 2007, he licensed the prestigious Florentine company Gibò to produce and distribute his top men's and women's line.

Seit 2003 steht Antonio Marras als Artistic Director der Damenmode bei Kenzo im Rampenlicht – eine Besetzung, die vielleicht das Traditionsbewusstsein widerspiegelt, das Kenzo Takada so wichtig war, als er das nach ihm benannte Label gründete. Mit seiner ersten Kollektion unter eigenem Namen, die er 1999 präsentierte, und seiner ersten Pret-à-porter-Linie für Herren im Jahr 2002 etablierte Marras sich sofort als eigenständiger internationaler Designer. Seiner Heimat Sardinien bleibt er eng verbunden, und er arbeitet auch weiterhin mit Familienangehörigen in Alghero zusammen. Diese Region und ihre Kultur üben einen starken Einfluss auf seine Entwürfe aus. Der 1961 geborene Marras bezieht von dort seine Cut & Paste-Ästhetik. Diese ist wiederum geprägt von hohem handwerklichem Niveau (wie arbeitsintensive und äußerst detailreiche Stickereien), zufälliger Dekonstruktion (wie in kostbare Stoffe gebrannte Löcher), extravaganten Brokaten neben unfertigen Säumen, dekonstruierten Formen aus Vintage-Stoffen und einem großen Repertoire von „Mistreatments": reißen, mattieren, verflecken, mit Salz verkrusten usw. Marras führt seinen

Ansatz zu einer logischen Konsequenz und kreiert eine Reihe von Prêt-à-porter-Unikaten aus Materialresten, die beim Designen seiner Hauptlinie übrig bleiben. Das sind Reste, wie sie ihn in seiner Kindheit im Stoffgeschäft seines Vaters umgaben. Obwohl er keine traditionelle Ausbildung hat, erkannte ein römischer Unternehmer sein Potenzial und ermöglichte ihm 1988 den Beginn seiner Designerkarriere. Im selben Jahr gewann er den Contemporary Linen Prize für ein Hochzeitskleid. 2006 publizierte die Fondazione Pitti Discovery die Monografie „Antonio Marras". Die Fondazione Sandretto Re Rebaudengo in Turin präsentierte anlässlich des zehnjährigen Jubiläums der Marke die Foto-ausstellung „Antonio Marras. Dieci anni dopo" (Antonio Marras. Zehn Jahre später). Im Mai 2007 war Marras erneut Eigentümer des Labels, das seinen Namen trägt. Gleichzeitig unterschrieb er eine Vereinbarung mit Interfashion über die Produktion und Vermarktung einer Zweitlinie, beginnend mit der Herbst/Winterkollektion 2008/2009. Im September 2007 erteilte er der angesehenen Modefirma Gibò in Florenz die Lizenz zur Produktion und zum Vertrieb seiner Premiumlinien für Herren und Damen.

Depuis 2003, Antonio Marras occupe les feux de la rampe en tant que directeur artistique des lignes pour femme de Kenzo : un poste qui reflète sans doute le sens de la tradition auquel Kenzo Takada accordait tant d'importance quand il concevait lui-même sa ligne éponyme. Après avoir lancé sa propre griffe en 1999 et sa première collection de prêt-à-porter pour homme en 2002, Marras s'était déjà imposé comme un styliste international à part entière. Il refuse de quitter sa Sardaigne natale, travaillant avec sa grande famille à Alghero, village dont la culture influence considérablement ses créations. C'est là que Marras (né en 1961) élabore son esthétique du « couper/coller », caractérisée par son immense savoir-faire artisanal (broderies méticuleuses fourmillant de détails), une destruction aléatoire (trous brûlés dans des tissus de luxe), des brocarts extravagants côtoyant des ourlets non finis, des formes déconstruites coupées dans des tissus vintage et un vaste répertoire de ce que Marras appelle des « maltraitances » : déchirures, feutrage, taches, incrustations au sel, etc. Antonio Marras adopte cette approche jusqu'à sa conclusion logique, créant une palette de pièces uniques mais prêtes à porter, taillées dans les coupons de tissu qu'il récupère en créant sa ligne principale : le genre de chutes au milieu desquelles il a grandi dans le magasin de tissus de son père. C'est un entrepreneur romain qui détecte le premier tout le potentiel de Marras, l'aidant à se lancer dans une carrière de styliste en 1988, sans formation préalable. La même année, il remporte le prix Contemporary Linen pour une robe de mariée. En 2006, la Fondazione Pitti Discovery publie la monographie « Antonio Marras » et, pour célébrer les dix ans de la marque, la Fondazione Sandretto Re Rebaudengo de Turin accueille l'exposition de photos « Antonio Marras. Dieci anni dopo » (Antonio Marras. Dix Ans Après). En mai 2007, Marras redevient propriétaire de la marque qui porte son nom. Au même moment, il signe un contrat avec Interfashion pour la production et la commercialisation sous licence d'une seconde ligne dès la saison automne/hiver 2008-2009. En septembre 2007, il octroie une licence à la prestigieuse entreprise florentine Gibò pour produire et distribuer sa collection de luxe pour homme et pour femme.

JOSH SIMS

PHOTOGRAPHY MANUEL YASON STYLING CHRISTINE FORTUNE MODEL HIDETOSHI NAKATA JULY 2005

PHOTOGRAPHY MANUEL VASON. STYLING CHRISTINE FORTUNE. MODEL FRANCESCA PICCININI. JULY 2005.

PHOTOGRAPHY TYRONE LEBON. STYLING JUDY BLAME. MODEL ISA. JUNE/JULY 2009.

What are your signature designs? Uniqueness, character and soul. A big part of every Antonio Marras collection is made of customised vintage pieces or handmade pieces **What is your favourite piece from any of your collection?** I can't answer, as we say in Italy every single piece is 'piezze 'e cuore' (a piece of my heart). They all are beloved sons **How would you describe your work?** Great luck! I can do a job that sums up all my passions: cinema, literature, photography, art, etc. **What's your ultimate goal?** I always work for today, I never think

about tomorrow **What inspires you?** Everything and nothing: a word that a friend told me on the phone, my grandmother's photo, an old child's shoe found on a market **Can fashion still have a political ambition?** Yes, of course! Everything is politics: choose to wear a particular T-shirt, decide not to wear furs, broach certain matters. Deciding how to live is politics **Who do you have in mind when you design?** I don't think; I go into a kind of trance **Is the idea of creative collaboration important to you?** It's essential! **Who has been the greatest influence**

on your career? A very little big Sardinian artist aged 85. She's called Maria Lai **How have your own experiences affected your work as a designer?** To me, private and working experiences are one single thing, they influence each other, there are no bounds or limits between them **Which is more important in your work: the process or the product?** They are both important! Of course, creative process is much more stimulating, alluring, full of pains, doubts, hesitations and then determinations and passions. When the collection is ready and

everything is over, I'm already thinking about something else! **Is designing difficult for you? If so, what drives you to continue?** Yes, it's difficult, but it is the only thing I love to do! **Have you ever been influenced or moved by the reaction to your designs?** I don't think so! **What's your definition of beauty?** What did my son Efisio say when he was four years old? What is beautiful, is beauty **What's your philosophy?** If it has to be, let it be! That means, never half-measures **What is the most important lesson you've learned?** Never take something for granted.

"I represent something for women. I've built up trust with them and that's important"
STELLA MCCARTNEY

Stella McCartney's stratospheric success story has only a little to do with her fabulous connections. Born in 1971, she graduated from Central Saint Martins in 1995. Her final-year collection was snapped up by the biggest names in retail (including Browns and Bergdorf Goodman) and a mere two years later she got the top job as creative director at Chloé. In 2001, McCartney left Chloé and relaunched her own eponymous line, this time backed by the Gucci Group. The first Stella McCartney store opened in New York's Meatpacking District in 2002, followed a year later by additional shops in London and Los Angeles. 2004 she got a Designer of the Year award in London. Like her late mother, Linda, she is serious about animal rights and refuses to use leather or fur in any of her designs. She also received a Women of Courage Award for her work with cancer charities. Whether working on experimental projects (such as the collaboration with artist Gary Hume in 2002 to produce handmade T-shirts and dresses), designing costumes for Gwyneth Paltrow's action movie 'Sky Captain' (2004) or enjoying the mainstream success of her two perfumes, McCartney is forever working a new angle. Summer 2005 saw her latest project unveiled, a collection of keep-fit wear designed in conjunction with Adidas, with a special collection for H&M launched later the same year. that has successfully grown to incorporate running, gym, yoga, tennis, swimming, dance, golf and winter sports. In November 2005, Stella worked on a special one-off collection for H&M that sold out worldwide in record time, and for spring/summer 2006 collaborated with the artist Jeff Koons on printed dresses and miniature chrome bunny accessories. Today the Stella McCartney label includes a luxury organic skincare line, a stunning lingerie range and a limited-edition travel collection with LeSportsac. In 2007, Stella won the Elle Style Award for Best Designer of the Year and The British Style Award for Best Designer of the Year. The appreciation continued worldwide, with Stella receiving the Green Designer of the Year at the ACE Awards in New York.

Stella McCartneys kometenhafter Aufstieg hat nur wenig mit ihren fabelhaften Connections zu tun. Die 1971 geborene Designerin machte 1995 ihren Abschluss am Central Saint Martins. Bereits die Kollektion ihres letzten Studienjahres wurde von einigen der größten Einzelhändler (unter anderem Browns und Bergdorf Goodman) ins Sortiment genommen. Nur zwei Jahre später erhielt sie den Spitzenjob Creative Director bei Chloé. 2001 verließ McCartney Chloé und unternahm einen Relaunch des nach ihr benannten Labels, diesmal allerdings mit Unterstützung des Gucci-Konzerns. Der erste Stella McCartney-Laden eröffnete 2002 im New Yorker Meatpacking District, ein Jahr später folgten weitere Geschäfte in London und Los Angeles. 2004 wurde McCartney in London mit einem Designer of the Year Award ausgezeichnet. Wie ihre verstorbene Mutter Linda engagiert sie sich sehr für den Tierschutz und weigert sich, Leder oder Pelz in ihren Entwürfen zu verwenden. Für die Unterstützung von Initiativen zum Schutz vor Krebs erhielt sie einen Women of Courage Award. Gleichgültig, ob es sich um eher experimentelle Projekte handelt (wie 2002 die Zusammenarbeit mit dem Künstler Gary Hume, wo es um die Produktion handgefertigter T-Shirts und Kleider ging), um Gwyneth Paltrows Kostüme in dem Actionfilm „Sky Captain" (2004) oder um die Freude am breiten Erfolg ihres

Parfüms – McCartney tut immer alles aus einer neuen Perspektive. Im Sommer 2005 präsentierte sie gemeinsam mit Adidas eine Kollektion Fitnesskleidung, die dank ihres Erfolges inzwischen die Sportarten Laufen, Yoga, Tennis, Schwimmen, Tanzen, Golf sowie Wintersport umfasst. Im November 2005 legte Stella McCartney eine Sonderkollektion bei H&M vor, die weltweit in Rekordzeit ausverkauft war. Für Frühling/Sommer 2006 tat sie sich für bedruckte Kleider und Miniaccessoires aus Chrom in Häschengestalt mit dem Künstler Jeff Koons zusammen. Heute umfasst das Label Stella McCartney eine luxuriöse Naturkosmetik-Linie, eine aufregende Lingerie-Kollektion sowie eine Sonderkollektion Reisegepäck bei LeSportsac. 2007 erhielt die Designerin den Elle Style Award als Best Designer of the Year sowie den British Style Award als Best Designer of the Year. Anerkennung findet sie allerdings auch weltweit, etwa mit der Auszeichnung als Green Designer of the Year im Rahmen der ACE Awards in New York.

Contrairement à ce que l'on pourrait penser, la success story planétaire de Stella McCartney n'a pas grand chose à voir avec son fabuleux réseau de relations. Née en 1971, elle sort diplômée de Central Saint Martins en 1995. Sa collection de fin d'études est immédiatement raflée par les plus grands noms de la vente (tels que Browns et Bergdorf Goodman). A peine deux ans plus tard, elle devient directrice de la création chez Chloé. En 2001, Stella McCartney quitte Chloé pour relancer sa ligne éponyme, cette fois-ci avec le soutien du groupe Gucci. En 2002, la première boutique Stella McCartney ouvre ses portes à New York dans le Meatpacking District, suivie un an plus tard par d'autres boutiques à Londres et Los Angeles. En 2004, elle remporte le Designer of the Year Award à Londres. Comme sa mère Linda aujourd'hui décédée, elle s'engage très sérieusement dans la défense des droits des animaux et se refuse à utiliser du cuir ou de la fourrure. Son travail auprès des associations de lutte contre le cancer lui a également valu un Women of Courage Award. Qu'elle travaille sur des projets expérimentaux (comme sa collaboration en 2002 avec l'artiste Gary Hume pour produire des T-shirts et des robes cousus main), qu'elle dessine les costumes du film d'action de Gwyneth Paltrow «Capitaine Sky et le monde de demain» (2004) ou qu'elle profite de l'immense succès de son parfum, Stella McCartney ne se lasse jamais d'explorer de nouvelles approches. Elle dévoile son nouveau projet à l'été 2005, une collection de sportswear conçue avec Adidas qui s'est depuis développée avec tant de succès qu'elle inclut désormais des tenues de course à pied, de fitness, de yoga, de tennis, de natation, de danse, de golf et de sports d'hiver. En novembre 2005, Stella McCartney conçoit une collection éphémère pour H&M qui s'écoule dans le monde entier en un temps record, tandis que pour la saison printemps/été 2006, elle collabore avec l'artiste Jeff Koons sur des robes imprimées et de minuscules accessoires chromés en forme de lapin. Aujourd'hui, la marque Stella McCartney comprend une gamme de cosmétiques biologiques de luxe, une étonnante ligne de lingerie et une collection d'articles de voyage en édition limitée avec LeSportsac. Stella remporte en 2007 l'Elle Style Award de Best Designer of the Year et le British Style Award dans la même catégorie. Le reste du monde lui prouve aussi sa reconnaissance, Stella ayant été récompensée du prix de Green Designer of the Year aux ACE Awards à New York. TERRY NEWMAN

PORTRAIT MARY MCCARTNEY DONALD. PHOTOGRAPHY DONALD CHRISTIE. STYLING GIANNIE COLLI. MODEL CHRISTINA KRUSE. OCTOBER 2002

PHOTOGRAPHY ALASDAIR MCLELLAN STYLING SOPHIA NEOPHITOU-APOSTOLOU

PHOTOGRAPHY PIERRE BAILLY STYLING CATTY ROGERING MODEL HANNAH HOLMAN AT FORD

PHOTOGRAPHY YELENA YEMCHUK. STYLING SORAYA DAYANI. MODEL FANNI. APRIL 2003.

What are your signature designs? Sexy trousers! **What's your favourite piece from any of your collections?** I don't have one. I love them all. Is that allowed? **How would you describe your work?** It hopefully covers all facets of a woman: sexy, feminine, humorous, confident and fucking cool **What's your ultimate goal?** I'm in the process, hopefully, of achieving it. My ultimate goal is to be happy. If my company succeeds and that means I'm happy, or if it doesn't but I'm still happy, it's all for the good **What inspires you?** My mum **Who do you have in mind when you design?** Me and my friends **Can fashion still have a political ambition?** Sure it can. You can take it as seriously as you want, but fashion on a daily basis is always political because it's people expressing themselves **Is the idea of creative collaboration important to you?** I think that collaborating with people, doing limited editions and one-off pieces, is really exciting. I'm increasingly interested in trying to make individual, special pieces rather than mass-producing things **Who has been the greatest influence on your career?** Just the customer. The girls that I know who wear my clothes. Only the cool ones, of course **Which is more important in your work: the process or the product?** The product. Because if the process is brilliant but the product's shit... who cares? **Is designing difficult for you? If so, what drives you to continue?** If I'd settled for being a cliché of myself and just making tons of money, it'd be fine. I've taken an option that's a bit more difficult and I'm pushing myself. But I love it. And I do it for the genuine reason that I think I have a place in the industry. I have a role; I represent something for women. I've built up trust with them and I think that's important. And I keep doing it because I'm totally a fucking glutton for punishment and am trying to prove myself, though to God knows who **Have you ever been influenced or moved by the reaction to your designs?** I had an event at a store to meet my clients. This woman came in who was about 75 years old and she was so stylish. And she said to me, "Your clothes make me so happy". And she really meant it. She wasn't a fashion person. She was a client. And I just thought, that's what it's all about, that is really what it's all about for me. I never would have thought a 75-year-old woman would wear my clothes. And she was fucking cool. And that definitely moved me **What's your definition of beauty?** Inner peace **What's your philosophy?** Be true to yourself, believe in yourself and shine on **What is the most important lesson you've learned?** Do unto others as you would have them do unto you.

"There is still a lot I want to achieve. There isn't any room for complacency in this head!"
ALEXANDER MCQUEEN

The Gothic sensibility of a Brothers Grimm fairytale is closer in spirit to Alexander McQueen's clothing than the fetish, gore and misogyny he's been accused of promoting. However dark McQueen's design, it still achieves a femininity that has seduced everyone from Björk to the Duchess of Westminster. The East End taxi driver's son, born in 1969, was apprenticed to the Prince of Wales' tailor Anderson & Sheppard on Savile Row, where he infamously scrawled obscenities into the linings of HRH's suits. He worked with Romeo Gigli, theatrical costumers Angels & Bermans and Koji Tatsuno before Central Saint Martins MA course director Bobby Hilson suggested he enrol. His 1992 'Jack the Ripper' graduation collection thrilled members of the British fashion press, none more so than Isabella Blow who bought the entire collection and adopted McQueen as one of her protégés. McQueen's bloodline of angular, aggressive tailoring inherited from MGM costume designer Adrian, Christian Dior and Thierry Mugler. His 'Highland Rape' and 'The Birds' collections used Mr Pearl corsetry to draw in the waist and exaggerate square shoulders and sharp pencil skirts. By 1996, he was named British Designer of the Year. 1996 also saw McQueen replace John Galliano as head of Givenchy haute couture. But by 2001 the Gucci Group had acquired a controlling stake in McQueen's own label and the designer left both Givenchy and LVMH. Since then, McQueen's eponymous label has dazzled Paris with bittersweet theatrical presentations. 2003 saw the launch of his first perfume, Kingdom, and a bespoke menswear collection produced by Savile Row tailor Huntsman; in 2004, his men's ready-to-wear was shown in Milan for the first time followed by 'McQueen' in 2005. By 2006 he launched McQ – Alexander McQueen, which is a denim-based ready-to-wear for women and men. His autumn/winter 2009 womenswear show was celebrating his ten-year anniversary and dedicated to his mum. Models paraded around a funeral pyre art installation showing looks constructed from past collections.

Die Kleidung von Alexander McQueen entspricht in ihrem Geist eher dem schauerlichen Reiz eines Märchens der Gebrüder Grimm als dem Fetischcharakter, der Blutrünstigkeit und der Frauenfeindlichkeit, die man ihm vorwirft. Wie düster die Entwürfe McQueens auch sein mögen, er erzielt damit dennoch eine Weiblichkeit, die Frauen angefangen bei Björk und bis hin zur Herzogin von Westminster ansprach. Der Sohn eines Taxifahrers aus dem Londoner East End wurde 1969 geboren und absolvierte seine Lehre beim Schneider des Prince of Wales, Anderson & Sheppard, in der Savile Row. Dort kritzelte er heimlich Obszönitäten in das Futter der Anzüge Seiner Königlichen Hoheit. Anschließend arbeitete er mit Romeo Gigli sowie den Kostümbildnern Angels & Berman und Koji Tatsuno, bevor ihm der Leiter des Magisterstudienganges Bobby Hilson vorschlug, sich am Central Saint Martins zu immatrikulieren. Mit seiner Abschlusskollektion „Jack the Ripper" entzückte er 1992 die britische Modepresse wie auch Isabella Blow, die die gesamte Kollektion kaufte und McQueen als Protegé unter ihre Fittiche nahm. McQueens kantige, geradezu aggressive Form der Schneiderei hat ihre Wurzeln beim MGM-Kostümdesigner Adrian, bei Christian Dior und Thierry Mugler. Für seine Kollektionen „Highland Rape" und „The Birds" benutzte er Korsetts von Mr Pearl, um die Taillen zu verschmälern und so die eckigen Schultern wie auch die scharf geschnittenen Bleistiftröcke zu

betonen. 1996 wurde er British Designer of the Year und trat die Nachfolge von John Galliano als Chef der Haute Couture bei Givenchy an. 2001 hatte der Gucci-Konzern allerdings schon die Kontrollmehrheit an McQueens eigenem Label erworben, und so verließ der Designer Givenchy und LVMH. Seit damals hat McQueen mit dem nach ihm benannten Label Paris schon mehrfach mit bittersüßen, theatralischen Präsentationen verwirrt. 2003 wurde mit Kingdom sein erstes Parfüm lanciert. Seine erste Prêt-à-porter-Kollektion für Herren war 2004 in Mailand zu sehen. 2005 folgte „McQueen", und 2006 präsentierte der Designer McQ – Alexander McQueen, eine Prêt-à-porter-Linie für Damen und Herren mit Schwerpunkt Denim. Mit seiner Show anlässlich der Damenkollektion für Herbst/Winter 2009, die seiner Mama gewidmet war, feierte McQueen zugleich sein Zehnjähriges. Dabei defilierten die Models um eine Installation in Gestalt eines Scheiterhaufens und präsentierten Outfits, die aus vergangenen Kollektionen kombiniert waren.

Souvent accusé de faire la promotion du fétichisme, d'un certain côté gore et de la misogynie, la mode d'Alexander McQueen est pourtant plus proche de la sensibilité gothique d'un conte de Grimm. Quelle que soit l'importance du côté obscur de McQueen dans son travail, il propose toujours une féminité qui séduit le plus grand nombre, de Björk à la Duchesse de Westminster. Né en 1969 d'un père chauffeur de taxi dans l'East End, il commence son apprentissage à Savile Row chez Anderson & Sheppard, tailleurs du Prince de Galles, où l'on raconte qu'il gribouillait des obscénités dans les doublures des costumes de Son Altesse Royale. Il travaille ensuite avec Romeo Gigli, les costumiers de théâtre Angels & Bermans ainsi que pour Koji Tatsuno, avant de suivre un cursus à Central Saint Martins sur les conseils de Bobby Hilson, son directeur d'études. En 1992, sa collection de fin d'études « Jack the Ripper » ravit les journalistes de mode britanniques et en particulier Isabella Blow qui, en achetant l'intégralité de sa collection, fait entrer McQueen dans le cercle de ses protégés. Les coupes signature de McQueen, viscéralement angulaires et brutales, lui ont été inspirées par Adrian, costumier de la MGM, par Christian Dior et Thierry Mugler. Ses collections « Highland Rape » et « The Birds » utilisaient des corsets de Mr Pearl pour cintrer la taille et exagérer les épaules carrées et les jupes droites aux lignes sévères. En 1996, il remporte le prix de British Designer of the Year. La même année, il est nommé directeur de la création haute couture chez Givenchy, où il succède à John Galliano. Mais en 2001, le Groupe Gucci acquiert une part majoritaire dans la propre griffe du créateur, qui décide de quitter Givenchy et LVMH. Depuis, la griffe éponyme de McQueen ne cesse d'éblouir le tout-Paris à travers des présentations grandiloquentes au style doux-amer. En 2003, le créateur lance son premier parfum, Kingdom, sa ligne de prêt-à-porter pour homme à Milan en 2004, suivie par la collection « McQueen » en 2005. L'année suivante, il présente McQ-Alexander McQueen, du prêt-à-porter féminin et masculin tournant autour du denim. Dédiée à sa mère, sa collection pour femme automne/hiver 2009 célèbre les dix ans de sa griffe : dans des looks construits à partir d'anciennes collections, les mannequins paradent autour d'une installation artistique évoquant un bûcher funéraire. JAMES SHERWOOD

PORTRAIT DERRICK SANTINI   PHOTOGRAPHY TOSH   FASHION DIRECTOR EDWARD ENNINFUL   AND KIDS BY THE MOONLIGHT 1949

PHOTOGRAPHY EMMA SUMMERTON. FASHION DIRECTOR EDWARD ENNINFUL. MODEL CLAUDIA SCHIFFER. SEPTEMBER 2008.

PHOTOGRAPHY DAVID LACHAPELLE. STYLING PATTI WILSON. MODEL JAMIE BOCHERT. SEPTEMBER 2002.

PHOTOGRAPHY KAYT JONES. STYLING BELÉN CASADEVALL. MODEL LIBERTY ROSS. NOVEMBER 2002

PHOTOGRAPHY LARRY DUNSTAN. STYLING REBECCA QUGA. SEPTEMBER 2002.

What are your signature designs? Signature pieces include the bumster, the frock coat, anything trompe-l'œil **What is your favourite piece from any of your collections?** The wooden fan kilts from spring/summer 1999, the red slide dress from spring/summer 2001, the jellyfish dress from autumn/winter 2002 **How would you describe your work?** Electric, eccentric **What's your ultimate goal?** To offer haute couture pieces as an integral part of the ready-to-wear collection **What inspires you?** I find a multitude of influences inspiring – homeless to the rich, vulgar to the common **Can fashion still have a political ambition?** Because fashion is so indicative of the political and social

climate in which we live, what we wear will always be a symptom of our environment **Who do you have in mind when you design?** A strong, independent woman who loves and lives fearlessly in equal measure **Is the idea of creative collaboration important to you?** Collaborations give me the opportunity to work with peers who I admire, as well as pushing myself creatively. What's the point otherwise? **Who has been the greatest influence on your career?** Anyone I come into contact with and find a connection with **How have your own experiences affected your work as a designer?** Working with the atelier at Givenchy showed me the possibilities that only haute couture can give a designer,

where craftsmanship suddenly becomes state of the art **Which is more important in your work: the process or the product?** Design development allows you to make mistakes; without screwing up once in a while, you can't ever move forward **Is designing difficult for you? If so, what drives you to continue?** I enjoy putting the whole picture together – from the initial design phase to the shows and the stores. It's rewarding to see the entire concept work in unison. There is still a lot I want to achieve, my mind works very quickly and there isn't any room for complacency in this head! **Have you ever been influenced or moved by the reaction to your designs?** When I watched Shalom

Harlow being spray-painted as the finale of my spring/summer 2000 show, I was very moved. She was so poetic and elegant that I could hear the audience gasp – it really moved me to hear such an immediate reaction to my work **What's your definition of beauty?** An image that combines opposing or unusual aesthetics **What's your philosophy?** To make a piece that can transcend any trend and will still hold as much presence in 100 years' time, when you find it in an antique store, as when you bought it in my store yesterday **What is the most important lesson you've learned?** How trust really works.

"I grew up with my parents' work"
ANGELA MISSONI · MISSONI

With a history that spans over 50 years, the house of Missoni is that rare phenomenon in fashion, an enduring force to be reckoned with. Established in 1953 by Rosita and Ottavio Missoni, what began as a small knitwear factory following the traditional Italian handicraft techniques has evolved into a world-famous luxury label whose technical innovation and free-thinking approach have redefined notions of knitwear. A fateful meeting with Emmanuelle Khanh in Paris resulted in an important early collaboration and the first Missoni catwalk show took place in Florence, in 1967. By 1970, the Missoni fusion of organic fabrics, a mastery of colour and instantly recognisable motifs – stripes, zig-zags, Greek keys and space-dyed weaves – saw the house become the last word in laid-back luxury. The layered mismatching of pattern and colour, mainly in the form of slinky knits, has become synonymous with Missoni, inspiring the American press to describe the look as "put-together". Since taking over design duties in 1997, Angela Missoni has imaginatively updated the brand, introducing florals and even denim without losing the essence of classic Missoni. After working alongside her mother, Rosita, for 20 years, in 1993, Angela Missoni produced her own collection, becoming Missoni's overall creative director when her parents retired a few years later. Angela has subtly transformed the beguiling feminine looks of the Missoni archive with tailored lines and sassy slim-line silhouettes. Working with world-class photographers such as Mario Testino, Mario Sorrenti and Mert Alas & Marcus Piggott, today Missoni attracts a new generation of devotees whilst maintaining the kudos of cool it established during its '70s heyday. The brand also boasts a Missoni fragrance in conjunction with Estée Lauder, two hotels (Hotel Missoni), in Edinburgh and Kuwait, a children's collection, furniture line and flagship stores in New York, Paris and Tokyo. In October 2006, Rosita, Angela and Margherita received 'Glamour' magazine's 'Women of the Year' award, celebrating their joint contribution to the fashion industry and their own timeless style.

Mit seiner über 50-jährigen Geschichte ist das Modehaus Missoni eines der seltenen Phänomene der Branche: eine beständige Kraft, mit der man rechnen muss. Aus der 1953 von Rosita und Ottavio Missoni gemäß der italienischen Handwerkstradition gegründeten kleinen Strickwarenfabrik entwickelte sich ein weltberühmtes Luxuslabel, dessen technische Innovationen und freimütiger Ansatz die Wahrnehmung von Strickwaren neu definierte. Ein schicksalhaftes Treffen mit Emmanuelle Khanh in Paris führte zu einer wichtigen frühen Zusammenarbeit. Die erste Missoni-Kollektion wurde dann 1966 präsentiert. 1970 war Missoni dank der Verbindung von Naturmaterialien, dem meisterhaften Umgang mit Farbe und unverwechselbaren Motiven – Streifen, Zickzack, griechische Mäander – zum Inbegriff des legeren Luxus avanciert. Die Lagen aus eigentlich nicht zusammenpassenden Mustern und Farben, vornehmlich aus hautengem Strick, wurden zum Synonym für Missoni und von der amerikanischen Presse als „put-together" tituliert. Seit sie das Familienunternehmen 1997 von ihren Eltern übernahm, hat Angela Missoni die Marke fantasievoll aktualisiert, etwa durch die Einführung von floralen Mustern und sogar Denim, ohne darüber den klassischen Missoni-Stil zu vernachlässigen. Nachdem sie 20 Jahre lang an der Seite ihrer Mutter Rosita gearbeitet hatte, produzierte Angela

Missoni 1993 ihre erste eigene Kollektion. Damit war der Weg zum Creative Director der Firma vorgezeichnet, als ihre Eltern sich einige Jahre später aus dem Geschäft zurückzogen. Angela Missoni transformiert auf subtile Weise die betörend femininen Looks aus dem Missoni-Archiv durch tadellos gearbeitete Linien und schicke, schmale Silhouetten. Dank der Zusammenarbeit mit Weltklassefotografen wie Mario Testino, Mario Sorrenti und Mert Alas & Marcus Piggott spricht Missoni heute eine neue Generation von Fans an, während man sich zugleich den in den 70ern erworbenen Ruhm bewahrt hat. Sehr erfolgreich ist die Marke auch mit einem Missoni-Duft bei Estée Lauder, zwei Hotels unter eigenem Namen in Edinburgh und Kuwait, einer Kinderkollektion, einer Möbellinie sowie Flagship-Stores in New York, Paris und Tokio. Im Oktober 2006 wurden Rosita, Angela und Margherita Missoni mit dem Preis Women of the Year der Zeitschrift Glamour für ihre gemeinsamen Verdienste um die Modebranche und für ihren persönlichen zeitlosen Stil geehrt.

Avec plus d'un demi-siècle d'histoire, la maison Missoni est un phénomène rare dans la mode, une force endurante absolument incontournable. Créée en 1953 par Rosita et Ottavio Missoni, ce qui a commencé avec une petite manufacture de tricot respectant les techniques artisanales italiennes traditionnelles s'est transformée en une griffe de luxe mondialement connue et dont l'innovation technique et la libre pensée ont redéfini la notion même de maille. Le destin de la petite maison est scellé lors d'une réunion fatidique avec Emmanuelle Khanh à Paris, première collaboration importante qui voit naître la première collection Missoni en 1966. En 1970, la fusion typique de Missoni entre tissus naturels, maîtrise de la couleur et motifs immédiatement identifiables (rayures, zigzags, motifs grecs et tissus à fils teints par zone) voit la griffe occuper l'avant-garde du luxe décontracté. A travers l'utilisation de tricots moulants, les superpositions de motifs et de couleurs dépareillés sont devenues synonymes de Missoni, incitant la presse américaine à qualifier ce look de « put-together ». Depuis qu'elle a repris l'affaire familiale de ses parents en 1997, Angela Missoni modernise la marque avec imagination, introduisant les motifs floraux et même le denim sans pourtant perdre de vue le style Missoni des origines. Après avoir travaillé pendant 20 ans aux côtés de sa mère Rosita, Angela Missoni produit en 1993 sa propre collection, une expérience bienvenue pour devenir directrice de la création de Missoni, lorsque ses parents prendront leur retraite quelques années plus tard. Angela Missoni transforme avec subtilité les looks étonnamment féminins des archives Missoni à travers de nouvelles coupes et des silhouettes élancées plutôt branchées. Avec des photographes mondialement célèbres comme Mario Testino, Mario Sorrenti et Mert Alas & Marcus Piggott, Missoni attire aujourd'hui une nouvelle génération de fans tout en préservant le côté cool qui a fait l'âge d'or de la marque dans les années 70. La marque a aussi lancé un parfum Missoni conçu en collaboration avec Estée Lauder, une collection pour enfant et une gamme de mobilier. De plus, elle a ouvert deux hôtels (Hotel Missoni) à Edinburgh et au Koweït, et possède des boutiques à New York, Paris et Tokyo. En octobre 2006, Rosita, Angela et Margherita ont reçu le prix de « Women of the Year » du magazine Glamour qui récompensait leur contribution à l'industrie de la mode et leur propre style intemporel.

AIMEE FARRELL

PHOTOGRAPHY ALEX HOERNER. STYLING GEORGE KOTSIOPOULOS. MODEL MICHELE HICKS. MARCH 2004.

What are your signature designs? Knit design: with fringes, bias-cuts, applications, inserts **What is your favourite piece from any of your collections?** My favourite changes all the time. I don't look back. In the spring/summer 2005 collection, I like the bouquet print lace dress with cream background, tulle inserts with raspberry knit ribbon edging **How would you describe your work?** It needs a 360° attention. I see it as a never-ending commitment **What's your ultimate goal?** I always look for perfection. So, until my last day at work, perfection will be my ultimate goal. Which is also why I dream to step out of the fashion business in five, six years… at that point, I would finally have time for myself **What inspires you?** Many different things, nothing especially. It can be a trip, a walk in town, a work of contemporary art, a classic or recent movie, the way one of my friends or one of my daughters put some pieces, shapes, colours together when they dress up. What mostly inspires me is the way they interpret and reinterpret the clothes I design. How they mix them with clothes they already have in their wardrobe, vintage pieces and other designers' clothes. How they express their personality. I guess I am trying to always have a type of natural attitude in mind when I think of a collection. A certain fresh, spontaneous way of being elegant… **Can fashion still have a political ambition?** Fashion is mirroring women's condition, it talks of the freedom most women have on this planet. It is a medium of expression and a channel of communication: the authority of fashion brands can be used to bring to the public attention crucial problems of our culture and society, to raise funds and to increase public participation **Who do you have in mind when you design?** My daughter Margherita is not my muse, but I often have a type like her in mind when I design. I look for a fresh, natural concept of elegance **Is the idea of creative collaboration important to you?** Absolutely, I don't like to be by myself. Talking, sharing and discussing ideas is quite necessary to me: I always work together with other people, the crew of my collaborators and assistants and occasionally some friends **Who has been the greatest influence on your career?** My mother especially. I have learnt my work by watching and then assisting her for years **How have your own experiences affected your work as a designer?** I grew up together with my parents' work: my personal experiences are therefore definitely, strictly connected with fashion design. That creative mood, that meeting of interesting people, that watching and listening to what my parents were doing, has certainly shaped me **Which is more important in your work: the process or the product?** They are strictly connected. I find both aspects very important and creative. I like to follow and control the entire process **Have you ever been influenced or moved by the reaction to your designs?** The public's positive reaction is always important and flattering. But I don't think it ever influences my next decisions in terms of design. I like to move forward **What's your definition of beauty?** The autumn sunsets' range of reds, oranges and pinks I can see in the landscape out of my window **What's your philosophy?** Practice. Improvement **What is the most important lesson you've learned?** I always feel I haven't learnt enough.

"My ultimate goal is to build a fashion house that outlives me"
ROLAND MOURET

When Roland Mouret (born 1961) set up his label in 1998, he was no newcomer to fashion. Then aged 36, the butcher's son from Lourdes had previous experience as a model, art director and stylist in Paris and London. While Jean Paul Gaultier, Paris 'Glamour' and i-D are namechecked on his stylist CV, he had little experience of making clothes, with only two years at fledgling label People Corporation under his belt. His first collection of 15 one-off pieces obviated the need for patterns. Instead, the critically acclaimed garments were put together using skilful draping and strategically placed hatpins. While his method may have become more refined with subsequent collections, Mouret's motto remains the same: "It all starts from a square of fabric." Inspired by folds, Mouret makes staggeringly beautiful clothes with the minimum of fuss. This formula has been hugely successful. His label is stocked all over the world in high-profile stores, including Harrods and Bergdorf Goodman. As well as the clothing line, it now includes rough diamond jewellery line RM Rough and the recently introduced cruise collection. Since 2003, the London-based designer has chosen to show in New York and this move has seen more Mouret on the red carpet. The fashion world is just as devoted as his celebrity clientele. Mouret's work has been acknowledged with a Vidal Sassoon Cutting Edge award and the Elle Style Awards named him British Designer of the Year in 2002. At the beginning of 2006, Roland Mouret left his company Roland Mouret Designs Ltd. and entered a new partnership later in the year with Simon Fuller's 19 Entertainment. His newly launched RM satellite collection was presented off schedule during haute couture in July 2007. A new collection – RM Bespoke Limited Edition – was next introduced in October 2008.

Als der 1961 geborene Roland Mouret 1998 sein Label gründete, war er in der Mode längst kein Newcomer mehr. Der damals 36-jährige Metzgerssohn aus Lourdes hatte bereits Erfahrungen als Model, Art Director und Stylist in Paris und London gesammelt. Während Jean Paul Gaultier, Paris Glamour und i-D in seiner Stylisten-Vita auftauchten, hatte er mit lediglich zwei Jahren beim Anfänger-Label People Corporation wenig Erfahrung in der Produktion von Kleidern. Bei seiner ersten Kollektion, die aus 15 Unikaten bestand, scherte er sich überhaupt nicht um Schnittmuster. Stattdessen wurden die von der Kritik hoch gelobten Kleider durch kunstvolle Drapierungen und strategisch platzierte Hutnadeln zusammengehalten. Und auch wenn sich seine Methoden in den folgenden Kol-

lektionen etwas verfeinert haben, bleibt Mourets Motto doch unverändert: „Alles beginnt mit einem quadratischen Stück Stoff." Von der Faltkunst animiert, erzeugt der Designer mit minimalem Aufwand umwerfend schöne Kleider. Diese Formel erwies sich als überaus erfolgreich. Die Modewelt verehrt ihn ebenso wie seine prominente Klientel. Seine Arbeit wurde bereits mit dem Vidal Sassoon Cutting Edge Award ausgezeichnet. Bei den Elle Style Awards war er 2002 British Designer of the Year. 2006 verließ Mouret sein Unternehmen Roland Mouret Designs Ltd. und ging eine Partnerschaft mit Simon Fullers 19 Entertainment ein. Seine neu dazugekommene Nebenkollektion RM wurde außerhalb des offiziellen Kalenders im Rahmen der Haute Couture im Juli 2007 vorgestellt. Im Oktober 2008 folgte mit RM Bespoke Limited Edition die nächste neue Kollektion.

Quand Roland Mouret (né en 1961) lance sa griffe en 1998, ce n'est déjà plus un débutant. Alors âgé de 36 ans, ce fils de boucher venu de Lourdes a déjà travaillé comme mannequin, directeur artistique et styliste à Paris et à Londres. Bien que Jean Paul Gaultier, le Glamour français et le magazine i-D figurent sur son CV de styliste, il ne possède pratiquement aucune expérience de la création de mode, avec seulement deux années de travail pour la bébé griffe People Corporation à son actif. Composée de 15 pièces uniques, sa première collection prouve qu'on peut créer des vêtements sans utiliser de patrons. En fait, ces pièces saluées par la critique sont assemblées à l'aide de drapés experts et d'épingles à chapeau stratégiquement placées. Bien qu'il ait affiné sa méthode au fil des collections, la devise de Mouret reste la même : « Tout commence à partir d'un carré de tissu. » Inspiré par les plis, Mouret propose des vêtements d'une beauté renversante et pourtant extrêmement simples, une formule qui s'avère largement gagnante. Et l'univers de la mode lui est tout aussi dévoué que ses célèbres clientes : son travail a été honoré d'un prix Vidal Sassoon Cutting Edge et les Elle Style Awards l'ont couronné British Designer of the Year en 2002. Début 2006, il ferme son entreprise Roland Mouret Designs Ltd. et conclut la même année un nouveau partenariat avec la société de production 19 Entertainment de Simon Fuller. Son tout dernier projet satellite, RM, a été présenté en marge des défilés haute couture en juillet 2007, avant le lancement de la nouvelle collection RM Bespoke Limited Edition en octobre 2008.

LAUREN COCHRANE

What are your signature designs? Draping, folding and the sensual relationship between fabric and the skin **How would you describe your work?** It is a necessity for me **What's your ultimate goal?** To build a fashion house that outlives me **What inspires you?** People's strengths and weaknesses **Can fashion still have a political ambition?** For me, fashion is more about social politics than a political ambition **Who do you have in mind when you design?** Skin, movement and memories **Is the idea of creative collaboration important to you?** Yes, because it challenges my own perceptions **Who has been the greatest influence on your career?** Many women and few men – from my grandmother, who first placed a needle in my hand, to my business partner, who allowed me to be not just a dressmaker **How have your own experiences affected your work as a designer?** My work allows me to provide without words the answers to my childhood questions **Which is more important in your work: the process or the product?** It is a bitter sweet relationship – you can't love without the reality of pain **Is designing difficult for you? If so, what drives you to continue**? Ask the same question to an athlete – yes, of course it is, but you have to continue, the way you have to keep breathing **Have you ever been influenced or moved by the reaction to your designs?** It's always emotional when my vision becomes part of the public domain **What's your definition of beauty?** Imperfect, unique, a raw diamond **What's your philosophy?** You are a good master when you are a good slave **What is the most important lesson you've learned?** Time needs time.

"The process and the product are completely intertwined in terms of our collections"
KATE & LAURA MULLEAVY · RODARTE

"And the winners are: Rodarte." In Zurich, November 2008, Kate and Laura Mulleavy won the prestigious Swiss Textile Award and a much needed injection of cash. Kate and Laura have been familiar names on the fashion awards nominations roster in the last few years: Ecco Domani Fashion Foundation Award (2005), nominated for CFDA Swarovski Emerging Womenswear Designer award (2006 and 2007), runner-up in the CFDA/Vogue Fashion Fund (2006) and winner of CFDA Swarovski Emerging Womenswear Designer award (2008). The two sisters, born in 1979 (Kate) and 1980 (Laura), grew up with unconventional parents in the post-hippie paradise of Santa Cruz, California, before studying liberal arts at the University of California, Berkeley. After graduation, the sisters moved back to their parents' home in Pasadena, where they founded Rodarte – named after their mother's Mexican maiden name. When 'American Vogue' editor Anna Wintour spotted their special talents in a Woman Wear Daily feature, the girls were airlifted to New York and presented their first runway collection in 2005, which was an instant success. Buyers from Barneys in New York to Colette in Paris were among the first support team. Their special mix of theatrical and cinematic fabrics, colours and artisan techniques combined with a naïve, almost amateur enthusiasm has created their own personal fan club. Somewhere between sci-fi salvage and culture, each collection launches a wave of copycats, which may amount to some idea of flattery. The sisters' confidence is growing with every accolade, opening up their shyness and opportunities to expand their international clientele. Their collection is currently available at over 40 of the world's premier fashion outlets.

„Und die Gewinner sind: Rodarte." In Zürich gewannen im November 2008 Kate und Laura Mulleavy den angesehenen Swiss Textile Award und die damit verbundene, dringend benötigte Finanzspritze. Die beiden waren in den letzten paar Jahren aber auch schon auf zahlreichen Nominierungslisten für Modepreise vertreten: Ecco Domani Fashion Foundation Award (2005), CFDA Swarovski Emerging Womenswear Designer Award (2006 und 2007), Zweitplatzierte beim CFDA/Vogue Fashion Fund (2006) und Gewinner des CFDA Swarovski Emerging Womenswear Designer Award (2008). Die beiden 1979 (Kate) und 1980 (Laura) geborenen Schwestern wuchsen im kalifornischen Post-Hippie-Paradies Santa Cruz auf, bevor sie an der University of California, Berkeley, Kunst studierten. Nach ihrem Abschluss zogen die beiden zurück in das Haus ihrer Eltern in Pasadena, wo sie Rodarte gründeten, das nach dem Mädchennamen ihrer mexikanischen Mutter benannt ist. Als die Herausgeberin der amerikanischen Vogue, Anna Wintour, durch ein Feature in ‚Woman Wear Daily' auf ihre herausragenden Talente aufmerksam wurde, ließ sie die Mädchen postwendend nach New York einfliegen. Ihre erste Catwalk-Kollektion 2005 war auf Anhieb ein Erfolg. Einkäufer von Barneys in New York und Colette in Paris zählten zu ihren ersten Förderern. Die besondere Mischung aus Materialien, Farben und handwerklicher Technik, die man üblicherweise für Theater- und Filmkostüme verwendet, kombiniert mit einer naiven, geradezu amateurhaften Begeisterung, hat den beiden Designerinnen einen ganz eigenen Fanclub beschert. Irgendwo zwischen Science-Fiction-Zweitverwertung und Hochkultur angesiedelt, sorgt jede Kollektion für eine Welle von Nachahmungen, die man ja durchaus als Kompliment verstehen kann. Mit jeder Auszeichnung wächst das Selbstvertrauen der Schwestern, die ihre Schüchternheit ablegen und zunehmend Gelegenheit zur Expansion auf dem internationalen Markt finden. Gegenwärtig ist ihre Kollektion in über 40 der besten Fashion Outlets überall auf der Welt verfügbar.

« Et le gagnant est : Rodarte ! » En novembre 2008 à Zurich, Kate et Laura Mulleavy ont remporté le prestigieux Swiss Textile Award, assorti d'une injection de cash dont elles avaient grand besoin. Ces dernières années, on a souvent entendu leurs noms dans les annonces de nominations aux prix de mode : Ecco Domani Fashion Foundation Award (2005), Swarovski Emerging Womenswear Designer Award du CFDA (en 2006 et 2007), finalistes du CFDA/Vogue Fashion Fund (2006) et lauréates du Swarovski Emerging Womenswear Designer du CFDA (2008). Nées en 1979 (Kate) et 1980 (Laura), les deux sœurs sont élevées par des parents anticonformistes dans le paradis californien post-hippie de Santa Cruz, puis suivent des études d'art à l'Université de Californie, Berkeley. Une fois diplômées, elles rentrent chez leurs parents à Pasadena, où elles créent leur griffe, baptisée Rodarte d'après le nom de jeune fille mexicain de leur mère. Quand Anna Wintour, rédactrice en chef du Vogue américain, repère leurs talents si particuliers dans un dossier de Woman Wear Daily, les filles gagnent leurs billets d'avion pour New York et présentent en 2005 une collection qui remporte un succès immédiat. Leurs supporters de la première heure incluent les acheteurs de Barneys à New York comme ceux de Colette à Paris. Leur mélange étonnant entre tissus de théâtre et de cinéma, couleurs et techniques artisanales, conjugué à leur enthousiasme naïf, voire amateur, leur vaut un véritable fan-club. A mi-chemin entre la récup' et la culture sci-fi, chaque collection déclenche une vague de copies, ce qui, dans une certaine mesure, est assez flatteur. A chaque témoignage de reconnaissance, les sœurs prennent davantage confiance en elles, sortent de leur coquille et saisissent toutes les chances d'étendre leur clientèle internationale. Leurs créations sont actuellement distribuées par plus de 40 enseignes de prestige dans le monde entier. TERRY JONES

PHOTOGRAPHY SØLVE SUNDSBØ. FASHION DIRECTOR EDWARD ENNINFUL. MODEL AGYNESS DEYN. MARCH 2009.

What are your signature designs? Our tulle draped dresses and spidery knits **How would you describe your work?** Delicate and transgressive **What's your ultimate goal?** To develop our aesthetic fully and conceptually **What inspires you?** Our early memories of California's redwood forests, orange poppies, tide pools, skater kids in Santa Cruz, surfers, Hare Krishnas, and Oakland punks **Can fashion still have a political ambition?** All forms of expression are political **Who do you have in mind when you design?** We design in terms of the inspiration that we are feeling at that moment. We never think of anyone specifically. Our last show was based off of Gordon Matta Clark's deconstructed homes and Frankenstein. The collection explored the process of building, ruin, and preservation **Is the idea of creative collaboration important to you?** Every aspect of our design process is a collaboration between Laura and I and the people that we work with **Who has been the greatest influence on your career?** Each other **How have your own experiences affected your work as designer?** We design from a personal place so in many ways everything is connected to us **Which is more important in your work: the process or the product?** The process and the product are completely intertwined **Is designing difficult for you? If so, what drives you to continue?** We love making clothes. **What's your definition of beauty?** Ballerinas and 'The Texas Chainsaw Massacre' **What's your philosophy?** Save the Polar Bears **What is the most important lesson you've learned?** To create with freedom.

"Both the process and the product are important. In a way, the process forms the product's soul"
RICHARD NICOLL

Richard Nicoll was born in London in 1977 to New Zealander parents. From the age of three, Nicoll grew up in the Australian city of Perth, where his ophthalmologist father raised him and his older sister. On leaving school, Nicoll returned to London and enrolled at Central Saint Martins, where he completed a BA in menswear. A brief period of hectic creativity ensued with Nicoll selling his own T-shirts through Paris store Colette and assisting the stylist Camille Bidault-Waddington. It was at this time that he first began collaborating on projects with i-D photographer Jason Evans, a partnership that remains intact to this day. (Evans produced a photographic slide show for Nicoll's spring/summer 2005 collection as part of London Fashion Week's Fashion East group show for new talent). In 2002, he completed and gained an MA in womenswear, back at Central Saint Martins; Italian design duo Dolce & Gabbana bought Nicoll's final collection and, following graduation, the young designer was awarded a bursary that enabled him to establish his own label. To date, Nicoll has shown twice as part of Fashion East (October 2004 and February 2005) and also during Osaka Fashion Week in Japan. Nicoll seems equally adept at fine drapery – as in his Madame Grès-inspired spring/summer 2005 collection – as he is at sophisticated tailoring, using Perspex and wood for unusual details. Print, too, is emerging as a bold design signature for this promising designer, lending his work an energetic Pop Art slant. Nicoll has progressively developed his personal style, winning the Fashion Forward award for the second time in 2007. His graphic simplicity combined with overt sexuality has increased his stockists worldwide. For autumn/winter 2009, Nicoll dived into the closet and incorporated corsetry, elastic and suspenders into the collection that combined with the classic gumshoe trenchcoat – from flesh tone to flasher mac and British tongue in cheek.

Richard Nicoll wurde 1977 als Kind neuseeländischer Eltern in London geboren. Ab seinem dritten Lebensjahr wuchs er mit seiner älteren Schwester bei seinem Vater, einem Augenarzt, im australischen Perth auf. Nachdem er die Schule beendet hatte, zog Nicoll zurück nach London und immatrikulierte sich am Central Saint Martins, wo er einen Bachelor im Fach Herrenmode erwarb. Darauf folgte eine kurze Phase hektischer Kreativität, in der Nicoll seine eigenen T-Shirts über das Pariser Kaufhaus Colette vertrieb und der Stylistin Camille Bidault-Waddington assistierte. Zu jener Zeit begann auch die projektbezogene Zusammenarbeit mit dem i-D-Fotografen Jason Evans, die bis heute andauert. (Evans produzierte eine Diaschau für Nicolls Kollektion Frühjahr/Sommer 2005, die bei der London Fashion Week im Rahmen von Fashion East, der Gruppenschau für neue Talente, gezeigt wurde.) 2002 machte Nicoll – wiederum am Central Saint Martins – noch seinen Master in Damenmode. Das italienische Designerduo Dolce & Gabbana kaufte seine Abschlusskollektion. Nach bestandenem Studium erhielt der Jungdesigner ein Stipendium, das es ihm ermöglichte, sein eigenes Label zu gründen. Nicoll hat bereits zweimal im Rahmen von Fashion East präsentiert (im Oktober 2004 und im Februar 2005) sowie bei der Osaka Fashion Week in Japan. Er scheint in der feinen Draperie – zu sehen in seiner von Madame Grès inspirierten Kollektion Frühjahr/Sommer 2005 – ebenso bewandert wie in der raffinierten Maßschneiderei, wo er Perspex und Holz für außergewöhnliche Details benutzt. Ein weiteres Markenzeichen dieses viel versprechenden Designers sind kräftige Muster, die seinen Arbeiten einen deutlichen Touch Pop-Art verleihen. Nicoll hat schrittweise seinen ganz eigenen Stil entwickelt und damit 2007 zum zweiten Mal den Fashion Forward Award gewonnen. Grafisch schlicht in Kombination mit explizit sexy – damit hat er sich Vertriebswege in alle Welt eröffnet. Für Herbst/Winter 2009 hat Nicoll tief im Kleiderschrank gegraben und Korsagen, elastische Bänder und Strapse in einer Kollektion gemixt, zu der auch der klassische Detektiv-Trenchcoat gehört – vom Hautfarbenen zum Exhibitionistenmantel also, und das mit britischer Ironie.

Richard Nicoll est né en 1977 à Londres de parents néo-zélandais. Dès l'âge de trois ans, il grandit dans la ville australienne de Perth auprès de son père ophtalmologiste et de sa grande sœur. Après le lycée, Nicoll revient à Londres pour étudier à Central Saint Martins, où il obtient un BA en mode masculine. S'ensuit une brève période de créativité mouvementée pendant laquelle Richard Nicoll vend ses T-shirts via la boutique parisienne Colette et assiste la styliste Camille Bidault-Waddington. C'est à cette époque qu'il commence à collaborer avec le photographe d'i-D Jason Evans, un partenariat toujours d'actualité (Evans a produit un diaporama photographique pour la collection printemps/été 2005 de Nicoll dans le cadre de l'exposition de groupe Fashion East dédiée aux nouveaux talents au cours de la London Fashion Week). En 2002, il décroche un MA en mode féminine de Central Saint Martins avec une collection de fin d'études achetée par le duo italien Dolce & Gabbana. Après l'obtention de son diplôme, le jeune créateur se voit remettre une bourse qui lui permet de fonder sa propre griffe. Richard Nicoll a effectué deux présentations dans le cadre de Fashion East (octobre 2004 et février 2005) et participé à la Semaine de la Mode d'Osaka au Japon. Il semble tout aussi adepte des beaux drapés, comme en témoigne sa collection printemps/été 2005 inspirée par Madame Grès, que des coupes sophistiquées, utilisant du Perspex et du bois pour créer des détails insolites. Les imprimés émergent également comme l'une des signatures audacieuses de ce couturier prometteur et confèrent à son travail un côté Pop Art plein d'énergie. Richard Nicoll a progressivement développé son propre style, couronné du Fashion Forward Award pour la seconde fois en 2007. Sa simplicité graphique et son sex-appeal assumé n'ont fait qu'augmenter le nombre de ses distributeurs à travers le monde. Pour l'automne/hiver 2009, Nicoll plonge dans ses placards pour associer corseterie, rubans élastiques et bretelles dans une collection qui fait aussi la part belle à l'indémodable trenchcoat de détective : entre couleur chair et imperméable d'exhibitionniste, c'est le triomphe du second degré à l'anglaise.

DAVID LAMB

What are your signature designs? I think it is too early for me to have formed any signatures, but I have been exploring a technique of twisting and knotting fabric around the body, most recently with the addition of outsized beads **What is your favourite piece from any of your collections?** It is a dress from my MA collection that was used by my friend Thom Murphy in a Dizzie Rascal video. It was pretty weird but oddly attractive and sexy. It's a salmon-coloured wool jersey stretch dress with engineered cut-outs and a stretch chiffon lining in tangerine with grey chiffon bloomers attached **How would you describe your work?** It is a bit like my best friend and my worst enemy at the same time **What's your ultimate goal?** Continued happiness **What inspires you?** My friends and an ideal of obtainable Utopia **Can fashion still have a political ambition?** Of course, but I think it falls on deaf ears. Maybe to have a social conscience is not really in harmony with the essence of the fashion industry **Who do you have in mind when you design?** I always start with a mood that reflects the way that I'm feeling at the time and apply it to my ideal subject, which is basically a hybrid of three of my friends **Is the idea of creative collaboration important to you?** I love collaborating because it keeps the work fresh and it's always more fun. You learn a lot about the essence of creativity from collaborating **Who has been the greatest influence on your career?** Well I'm pretty inspired by anyone who has the courage to make original work with conviction and can retain a strong sense of humility and consideration for other people (I like Issey Miyake's and Jil Sander's approach) **How have your own experiences affected your work as a designer?** It's impossible to say **Which is more important in your work: the process or the product?** They are both important but, at the end of the day, the life of the product only really begins when the process is finished. In a way the process forms the product's soul **Is designing difficult for you? If so, what drives you to continue?** Sometimes it is really difficult and sometimes it is easy, but I think that if you are a designer, you don't have a choice, it is fundamentally part of you **Have you ever been influenced or moved by the reaction to your designs?** Well, it's obviously encouraging if people like what you do **What's your definition of beauty?** Happiness **What's your philosophy?** To deal with the fundamental elements of life and to try to instil those into a product that reflects a purity of design **What is the most important lesson you've learned?** Not to take life too seriously and to treat other people well.

"Ape shall never kill Ape"
NIGO • A BATHING APE

Nigo is the independent entrepreneur, businessman, graphic designer, figurehead, president, CEO of Tokyo-based clothing brand A Bathing Ape. Named after the 1968 film 'Planet of the Apes', the name 'BAPE' is short for 'A Bathing Ape In Lukewarm Water'. BAPE is a modern lifestyle brand with its own hair salon, kids store, café, TV channel, music store and wrestling franchise in Japan. By producing high-end, well-designed luxurious apparel (all in extremely limited quantities), Nigo single-handedly revolutionised streetwear. Nigo (or Tomoaki Nagao, as he was then known) moved to Tokyo to study fashion journalism at the world-renowned Bunka Fukuso Gakuin fashion college and with his best friend Jonio (Jun Takahashi from Undercover) became two prominent 'cool hunters' on the scene and soon launched their own store named Nowhere, which sold their Undercover and A Bathing Ape brands and which has since been relaunched as a Pop Up Shop in Rei Kawakubo's Dover Street Market in London. Items were so exclusive that people were soon queuing up round the block to secure their chosen piece. Standalone BAPE stores followed, with neon signing, moving conveyor belts, BAPE camo, plastic and chrome fittings being their futuristic retail experience. Soon BAPE expanded into Nagoya and Osaka before launching overseas with the Busy Workshop opening in London in 2001. Bape now has 22 stores worldwide including Japan, Hong Kong, London, New York, Taipei and Los Angeles and Nigo has joint ownership of Billionaire Boys Club with Pharrell Williams. His continued re-appropriation of classic items and Americana, from jackets to jeans, hoodies to tees, is considered with the highest care and the utmost love and attention. By keeping their taste levels at the highest, impeccable standards, by never advertising the brand, by shying of paid celebrity endorsement, Nigo has kept interest in his brand on the ever ascendant whilst being championed by leading musical talents.

Nigo ist der unabhängige Entrepreneur, Geschäftsmann, Grafikdesigner, Aushängeschild, Präsident und CEO des Textillabels A Bathing Ape mit Sitz in Tokio. Benannt nach dem Film „Planet der Affen" von 1968 ist BAPE eigentlich die Abkürzung für ‚A Bathing Ape In Lukewarm Water'. BAPE ist eine moderne Lifestyle-Marke mit eigenem Friseursalon, Kinderboutique, Café, TV-Kanal, Musikladen und Wrestling-Lizenz in Japan. Mit der Produktion von gut designter Luxuskleidung (stets in extrem begrenzter Stückzahl) hat Nigo im Alleingang die Streetwear revolutioniert. Nigo (oder Tomoaki Nagao, wie er damals noch hieß) war ursprünglich nach Tokio gekommen, um an der weltberühmten Mode-Uni Bunka Fukuso Gakuin Modejournalismus zu studieren und wurde gemeinsam mit seinem besten Freund Jonio (Jun Takahashi von Undercover) zum prominenten „Cool Hunter" der Szene. Bald machten die beiden ihren eigenen Laden unter dem Namen Nowhere auf und verkauften dort ihre Marken Undercover und A Bathing Ape. Inzwischen wurde der Laden als ein ‚Pop Up Shop' in Rei Kawakubos Dover Street Market in London relaunched. Die dort angebotenen Artikel waren so exklusiv, dass die Leute bald bis auf die Straße anstanden, um sich die begehrten Stücke zu sichern. Also folgten eigenständige BAPE-Stores mit Neonschildern, Fließband, BAPE-Camouflage-Muster und

Umkleiden aus Plastik und Chrom für ein futuristisches Einkaufserlebnis. Bald expandierte BAPE nach Nagoya und Osaka, bevor man mit der Eröffnung von Busy Workshop 2001 in London auch in Europa auftrat. Heute betreibt BAPE weltweit 22 Läden, unter anderem in Japan, Hongkong, London, New York, Taipeh und Los Angeles, während Nigo sich mit Pharrell Williams die Eigentümerschaft am Billionaire Boys Club teilt. Seine fortgesetzte Aneignung von klassischen Kleidungsstücken und Americana, von Jacken bis Jeans, von Kapuzensweatern bis zu T-Shirts, erfolgt mit höchster Sorgfalt, größter Liebe und Aufmerksamkeit. Weil sein Geschmacksniveau immer höchsten, tadellosen Ansprüchen genügen musste, er das Label nie beworben hat und gleichzeitig vor bezahlter Unterstützung durch Prominente zurückschreckte, hat Nigo dafür gesorgt, dass das Interesse an seiner Marke stetig wächst. Inzwischen wird sie von führenden Stars der Musikbranche favorisiert.

Nigo est à la fois le fondateur, l'homme d'affaires, le graphiste, la figure de proue et le PDG de la marque tokyoïte A Bathing Ape. Choisi en référence au film de 1968 « La Planète des Singes » le nom « BAPE » est une forme abrégée de « A Bathing Ape In Lukewarm Water ». BAPE est une marque de lifestyle moderne avec son propre salon de coiffure, sa boutique pour enfant, son café, sa chaîne de télévision, son magasin de disques et même sa propre licence de catch au Japon. En produisant des vêtements haut de gamme, luxueux et bien coupés (toujours en quantités extrêmement limitées), Nigo a révolutionné à lui seul le streetwear. Nigo (ou Tomoaki Nagao, son nom d'alors) s'installe à Tokyo pour étudier le journalisme de mode dans la célèbre école Bunka Fukuso Gakuin, où il rencontre son meilleur ami Jonio (Jun Takahashi d'Undercover). Ces deux éminents « chasseurs de cool » ouvrent vite leur propre boutique, Nowhere, pour présenter leurs marques Undercover et A Bathing Ape, un projet d'ailleurs récemment relancé sous forme de « pop-up store » dans le Dover Street Market londonien de Rei Kawakubo. Les articles qu'ils vendent sont si exclusifs que les gens font la queue tout autour de l'immeuble pour être sûrs d'obtenir le collector qu'ils convoitent. Peu de temps après, il ouvre des boutiques BAPE futuristes faites de néons, de tapis roulants, du fameux camo BAPE et d'aménagement en plastique et chrome. Rapidement, BAPE conquiert Nagoya et Osaka, puis se lance à l'étranger avec l'ouverture du Busy Workshop à Londres en 2001. BAPE possède aujourd'hui 22 boutiques dans le monde, notamment au Japon, à Hong Kong, à Londres, New York, Taipei et Los Angeles. Nigo est aussi le cofondateur de la marque Billionaire Boys Club avec Pharrell Williams. Sa constante réappropriation des classiques et de l'Americana, des blousons aux jeans, des sweats à capuche aux T-shirts, repose sur une attention immense et un maximum d'amour pour ce qu'il fait. En privilégiant toujours le meilleur goût et des normes de qualité irréprochables, sans jamais faire de publicité et refusant tout contrat de promotion avec des célébrités, Nigo voit sans cesse augmenter l'intérêt suscité par sa griffe, soutenue par les plus grandes stars de la musique.

BEN REARDON

What are your signature designs? The logo of A Bathing Ape and the Ape Camouflage pattern What is your favourite piece from any of your collections? I like all the items How would you describe your work? Fun amusement What's your ultimate goal? I do not set a goal What inspires you? My life Can fashion still have a political ambition? No, I don't think so Who do you have in mind when you design? Myself Is the idea of creative collaboration important to you? Yes, I guess it is important Who has been the greatest influence on your career? Pharrell Williams How have your own experiences affected your work as a designer? Yes, all experiences have been affecting my work Which is more important in your work: the process or the product? Both Is designing difficult for you? If so, what drives you to continue? It is not difficult – as all is inspiration and casual ideas Have you ever been influenced or moved by the reaction to your designs? Nothing in particular crosses my mind as an answer to this What's your definition of beauty? Nothing in particular What's your philosophy? Ape shall never kill Ape What is the most important lesson you've learned? Nothing in particular.

"I aim to create fashion that is neutral in such a way that each person can add his or her own personality to it"
DRIES VAN NOTEN

Dries Van Noten's culturally diverse style has made him one of the most successful of the 'Antwerp Six' designers who arrived at the London collections back in March 1986. His signature full skirts, soft jackets and scarves are embroidered or beaded using the traditional folkloric techniques of India, Morocco or eastern Europe – whichever far-flung culture has caught his attention that season. Born in Antwerp, Belgium, in 1958 to a family of fashion retailers and tailors, Van Noten enrolled at the city's Royal Academy in 1975; to support his studies, he worked both as a freelance designer for various commercial fashion companies and as a buyer for his father's boutiques. Following the legendary group show in London, Van Noten sold a small selection of men's shirts to Barneys in New York and Whistles in London; these stores then requested that he make smaller sizes, for women. In the same year, Van Noten opened his own tiny shop in Antwerp, subsequently replaced by the larger Het Modepaleis in 1989. In 1991, he showed his menswear collection in Paris for the first time; a womenswear line followed in 1993. Van Noten is perhaps the most accessible of the Belgian designers, but his theory of fashion is far from conventional. He prefers to design collections 'item by item', offering his clients a sense of individuality, rather than slavishly creating a collection around one silhouette or a single theme. In 2004, he celebrated his 50th fashion show with a dinner in Paris where models walked along dining tables wearing his spring/summer 2005 collection; the anniversary was also marked with the publication of a book, 'Dries Van Noten 01-50'. He now has three stores and around 500 outlets worldwide. In March 2009, the Belgian designer opened a boutique in Tokyo to complement his flagship in Saint-Germain close to the Académie des Beaux-Arts de Paris and bringing the total number of Dries Van Noten stores worldwide to nine.

Dries van Notens multikultureller Stil hat ihn zu einem der erfolgreichsten Designer der „Antwerp Six" gemacht, die erstmals bei den Londoner Kollektionen 1986 in Erscheinung traten. Seine Markenzeichen sind lange Röcke, weiche Jacken und Schals, oft bestickt oder perlenverziert mit den traditionellen volkstümlichen Techniken Indiens, Marokkos oder Osteuropas – je nachdem, welches Land in der jeweiligen Saison seine Aufmerksamkeit besonders gefesselt hat. 1958 wurde van Noten im belgischen Antwerpen in eine Familie geboren, die vom Einzelhandel mit Mode und von der Schneiderei lebte. Die Ausbildung an der Royal Academy seiner Heimatstadt begann er 1975. Um sich sein Studium zu finanzieren, arbeitete er zum einen als selbstständiger Designer für verschiedene kommerziell ausgerichtete Modefirmen, zum anderen als Einkäufer für die Läden seines Vaters. Nach der legendären gemeinsamen Modenschau in London verkaufte van Noten eine kleine Auswahl von Herrenhemden an Barneys, New York, und Whistles, London. Genau diese Läden verlangten bald Hemden in kleineren Größen – für Damen. Noch im selben Jahr eröffnete van Noten auch ein winziges eigenes Geschäft in Antwerpen, aus dem er dann 1989 in Het Mode-

paleis – bis heute sein Flagship-Store – umzog. 1991 präsentierte er erstmals eine Herrenkollektion in Paris; die Damenlinie folgte 1993. Obwohl sein Verständnis von Mode alles andere als konventionell ist, gelten van Notens Kreationen als die tragbarsten aller belgischen Designer. Er zieht es vor, seine Kollektionen „Stück für Stück" zu kreieren, was seinen Kunden mehr Raum für Individualität lässt, anstatt sklavisch um eine Silhouette oder ein einziges Thema herum zu entwerfen. Im Jahr 2004 feierte der Designer seine 50. Modenschau mit einem Dinner in Paris, bei dem die Models in seiner Kollektion Frühjahr/Sommer 2005 über die Tische flanierten. Aus Anlass dieses Jubiläums kam auch das Buch „Dries Van Noten 01–50" heraus. Im März 2009 eröffnete der belgische Designer eine Boutique in Tokio, quasi als Gegenstück zu seinem Flagship-Store im Pariser Saint-Germain, nahe der Académie des Beaux-Arts. Damit stieg die Zahl der Dries Van Noten Stores weltweit auf neun.

Parmi les jeunes créateurs du «Antwerp Six» qui ont débarqué aux collections de Londres en mars 1986, Dries Van Noten, grâce à son style culturellement éclectique, est l'un de ceux qui ont rencontré le plus de succès. Selon la culture lointaine qui l'inspire pour la saison, il brode et perle les jupes amples, les vestes souples et ses écharpes inimitables à l'aide de techniques folkloriques traditionnelles venues d'Inde, du Maroc ou d'Europe de l'Est. Né en 1958 à Anvers dans une famille de tailleurs et de commerçants spécialisés dans l'habillement, Van Noten entre à l'Académie Royale de la ville en 1975; pour financer ses études, il travaille à la fois comme créateur free-lance pour diverses griffes commerciales et comme acheteur pour les boutiques de son père. A l'issue du défilé londonien légendaire des Six d'Anvers, Van Noten vend une petite collection de chemises pour homme au grand magasin Barneys de New York et à Whistles à Londres; les deux lui demanderont ensuite de fabriquer des tailles plus petites, pour les femmes. La même année, Van Noten ouvre une minuscule boutique à Anvers, remplacée en 1989 par le plus important Het Modepaleis, qui reste aujourd'hui sa boutique phare. En 1991, il présente pour la première fois sa collection pour homme à Paris, suivie d'une ligne pour femme en 1993. Van Noten est sans doute le plus accessible des créateurs belges, mais sa théorie de la mode n'a pourtant rien de conventionnel. Pour offrir à ses clients un certain sens de l'individualité, il préfère dessiner ses collections «pièce par pièce» plutôt que de concevoir servilement ses lignes autour d'une seule silhouette ou d'un même thème. En 2004, il célèbre son 50ᵉ défilé lors d'un dîner parisien où les mannequins paradent sur les tables, vêtues de sa collection printemps/été 2005; cet anniversaire est également marqué par la sortie d'un livre, «Dries Van Noten 01–50». En 2009, le créateur belge ouvre une grande boutique à Tokyo, qui s'ajoute à celle de Saint-Germain-des-Prés non loin de l'Académie des Beaux-arts de Paris et porte le nombre de points de vente Dries Van Noten à neuf à travers le monde.   SUSIE RUSHTON

PHOTOGRAPHY EMMA SUMMERTON. FASHION DIRECTOR EDWARD ENNINFUL. MODEL RAQUEL ZIMMERMANN. MARCH 2008.

What are your signature designs? Prints, colours and fabrics converging in good designs **What is your favourite piece from any of your collections?** My favourite pieces are those that I can associate with personal memories or people, ranging from a simple T-shirt to a very elaborate piece **How would you describe your work?** I start from the fabrics and I aim to create fashion that is neutral in such a way that each person can add his or her own personality to it. It's about fashion that doesn't overwhelm your own personality **What's your ultimate goal?** To create beautiful things **What inspires you?** Everything that surrounds me. This can be a flower, a painting or a human being **Can fashion still have a political ambition?** The atmosphere of a collection often reflects what's going on around you. I believe you can manifest yourself and express your ideas through the way you dress, but after all, it remains just clothes **Who do you have in mind when you design?** I don't have some mental image of a Dries Van Noten man or woman. What's in my mind is the individual garment I'm working on, but I also wonder how people are going to wear it or combine it with other garments. Because finally, you create fashion not for the catwalk, but to be worn **Is the idea of creative collaboration important to you?** Creativity is at its best when it's an interaction between different people **Who has been the greatest influence on your career?** All that I do now is a result of my education and of people sharing with me the things they love **How have your own experiences affected your work as a designer?** It's difficult, if not impossible, to separate my private and professional life. My work is obviously influenced and inspired by the constant interplay between both **Which is more important in your work: the process or the product?** The product, that's what people get to see. But I enjoy the process more **Is designing difficult for you? If so, what drives you to continue?** It's not difficult, as long as it's not limited to working on the collections only. It's the mixture of different elements that drives me, ranging from the business aspect to the design process and the artistic input **Have you ever been influenced or moved by the reaction to your designs?** You have to take into account the reactions to your work. Sometimes, I have been stimulated more by negative reactions. Paradoxically enough, these can give you a hint that you're moving on in the right direction **What's your definition of beauty?** Beauty is a most personal thing **What's you philosophy?** Enjoy your life, fashion is not that important **What's the most important lesson you've learned?** Fashion is not so important.

"The clothes we wear should underline the personality of the individual who wears them"
LUCAS OSSENDRIJVER • LANVIN

Born and raised in the Netherlands, Lucas Ossendrijver is today's undisputed king of menswear. Since joining Lanvin as Alber Elbaz's counterpart in 2005, his collections have slowly collected legions of fans who subscribe to the Lanvin aesthetic of fragility and lived-in quality. Evolution, not revolution, is a word that regularly comes up in interviews with Ossendrijver. Despite Lanvin not having a menswear archive for him to refer to – even though the company had produced men's tailored pieces in 1901 – Ossendrijver has powered ahead to mark Lanvin menswear with his signature pairing of trainers with a tux, this laidback attitude to luxury a manifestation of the understated yet self-confident Dutch sensibility. Ossendrijver also brought to Lanvin his extensive experience. A compatriot of Viktor & Rolf at the Arnhem Institute for the Arts, Ossendrijver briefly designed womenswear for the French brand Plein Sud before working as a freelance designer for Kenzo Homme (1997–2000) followed by a brief spell working with Kostas Murkudis. Until right before landing the position at Lanvin, Ossendrijver was head designer at Dior Homme Classic line and had previously worked for Hedi Slimane. In the time that Ossendrijver has been at Lanvin, the company has collaborated with Acne and rebranded the classic non-fashion menswear line as Lanvin 15 Faubourg.

Der in den Niederlanden geborene und aufgewachsene Lucas Ossendrijver ist heute der unumstrittene König der Herrenmode. Seit er 2005 als Alber Elbaz' Widerpart zu Lanvin kam, haben seine Kollektionen nach und nach Legionen von Fans akquiriert, die sich Lanvins fragiler Ästhetik und behaglicher Qualität verschrieben haben. Evolution, nicht Revolution, ist ein Ausdruck, der in Interviews mit Ossendrjver regelmäßig benutzt wird. Und obwohl Lanvin über kein Menswear-Archiv verfügt, aus dem er schöpfen könnte – auch wenn das Unternehmen schon 1901 Herrenkleidung maßschneiderte – hat sich Ossendrijver ins Zeug gelegt, um der Herrenmode von Lanvin seinen Stempel aufzudrücken: Turnschuhe zum Smoking. Diese lässige Haltung gegenüber Luxus wirkt wie eine Manifestation der zurückhaltenden, aber zugleich selbstbewussten niederländischen Befindlichkeit. Ossendrijver brachte bei Lanvin auch seine umfassende Erfahrung ein. Der Landsmann von Viktor & Rolf am Arnhem Institute for the Arts entwarf kurze Zeit Damenmode für die französische Marke Plein Sud, bevor er als selbstständiger Designer für Kenzo Homme arbeitete (1997–2000). Darauf folgte ein kurzes Intermezzo bei Kostas Murkudis. Bevor er schließlich seine jetzige Position bei Lanvin einnahm, war Ossendrijver Chefdesigner der Linie Dior Homme Classic, davor hatte er auch noch für Hedi Slimane entworfen. Seit Ossendrijver dort ist, hat das Unternehmen Lanvin mit Acne kooperiert sowie der klassischen, von aktuellen Trends unabhängigen Herrenlinie unter dem Namen Lanvin 15 Faubourg ein neues Image verliehen.

Né et élevé aux Pays-Bas, Lucas Ossendrijver est aujourd'hui le roi incontesté de la mode pour homme. Depuis son arrivée chez Lanvin aux côtés d'Alber Elbaz en 2005, ses collections attirent progressivement des légions de fans qui s'approprient avec joie l'esthétique délicate et la qualité éprouvée de la maison. Dans les interviews données par Ossendrijver, le mot évolution, et non révolution, revient régulièrement. Lanvin ne possède pas d'archives de mode masculine dont il pourrait s'inspirer – bien que la maison ait produit des costumes sur mesure en 1901 – mais Ossendrijver a dynamisé la collection pour homme avec sa juxtaposition caractéristique du jogging et du smoking, cette attitude relax du luxe qui révèle une sobriété néerlandaise néanmoins pleine d'assurance. Ossendrijver apporte aussi à Lanvin sa longue expérience du métier. Diplômé de l'Arnhem Institute for the Arts comme ses compatriotes Viktor & Rolf, Ossendrijver commence par créer des vêtements pour femme pour la marque française Plein Sud pendant une brève période, travaille ensuite comme styliste free-lance pour Kenzo Homme (1997–2000), avant une collaboration de courte durée avec Kostas Murkudis. Juste avant d'être nommé chez Lanvin, Ossendrijver était styliste principal de la ligne Dior Homme Classic, après avoir travaillé pour Hedi Slimane. Depuis qu'il est chez Lanvin, la maison a collaboré avec Acne et relancé sa ligne pour homme ultra classique sous la griffe Lanvin 15 Faubourg.

KAREN LEONG

What are your signature designs? Sportswear-influenced tailoring and trainers **What is your favourite piece from any of your collections?** A black cotton drawstring parka from the spring/summer 2008 collection **How would you describe your work?** Emotional clothing; clothes with a 'soul'. The clothes we wear should underline the personality of the individual who wears them **What's your ultimate goal?** To make people dream and make their lives a little bit nicer **What inspires you?** The people I work with, friends and work **Can fashion still have a political ambition?** In menswear, there are a lot of 'dress codes'. I hope men will feel freer in order to dress more as individuals and less uniform. What is also important to keep in mind is that fashion is also supposed to be 'fun' **Who do you have in mind when you design?** I see the studio as a laboratory; where we test and try out new ideas. So it is the people around me and the people with whom I work who I have in mind **Is the idea of creative collaboration important to you?** Yes! Because by exchanging with other people, you learn and progress **Who has been the greatest influence on your career?** Helmut Lang, Hedi Slimane and, of course, Alber! **How have your own experiences affected your work as a designer?** I believe, as a designer, you always draw on your own experiences. However, it is not always conscious **Which is more important in your work: the process or the product?** Both! Without the process, there is no product **Is designing difficult for you? If so, what drives you to continue?** Yes, it is a difficult process. You have lots of possibilities and not always the answers. Nothing is instant, but this is also the challenge. You want to do better after each collection **Have you ever been influenced or moved by the reaction to your designs?** It is always surprising to see people wear the clothes in the street and the way they make them their own. I always find this quite touching **What is your definition of beauty?** Imperfection and personality **What's your philosophy?** Staying true to myself and enjoying what I do **What is the most important lesson you've learned?** To go for what I believe in and let go of everything that is not important. Follow my intuition.

"I'd describe my work as Frankenstein and Garbo, falling in love in a leather bar"
RICK OWENS

Rick Owens (born 1961) stands alone in the international fashion industry. He is that rare thing: an LA designer. Owens' draped, dark and perfectly cut aesthetic is the antithesis of the sunshine-saturated, bleached-teeth image of LA. Born in the city, Owens grew up in Porterville, a small town in California. Moving back to LA in 1984 after high school, he studied painting at the Otis Parsons Art Institute, but dropped out after two years and began to pursue his career in fashion. However, he rejected fashion college and instead studied pattern cutting at a trade school. In 1988, he took a job in LA's Garment District, where he earned his keep as a pattern cutter for six years. In 1994, Owens set up his own label and began selling his small collections through Charles Gallay, an up-and-coming boutique. Nineties pop culture and Hollywood's red carpet influenced his designs, resulting in bias-cut gowns and trailer park vests. Owens playfully describes his darkly chic clothes as 'glunge' – a mix of glamour and grunge. Rather than show on a catwalk, he instead travelled the world throughout the '90s presenting his clothes to fashion buyers and developing an impressive client list that includes Madonna and Courtney Love. His reputation continued to grow by word of mouth and in 2002, American 'Vogue' offered to sponsor his autumn/winter collection, his first on a runway. In the same year, Owens won the Perry Ellis Emerging Talent Award from the Council of Fashion Designers of America (CFDA). Moving to Paris in 2003 after scoring an artistic director contract with fur house Revillon. Today the Rick Owens label includes two diffusion lines alongside the main collection: Rick Owens Lilies, a collection of simple, stunning basics and DRKSHDW, a denim collection: Owens also designs furniture and his own fur collection entitled Palais Royal. In 2007, Owens was awarded the Cooper-Hewitt National Design Award for outstanding achievement and The Rule Breakers Award from The Fashion Group International. Today he owns a number of global stores.

Der 1961 geborene Rick Owens ist eine Ausnahme in der internationalen Modeindustrie, denn er gehört einer seltenen Spezies an: Er ist ein Designer aus Los Angeles. Seine verhüllende, düstere und perfekt geschnittene Ästhetik ist das Gegenteil des gängigen Images von L.A. mit Sonne bis zum Abwinken. In Los Angeles geboren, wuchs Owens in der kalifornischen Kleinstadt Porterville auf. 1984 zog er nach dem High-School-Abschluss zurück in die Großstadt und studierte am Otis Parsons Art Institute Malerei. Zwei Jahre später brach er diese Ausbildung ab und begann an seiner Karriere als Modedesigner zu arbeiten. Er tat dies jedoch nicht an einer Modeschule, sondern entschied sich für das Musterschneiden an einer Handelsschule. 1988 suchte er sich einen Job als Musterschneider im Garment District von Los Angeles, womit er sechs Jahre lang seinen Lebensunterhalt bestritt. Dann gründete er 1994 sein eigenes Label und begann, seine kleinen Kollektionen über die angesagte Boutique Charles Gallay zu verkaufen. Die Popkultur der 1990er-Jahre und der Glamour Hollywoods beeinflussten seine Entwürfe und sorgten für diagonal geschnittene Roben und Trailer-Park-Westen. Owens nennt seine Kleider mit dem düsteren Schick ironisch „glunge" – eine Mixtur aus Glamour und Grunge. Anstatt sie auf dem Laufsteg zu zeigen, reiste der Designer in den 1990er-Jahren lieber kreuz und quer durch die Welt und präsentierte seine Mode den Käufern direkt, was ihm

eine respektable Kundenliste mit Namen wie Madonna und Courtney Love einbrachte. Seine Reputation wuchs vornehmlich durch Mundpropaganda, bis 2002 die amerikanische Vogue anbot, seine Herbst/Winterkollektion – die erste auf dem Catwalk – zu sponsern. Im gleichen Jahr verlieh das Council of Fashion Designers of America (CFDA) Owens den Perry Ellis Emerging Talent Award. Als ihn das Pelzhaus Revillon als künstlerischen Leiter unter Vertrag nahm, zog Owens 2003 nach Paris. Heute umfasst das Label Rick Owens außer der Hauptkollektion zwei Nebenlinien: Rick Owens Lilies, eine Auswahl einfacher, aber dennoch überraschender Basics, sowie die Jeanskollektion DRKSHDW. Owens entwirft auch Möbel und zudem eine Pelzkollektion unter dem Namen Palais Royal. 2007 erhielt Owens den Cooper-Hewitt National Design Award für herausragende Leistungen sowie den Preis The Rule Breakers von The Fashion Group International. Heute gehören ihm eine Reihe von Läden in der ganzen Welt.

Rick Owens (né en 1961) apparaît comme un franc-tireur dans l'industrie de la mode internationale car il fait figure de véritable rareté : c'est un créateur de Los Angeles. L'esthétique drapée, sombre et parfaitement coupée d'Owens se trouve à l'antithèse de l'image saturée de soleil et de dents blanches si typique de Los Angeles. Né à L.A., Owens grandit à Porterville, une petite ville de Californie. Après le lycée, il revient à Los Angeles en 1984 pour étudier la peinture à l'Otis Parsons Art Institute, qu'il quitte au bout de deux ans pour se lancer dans la mode. Toutefois, il rejette les formations en mode proposées par les universités, préférant étudier la coupe de patrons dans un collège technique. En 1988, il décroche un job dans le Garment District de L.A., où il gagne sa vie en tant que traceur de patrons pendant six ans. En 1994, Owens crée sa propre griffe et commence à vendre ses petites collections par le biais de Charles Gallay, la boutique montante de l'époque. La culture pop et le glamour hollywoodien des années 90 influencent ses créations et s'expriment à travers des robes coupées en biais et des débardeurs d'inspiration white trash. Owens qualifie avec humour ses vêtements chic et sombres de « glunge », mélange de glamour et de grunge. Au lieu de présenter son travail de façon formelle, il voyage dans le monde entier tout au long des années 90 pour présenter ses vêtements aux acheteurs et se constituer ainsi une impressionnante liste de clientes, parmi lesquelles Madonna et Courtney Love. Le bouche-à-oreille contribue à asseoir sa réputation et en 2002, le Vogue américain lui propose de sponsoriser sa collection automne/hiver, la première qu'il présente sur un vrai podium de défilé. La même année, Owens remporte le prix Perry Ellis remis aux jeunes talents par le CFDA (Council of Fashion Designers of America). En 2003, il s'installe à Paris après avoir été nommé directeur artistique du fourreur Revillon. Outre la collection principale, la griffe Rick Owens comprend désormais deux lignes de diffusion : Rick Owens Lilies, une gamme de basiques simples et étonnants et DRKSHDW, une collection en denim. Owens dessine également des meubles et sa propre collection de fourrures, Palais Royal. En 2007, il a reçu le Cooper-Hewitt National Design Award qui couronne des réalisations exceptionnelles, ainsi que le prix The Rule Breakers de Fashion Group International. Il possède aujourd'hui de nombreuses boutiques à travers le monde. LAUREN COCHRANE

PHOTOGRAPHER IN-CHIEF PAOLO ROVERSI. FASHION DIRECTOR EDWARD ENNINFUL. MODEL AGYNESS DEYN. SPRING 2008.

What are your signature designs? I suppose I'm best known for narrow jackets with small shoulders and long narrow sleeves, worn over draped jerseys in grey and beige, washed and aged leathers and cashmeres **What is your favourite piece from any of your collections?** I once had Lemarie, the famous French feather house, turn pearl-grey vulture feathers into a coat that was like wearing a fog… **How would you describe your work?** Frankenstein and Garbo falling in love in a leather bar… **What's your ultimate goal?** Frankly, I try to appreciate where I am; I have a lot to learn and a lot to improve, but being in a position where I'm able to create is more than my fair share **What inspires you?** I recharge my batteries by looking at architecture and furniture designers: Oscar Niemeyer, Piero Portaluppi, Le Corbusier, Carlo Mollino, Joe Colombo, Jean-Michel Frank, are always soothing favourites **Can fashion still have a political ambition?** I've always seen fashion as a response, reaction or protest to social conditions. I'd have a hard time considering it more… **Who do you have in mind when you design?** Someone with a practical attitude; who's experienced the joy and damage that life has to offer and found a good-humoured balance there **Is the idea of creative collaboration important to you?** I sincerely wish I could collaborate, but I was always such a loner. I'm afraid I'm more comfortable being a cruel dictator **Who has been the greatest influence on your career?** I had great mentors in legendary retailing pioneers who helped me out at the beginning – Charles Gallay and Maxfield in LA, Linda Dresner in New York and Maria Luisa in Paris… people with an adventurous eye who really support this business **How have your own experiences affected your work as a designer?** Everything I do is completely autobiographical; wreckage and stillness **Which is more important in your work: the process or the product?** Without the product, it's just self-indulgence **Is designing difficult for you? If so, what drives you to continue?** I'm lucky I know what I want to do and have a place to do it. I have no patience with sensitive torture artists **Have you ever been influenced or moved by the reaction to your designs?** I remember a shy woman, uncomfortable with her body, blossoming in front of her husband while trying some things on **What's your definition of beauty?** Anyone, anyone, anyone can be wildly attractive. Fitness, grooming and an open heart can do way more than any designer dress **What's your philosophy?** A million years from now no one will care, so get over yourself **What is the most important lesson you've learned?** We're all freaks.

"The idea of creating something new out of nothing every season drives me"
BRUNO PIETERS · HUGO BOSS

Born 1977 in Bruges, Belgium, Bruno Pieters – like so many of his other fellow fashion designer compatriots – studied at the Royal Academy in Antwerp. One of his lecturers, Hieron Pessers (who also taught Kris Van Assche and Bernhard Willhelm), greatly influenced the young Pieters' sartorial technique. A perfectionist, Pieters cites craftsmanship and technique as the cornerstone of his design sensibilities; he is also not afraid to experiment with shape and proportion. After graduating in 1999, Pieters worked for Maison Martin Margiela and Christian Lacroix before launching his own-name label in 2001. In July that same year, Pieters presented a couture collection inspired by the '50s New Look suit during Paris couture week. Since 2003, Pieters has been the creative director of Belgian luxury brand Delvaux. In 2006, competing against Anne Valérie Hash and Jonathan Saunders, Pieters bagged the Swiss Textile Awards. In the following year, he was announced as winner of the Andam Award. Since June 2007, Pieters has been the art director of Hugo Boss' diffusion line Hugo. The Antwerp-based Pieters divides his time between the Belgian city and Metzingen, Germany, the heaquarters of Hugo Boss.

Der 1977 in Brügge geborene Bruno Pieters hat wie so viele seiner belgischen Kollegen an der Royal Academy of Fine Arts in Antwerpen studiert. Einer seiner Dozenten, Hieron Pessers (der auch Kris Van Assche und Bernhard Willhelm unterrichtet hat), nahm großen Einfluss auf die Schneiderkunst von Pieters. Als Pefektionist bezeichnet dieser handwerkliches Können und Technik als die Grundpfeiler seiner Fähigkeiten als Designer. Er scheut sich aber auch nicht, mit Form und Proportion zu experimentieren. Nach seinem Studienabschluss 1999 arbeitete Pieters für Maison Martin Margiela und Christian Lacroix, bevor er 2001 ein Label mit seinem eigenen Namen startete. Im Juli desselben Jahres präsentierte er im Rahmen der Pariser Couture-Woche eine vom New Look der 50er-Jahre inspirierte Couture-Kollektion. Seit 2003 ist Pieters Creative Director der belgischen Luxusmarke Delvaux. 2006 gewann er gegen Anne Valérie Hash und Jonathan Saunders den Swiss Textile Award. Im darauffolgenden Jahr war er Preisträger des Andam Award. Seit Juni 2007 ist Pieters Art Director der Nebenlinie Hugo bei Hugo Boss. So teilt der Designer seine Zeit zwischen seinem Wohnsitz in Antwerpen und dem Hauptquartier von Hugo Boss in Metzingen.

Né à Bruges en 1977, le Belge Bruno Pieters – comme nombre de ses compatriotes créateurs de mode – a fait ses études à l'Académie Royale d'Anvers. L'un de ses professeurs, Hieron Pessers (dont Kris Van Assche et Bernhard Willhelm ont également suivi les cours), a grandement influencé la technique de couturier du jeune Pieters. Perfectionniste, il considère l'artisanat et la technique comme les pierres angulaires de sa créativité, mais n'a pas peur d'expérimenter dans le domaine des formes et des proportions. Après l'obtention de son diplôme en 1999, il travaille chez Maison Martin Margiela et Christian Lacroix avant de lancer sa griffe éponyme en 2001. En juillet de la même année, Bruno Pieters présente aux défilés parisiens une collection haute couture inspirée du tailleur New Look des années 50. Depuis 2003, il est directeur de la création de la marque de luxe belge Delvaux. En 2006, Pieters rafle le Swiss Textile Award devant Anne Valérie Hash et Jonathan Saunders. L'année suivante, il gagne le Andam Award. Depuis juin 2007, Bruno Pieters est le directeur artistique de la ligne de diffusion Hugo chez Hugo Boss. Il partage son temps entre Anvers et la ville allemande de Metzingen, quartier général d'Hugo Boss.

KAREN LEONG

What are your signature designs? Construction and tailoring. I sometimes consider myself more as a tailor then a designer **What is your favourite piece from any of your collections?** I don't have a favourite, but if I had to choose it would be the black suit from my very first couture collection in 2001 **How would you describe your work?** Tailored, architectural and melancholic **What 's your ultimate goal?** I would like to continue and retain the freedom I still have **What inspires you?** Life **Can fashion still have a political ambition?** Probably not as obviously as it did in the past. Fashion, like politics today, has become very democratic, combined with a lot of image making **Who do you have in mind when you design?** I work more on intuition. I design what I believe is new and interesting **Is the idea of creative collaboration important to you?** I love working with the amazing composer Senjan Jansen on the music for the shows. I think we truly understand each other **Who has been the greatest influence on your career?** The stylist I have worked with for years now, he's very supportive and always pushes me to go further. We've become good friends **How have your own experiences affected your work as a designer?** Usually the seasons I've felt happiest have produced the best collections. It's very connected I believe **Which is more important in your work: the process of the product?** You need the process to get the result. Lately I try to enjoy the process more and do everything with more awareness **Is designing difficult for you? If so what drives you to continue?** It's not difficult so far. The idea of creating something new out of nothing every season drives me **Have you ever been influenced or moved by the reaction to your designs?** I'm very sensitive to the reaction to my work, but I'm not often influenced by it. I usually know what I will do the next season even before I show a collection **What's your definition of beauty?** Being in a state of absolute presence and acceptance with all **What's your philosophy?** The only moment that matters is now, the past is over, the future hasn't happened yet **What is the most important lesson you have learned?** To trust my instincts and follow my intuition, always.

"Because it's Saint Laurent, I think about silhouette, imagery and how I can refer to the past we have"
STEFANO PILATI · YVES SAINT LAURENT

One of the most provocative designers working this century, Stefano Pilati has forged an identifiable design signature since taking over the reins as creative director of Yves Saint Laurent in 2004. Born in Milan in 1965, Pilati's introduction into the fashion industry was part and parcel of growing up in a family of stylish women and a city where the fashion scene was thriving. From a seasonal job at the Milan shows, Pilati interned at Nino Cerruti before joining Giorgio Armani in 1993. It was here, during an 18-month stint in Armani's menswear studio – where he developed his knowledge of fabric research and development, skills he continues to perfect to this day – that Pilati's talent caught the attention of the Prada Group. In 1995, he left Armani and began working for Miu Miu and Jil Sander, where he remained for five years. In 2000, he joined Yves Saint Laurent to design women's ready-to-wear; this swiftly went on to include the men's collections as well. In 2002, Pilati was promoted to head of design for all Yves Saint Laurent product lines, including accessories, before receiving the recognition he rightly deserved and being appointed creative director of the label in 2004. Making a distinct departure from Tom Ford's high-sexed imagery, Pilati has since redefined the silhouette of the YSL woman and taken the brand slap bang into the 21st century. Under his guidance, YSL today treads the right balance between elegance and modernism, delivering clothes that are at once beautiful, comfortable and modern, while still catering for exactly what the Parisian chic women demand from YSL. As well as the mainline women's and men's collections, and a massive overhaul of all the stores to reflect his own aesthetic, Pilati has introduced Edition Unisex, an elegant, casual, tailored collection of men's clothing designed for women and Edition 24, a 50-piece line, that helps fulfil the brand's promise of not only inciting desire, but serving women with a complete wardrobe for modern life.

Als einer der provozierendsten Designer dieses Jahrhunderts hat Stefano Pilati sich seit seiner „Regierungsübernahme" als Creative Director bei Yves Saint Laurent 2004 eine unverkennbare Handschrift zugelegt. Der 1965 in Mailand geborene Pilati fand den Zugang zur Modebranche nicht zuletzt dadurch, dass er in einer Familie mit lauter eleganten Frauen und in einer Stadt mit fruchtbarer Modeszene aufwuchs. Aus einem Gelegenheitsjob bei den Mailänder Modenschauen wurde ein Praktikum bei Nino Cerruti, bevor er 1993 bei Giorgio Armani anfing. Dort eignete er sich während seiner 18 Monate in Armanis Atelier für Herrenmode Kenntnisse in Materialkunde an, die er bis heute weiterentwickelt. Und dort fiel sein Talent auch der Prada-Gruppe ins Auge. So verließ er 1995 Armani und begann, für Miu Miu und Jil Sander zu arbeiten. Nach fünf Jahren in dieser Position stieg er 2000 bei Yves Saint Laurent ein, um die Prêt-à-porter-Linie für Damen zu entwerfen, wobei er allerdings blitzschnell auch die Verantwortung für die Herrenkollektionen übernahm. 2002 wurde Pilati zum Chefdesigner aller Produktlinien von Yves Saint Laurent, inklusive Accessoires, erkoren, bevor man ihm die rechtmäßig gebührende Anerkennung

zukommen ließ und ihn 2004 zum Creative Director des gesamten Labels machte. Als deutliche Abkehr von Tom Fords sexuell aufgeladener Symbolik hat Pilati seither die Silhouette der Frau bei YSL neu definiert und die Marke auf einen Schlag ins 21. Jahrhundert versetzt. Unter seiner Führung hat YSL heute den idealen Ausgleich zwischen Eleganz und Modernität gefunden und liefert Kleidung, die schön, bequem und zeitgemäß zugleich ist und noch dazu genau dem entspricht, was die schicken Pariserinnen von YSL erwarten. Außer sich um die zentralen Kollektionen für Damen und Herren und um eine General-überholung aller Läden nach seinen persönlichen ästhetischen Vorstellungen zu kümmern, hat Pilati inzwischen auch die Edition Unisex eingeführt. Die elegante, lässig geschneiderte Kollektion besteht aus Herrenbekleidung für Damen. Und schließlich wäre da noch die Edition 24, eine 50-teilige Linie, die das Versprechen der Marke einlöst, nicht nur Sehnsüchte zu wecken, sondern Frauen mit einer kompletten Garderobe für den modernen Alltag auszustatten.

Stefano Pilati, l'un des plus grands provocateurs de la mode du nouveau siècle, s'est forgé une signature très identifiable depuis qu'il a repris les rênes d'Yves Saint Laurent en 2004 au poste de directeur de la création. Né à Milan en 1965, l'arrivée de Pilati dans l'industrie de la mode est intrinsèquement liée au fait d'avoir grandi parmi des femmes élégantes dans une ville où la mode florissait. Grâce à un petit job sur les défilés de Milan, Pilati obtient un stage chez Nino Cerruti, puis intègre la maison Giorgio Armani en 1993. Au cours des 18 mois qu'il passe dans l'atelier de mode masculine d'Armani – où il développe ses connaissances sur la recherche et le développement de tissus, des compétences qu'il continue de perfectionner à ce jour – le talent de Pilati attire l'attention du Groupe Prada. En 1995, il quitte Armani et travaille pendant cinq ans pour Miu Miu et Jil Sander. En 2000, il entre chez Yves Saint Laurent comme styliste de prêt-à-porter féminin et se voit rapidement confier les collections pour homme aussi. En 2002, Pilati est promu directeur de la création de toutes les lignes de produits Yves Saint Laurent, notamment les accessoires. En 2004, il reçoit la reconnaissance qu'il mérite amplement en étant nommé directeur de la création de la marque. En nette opposition avec l'image ultra sexy véhiculée par Tom Ford, Stefano Pilati a depuis redéfini la silhouette de la femme YSL et propulsé la marque en plein dans le XXIᵉ siècle. Sous sa direction, YSL trouve aujourd'hui le bon équilibre entre élégance et modernisme. La maison propose des vêtements à la fois beaux, confortables et contemporains tout en livrant aux Parisiennes chics exactement ce qu'elles attendent d'YSL. Outre les principales collections pour femme et pour homme, et un vaste relooking de toutes les boutiques afin qu'elles reflètent sa propre esthétique, Pilati a lancé Edition Unisex, une collection de tailleurs élégants et décontractés inspirée par la mode masculine, ainsi qu'Edition 24, une ligne de 50 pièces qui aide la marque à tenir ses promesses, c'est-à-dire susciter le désir tout en offrant aux femmes une garde-robe complète adaptée à la vie moderne.

HOLLY SHACKLETON

What are your signature designs? Intuition, coherence, mathematics, passion **What is your favourite piece from any of your collections?** All of them **How would you describe your work?** Intense. Vitally unnecessary. All of myself **What's your ultimate goal?** To be immortal **What inspires you?** Anything from reality to fiction, from the natural to the artificial **Can fashion still have a political ambition?** I hope so. This depends on the strength of the fashion message and how receptive its audience is **Who do you have in mind when you design?** I design to fulfill a sense of loneliness … and as a cure to relativism **Is the idea of creative collaboration important to you?** Yes, as long as the collaborators are efficient **Who has been the greatest influence on your career?** Giorgio Armani, Miuccia Prada, Yves Saint Laurent **How have your own experiences affected your work as a designer?** On every angle, approach, layer and level **What is more important in your work: the process or the product?** The process isn't important if it doesn't translate into a product **Is designing difficult for you? If so, what drives you to continue?** Designing isn't 'difficult' per se – it is actually very interesting – and I will continue with an awareness of the privilege I have in expressing myself through it **Have you ever been influenced or moved by the reaction to your designs?** Always **What's your definition of beauty?** Pure nature **What's your philosophy?** What goes around, comes around **What is the most important lesson you've learned?** Don't trust anyone other than yourself.

"My work is about the female body and, ultimately, my clothes are about making women feel and look beautiful" ZAC POSEN

Zac Posen, at only 29 years of age, has already earned a place in fashion history. His leather dress, designed for the 'Curvaceous' exhibition at the Victoria & Albert Museum, was awarded the V&A Prize and acquired for the museum's permanent collection (2001). This event marked the beginning of great things for the young New York native. Born in 1980, the son of a painter, Posen enrolled in the pre-college programme at the Parsons School of Design, later joining Saint Ann's School for the Arts in Brooklyn. His fashion studies led him to Central Saint Martins in 1999, where he embarked on a BA in womenswear. However, he soon packed in his studies in order to start his own label, which was an immediate success. His glamorous signatures include bias-cut gowns, fishtail hemlines and a passion for screen-siren style. His talent was swiftly recognised by the fashion industry: he was a finalist for the ENKA International Fashion Design Award in 2002 and a nominee for the CFDA Award for new talent in both 2002 and 2003 before winning the Perry Ellis Award in 2004. That year proved to be a groundbreaking period for Posen. In April, Sean John, the fashion company backed by Sean 'Puff Daddy' Combs, announced it was making a long-term investment in Posen's label. However, it is Posen who continues to steer the label creatively, driving it forward with his vision of a strong, feminine silhouette. With Sean John's financial backing, the days when he was forced to fund his first catwalk show with the £14,000 prize from a fashion competition are a distant memory. Freed from monetary restraints, and with his sister (Alexandra Posen) leading his Tribeca studio, he is now able to concentrate on expanding his ready-to-wear collection and developing his accessories line.

Mit seinen gerade mal 29 Jahren hat Zac Posen seinen Platz in der Modegeschichte schon sicher. Das Lederkleid, das er für die Ausstellung „Curvaceous" im Victoria & Albert Museum entworfen hat, wurde mit dem V&A Prize ausgezeichnet und für die Dauerkollektion des Museums angekauft. Dieses Ereignis markierte für den gebürtigen New Yorker den Beginn einer großartigen Karriere. Geboren wurde er 1980 als Sohn eines Malers. An der Parsons School of Design nahm er am Pre-College-Programm teil, später schrieb er sich an der Saint Ann's School for the Arts in Brooklyn ein. Im Rahmen seines Modestudiums begann er 1999 den Bachelor-Studiengang Damenmode am Central Saint Martins in London. Bald schon brach er die Ausbildung jedoch ab, um sich voll auf die Gründung seines eigenen Labels zu konzentrieren, das sofort ein Erfolg war. Zu seinem typischen glamourösen Stil gehören diagonal geschnittene Roben, Schleppen und ganz allgemein die Liebe zum Stil der Leinwand-Diven. Sein Talent wurde innerhalb der Branche rasch erkannt: Beim ENKA International Fashion Design Award 2002

gehörte Posen zu den Finalisten; beim CFDA-Preis für neue Talente war er 2002 und 2003 nominiert; 2004 gewann er schließlich den Perry Ellis Award. Jenes Jahr sollte ohnehin ein sehr bewegendes für Posen werden. Im April vermeldete Sean John, das Modeunternehmen von Sean „Puff Daddy" Combs, eine längerfristige Investition in Posens Label. Die kreative Richtung gibt allerdings weiterhin der Designer selbst vor, und zwar mit seiner Vision von einer starken, femininen Silhouette. Mit der finanziellen Unterstützung von Sean John sind die Zeiten, als er seine erste Catwalk-Show mit den bei einem Modewettbewerb gewonnenen 14.000 Pfund bestreiten musste, nur noch Erinnerung. Finanzieller Beschränkungen enthoben und gemeinsam mit seiner Schwester Alexandra Posen, die sein Tribeca-Atelier leitet, kann Posen sich nun auf den Ausbau seiner Prêt-à-porter-Kollektion und die Entwicklung einer Accessoire-Linie konzentrieren.

A 29 ans seulement, Zac Posen a déjà gagné sa place au panthéon de la mode. La robe en cuir qu'il a dessinée pour l'exposition « Curvaceous » du Victoria & Albert Museum lui a valu le V&A Prize et fait désormais partie de la collection permanente du musée. Cet événement marque le début d'une grande carrière pour ce jeune New-Yorkais. Né en 1980 d'un père peintre, Zac Posen s'inscrit à la prépa de la Parsons School of Design avant de partir pour la Saint Ann's School for the Arts de Brooklyn. En 1999, il débarque à Central Saint Martins où il entame un BA en mode féminine. Il interrompt ses études prématurément pour lancer sa propre griffe et rencontre un succès immédiat. Son style glamour et caractéristique se distingue par ses robes coupées en biais, ses ourlets en queue de poisson et une passion pour les sirènes du grand écran. Le monde de la mode ne tarde pas à reconnaître son talent : finaliste de l'ENKA International Fashion Design Award en 2002, nominé par le CFDA dans la catégorie nouveau talent en 2002 et 2003, il finit par remporter le prix Perry Ellis en 2004, une année révolutionnaire pour le jeune créateur. En avril, Sean John, la marque de Sean « Puff Daddy » Combs, décide d'investir à long terme dans la griffe de Posen. Malgré toutes ces réussites, il continue à diriger sa griffe avec créativité et la fait évoluer grâce à sa vision d'une silhouette féminine prononcée. Fort du soutien de Sean John, la période où il était contraint de financer son premier défilé avec les 14 000 livres gagnées dans un concours de mode n'est plus qu'un lointain souvenir. Libéré de toute contrainte économique et soutenu par sa sœur (Alexandra Posen) qui dirige son atelier de Tribeca, il peut désormais se concentrer sur l'extension de sa collection de prêt-à-porter et sur le développement de sa ligne d'accessoires.

KAREN LEONG

What are your signature designs? My signature designs are anatomical in their inspiration, and architectural in construction. They also incorporate movement and flair to accentuate a woman's personality **What is your favourite piece from any of your collections?** My favourites keep changing as my work evolves. The pieces that have really thrilled me have included: the cape skirt from Artemis, the snap gown and the papyrus dress from Circe, the Kaleidoscope dress from Leagues and Fathoms, the overall chic simplicity of the Sargasso collection, the Blixen gown and all of the knits from my resort and spring collections. Some of my ultimate favourites are the custom pieces I have designed for my private clients. There is nothing better than creating something special for an individual personality **How would you describe your work?** I make timeless clothing for feminine, strong, intelligent women. I pay enormous attention to design detail and artistry of construction in my clothing. I am drawn to textures and designs that are both ancient and futuristic. My work is about the female body and, ultimately, my clothes are about making women feel and look beautiful. It's about creating a cool and glamorous lifestyle **What's your ultimate goal?** Wanting to make women feel strong, sexy, romantic and confident by creating the classics of the future **What inspires you?** Sensuality, life, craft and craftsmanship and, most of all, the incredible women that surround me **Who do you have in mind when you design?** I love women of all ages, sizes and personalities – I am surrounded by them – and I keep them in mind when I design **Is the idea of creative collaboration important to you?** This is a collaborative business by nature. My work incorporates the genius of many experts, from the manufacturers of my materials, to my patternmakers and sewers. Within the creative studio, it is the variety of voices that lends depth and complexity to a collection **Who has been the greatest influence on your career?** My family **Is designing difficult for you?** The creative process is always tumultuous and intense, but that's what keeps me going and keeps me fulfilled **Have you ever been influenced or moved by the reaction to your designs?** I love doing trunk shows and seeing women react to and inhabit my designs. I also love hearing stories from my clients of the experiences that they have had while wearing my clothes. For me, it's all about making women feel wonderful and expressive **What's your definition of beauty?** A woman who is intelligent, feminine, provocative, imaginative, playful and has a good sense of humour **What is the most important lesson you have learned?** Perseverance.

"When people think of fashion, they always prefer to see the crazy side, the clichéd side of it. But I think that's wrong. Fashion is an important part of a woman's life"
MIUCCIA PRADA • PRADA + MIU MIU

In 1971, Miuccia Prada entered the family business. Twenty years later, the highly traditional leather goods company had changed beyond all recognition. The innovation of something as simple as a nylon bag meant there was no looking back: Prada was on the way to redefining luxury, subtlety and desirability in fashion. Prada the company – led by the designer and her husband, Patrizio Bertelli, who started work with Prada in 1977 and is now CEO of the Prada Group – seems to have an uncanny ability to capture the cultural climate in fashion. This sensitivity has been unashamedly teamed with commercial savvy, which has made the brand's influence over the past decade vast and its growth enormous. From bags and shoes to the first womenswear collection (1988), the Miu Miu line for the younger customer (1993), menswear (1994), Prada Sport (1997) and Prada Beauty (2000), all are directly overseen by Miuccia Prada herself. Yet, unlike many other Leviathan brands, there is something both unconventional and idiosyncratic in Miuccia Prada's aesthetic. Much of this may be down to her contradictory character. Born in Milan in 1950, Miuccia Prada studied political science at the city's university and was a member of Italy's Communist Party, yet is said to have worn Yves Saint Laurent on the barricades. The designer, who has made The Wall Street Journal's '30 Most Powerful Women in Europe' list, also spent a period studying to be a mime artist. These dualities have led to her expert ability in balancing the contrary forces of art and commerce within the superbrand, sometimes quite literally: Prada has its own art foundation and has collaborated with the architect Rem Koolhaas on stores in New York (2001) and Los Angeles (2004). From the late '90s, the Prada Group embarked upon a policy of rapid expansion, purchasing brands including Azzedine Alaïa, Helmut Lang and Church & Co. Every presentation of men, women and Miu Miu collection continues to reflect the diverse cultural interests of Miuccia Prada. With associated projects her collaboration with Rem Koolhaas is a constant inspiration.

1971 trat Miuccia Prada in das Familienunternehmen ein. Zwanzig Jahre danach hat sich die bis dahin eher traditionelle Lederwarenfabrik bis zur Unkenntlichkeit verändert. Etwas so Simples wie eine Nylonhandtasche markierte den Neuanfang. Prada gab den Begriffen Luxus, Raffinesse und Begehrlichkeit in Sachen Mode eine neue Bedeutung. Unter der Leitung der Designerin und ihres Mannes Patrizio Bertelli, der 1977 in das Unternehmen eintrat und heute Chef des Konzerns ist, beweist Prada einen untrüglichen Instinkt, wenn es darum geht, aktuelle Modeströmungen aufzunehmen. Dieses Gespür sorgte, gepaart mit dem nötigen Geschäftssinn, in den letzten zehn Jahren für das ungeheure Wachstum und den enormen Einfluss der Marke. Von den Taschen und Schuhen, der ersten Damenkollektion, dem Label Miu Miu für jüngere Kundinnen (1993) über Männermode (1994) und die Linie Prada Sport (1997) bis hin zu Prada Beauty (2000) unterstehen alle Bereiche nach wie vor Miuccia Prada. Doch im Unterschied zu anderen großen Marken ist Miuccia Pradas Ästhetik höchst unkonventionell und individuell. Vieles davon mag auf ihren ungewöhnlichen Werdegang zurückzuführen sein. 1950 in Mailand geboren, studierte Miuccia Prada in ihrer Heimatstadt Politikwissenschaft und war Mitglied der Kommu-

nistischen Partei. Doch angeblich trug sie selbst auf den Barrikaden Yves Saint Laurent. Die vom Wall Street Journal zu einer der „30 mächtigsten Frauen Europas" gekürte Geschäftsfrau absolvierte auch eine Ausbildung als Pantomime. Ihre Vielseitigkeit mag dazu beitragen, dass es ihr immer wieder hervorragend gelingt, Kunst und Kommerz unter dem Dach der Supermarke miteinander zu versöhnen. Und das ist gelegentlich durchaus wörtlich zu verstehen: So betreibt Prada eine eigene Kunststiftung und ließ die Läden in New York (2001) und Los Angeles (2004) vom Stararchitekten Rem Koolhaas gestalten. Seit Ende der 1990er-Jahre setzt der Prada-Konzern auf rasche Expansion und kaufte in diesem Zuge Marken wie Azzedine Alaïa, Helmut Lang oder Church & Co. auf. Jede Präsentation einer Herren-, Damen- oder Miu-Miu-Kollektion spiegelt nach wie vor Miuccia Pradas vielfältige kulturelle Interessen. In den dazugehörigen Projekten dient ihr Rem Koolhaas als stetiger Quell der Inspiration.

Miuccia Prada rejoint l'entreprise familiale en 1971. 20 ans plus tard, ce maroquinier ultra-classique a subi une transformation si radicale qu'il en est devenu méconnaissable. Une innovation telle que le sac en nylon prouvait bien que la maison ne regardait plus en arrière : Prada était sur le point de redéfinir le luxe, la subtilité et les avantages de la mode. Patrizio Bertelli, mari de Miuccia mais également directeur de l'entreprise, designer et actuel PDG du groupe Prada, avait commencé à travailler pour la maison en 1977. La société semble douée d'une étrange facilité à capter le climat culturel de la mode. Cette intuition se mêle sans complexe à un esprit de conquête commerciale qui n'a fait qu'augmenter l'influence de la marque ces dix dernières années et lui a permis d'enregistrer une croissance vertigineuse. Des chaussures aux sacs en passant par la première collection de vêtements pour femme (1988), la ligne Miu Miu pour les jeunes (1993), la ligne masculine (1994), Prada Sport (1997) et Prada Beauty (2000), tout est directement supervisé par Miuccia Prada en personne. Contrairement à la plupart des géants de la mode, l'esthétique de Miuccia Prada se distingue par son anti-conformisme très caractéristique. Cette ambivalence repose en grande partie sur l'esprit de contradiction de Miuccia. Née en 1950 à Milan, elle étudie les sciences politiques à l'université de la ville et s'inscrit au Parti Communiste Italien, n'hésitant pas à monter sur les barricades habillée en Yves Saint Laurent. La créatrice, incluse dans la liste des « 30 femmes les plus puissantes d'Europe » du Wall Street Journal, a également suivi une formation pour devenir mime. Ces dualités lui ont permis de réconcilier les forces contradictoires de l'art et du commerce au sein de la « supermarque », parfois même au pied de la lettre : Prada possède sa propre fondation artistique et a collaboré avec l'architecte Rem Koolhaas à la création des boutiques de New York (2001) et de Los Angeles (2004). Dès la fin des années 90, le Groupe Prada a adopté une politique d'expansion rapide, rachetant des marques telles qu'Azzedine Alaïa, Helmut Lang et Church & Co. Chaque présentation des collections pour homme, pour femme et Miu Miu continue à refléter la diversité des passions culturelles de Miuccia Prada. Avec des projets communs Rem Koolhaas demeure une constante source d'inspiration.

JO-ANN FURNISS

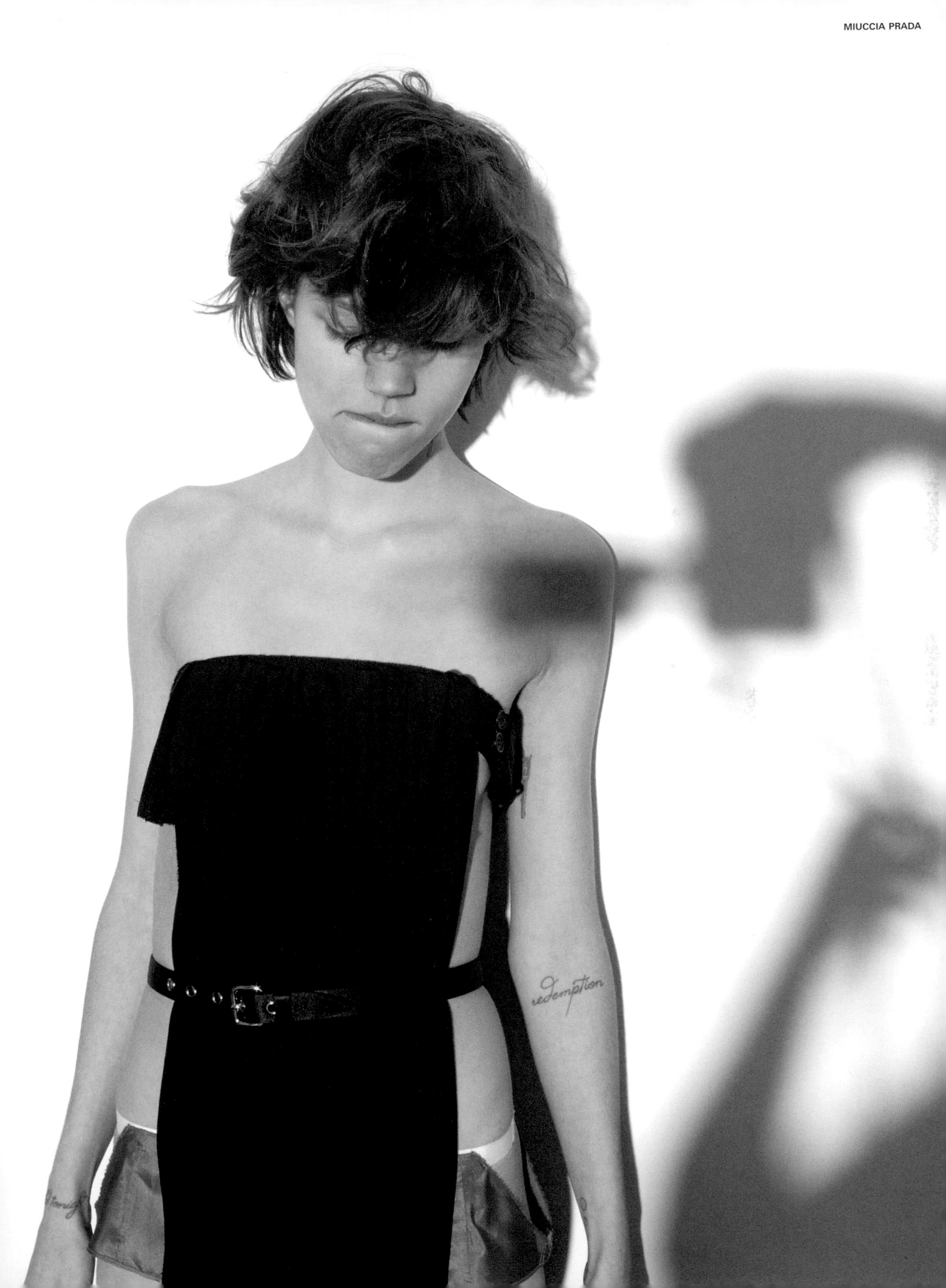

How would you describe your work? To have to express in a simple, banal object, a great complexity about women, aesthetics and current times **What's your ultimate goal?** To do my work as well as I can **What inspires you?** At the moment, I am intrigued by the increasingly ambiguous boundary between what is real and what is unreal, or what is beauty and what is fake, which we can no longer tell **Can fashion still have a political ambition?** I try to express the contemporary woman and do it through fashion because that's my instrument. When people think of fashion, they always prefer to see the crazy side, the clichéd side of it. But I think that's wrong. Fashion is an important part of a woman's life **Who do you have in mind when you design?** I do not have anyone in mind, there isn't just one. I am a complicated person: I am different people at different times. So I do not have one woman in mind. Prada and Miu Miu are the opposite of that idea because it's just not one thing **Is the idea of creative collaboration important to you?** Working as a designer allows me to have a lot of connections and relationships that can turn into important collaborations. Working on projects with artists, architects, directors, philosophers and creative people in general feeds my interests and my need of better understanding the complexity of the world we live in **How have your own experiences affected your work as a designer?** Of course, I am what I feel, see, listen, read and meet. My fashion is a reflection of myself **Which is more important in your work: the process or the product?** It is difficult to say, because the two things cannot be separated. The product is the process itself. Depending on the kind of product I have in mind, I use a different process: a couture process when I want to refer to that; more schizophrenic when I want to express something naïve…. My research for the new pushes me to invent every time a different process, and that is one of the things I like more **Is designing difficult for you? If so, what drives you to continue?** Designing, if you want to push boundaries, is not easy. I like to embrace the complexity and choose one theme through which I try to express it **Have you ever been influenced or moved by the reaction to your designs?** Not by the reaction, but by the reason for the reaction. You have to balance creativity with an understanding of what happens around you and the reality is that selling is the only way to prove that what you are doing makes sense to people.

"I don't find designing difficult, it's everything else that goes with it that's hard"
GARETH PUGH

Gareth Pugh is the Sunderland-born designer currently hammering a nail into the coffin of conventional fashion. When he graduated from Central Saint Martins in 2003, his red-and-white striped inflatable balloon costume was photographed by Nicola Formichetti for the cover of 'Dazed & Confused' in February 2004. He showed his fantastical creations in the London clubs and assisted Rick Owens at luxury furrier Revillon before receiving an invitation to show at Fashion East during London Fashion Week, where Casey Spooner walked the final look which lit up to screams and thunderous applause from an audience, who felt lucky to be there at the right time to witness the birth of a new and important voice in British fashion. Pugh soon received commissions from Kylie Minogue to design for her Showgirls tour, collaborated with Judy Blame, Nick Knight, Fischerspooner, Moët, MTV, a commercial for HSBC and i-D. BoomBox threw a party in his honour, 'Elle' crowned him Young Designer of the Year, he modelled for Arena Homme Plus, made bespoke clothes for Beth Ditto, styled for every magazine of note, featured in exhibitions including the V&A and The Metropolitan Museum of Art, was photographed by Bruce Weber and Mario Testino, designed a Christmas tree for Topshop, guest edited 'Time Out' and designed his own Ken doll. On top of all this, he has carved out his bleak yet elegant, aggressive but luxurious unflinching vision of how to dress in the modern world. Each season, Pugh explores the same recurring themes, including inflatables, fur, leather, triangles PVC and black, black and more black, quickly establishing his voice as strong and severe. Showing in Paris since September 2008, Pugh showed his first menswear collection in January 2009, which mirrored and complemented his womenswear and featured clothing punctured with nails.

Gareth Pugh ist der in Sunderland geborene Designer, der gegenwärtig einen Nagel in den Sarg der konventionellen Mode hämmert. Nach seinem Abschluss am Central Saint Martins im Jahr 2003 wurde sein rot-weiß-gestreiftes aufblasbares Ballonkostüm von Nicola Formichetti für das Cover von „Dazed & Confused" im Februar 2004 fotografiert. Er zeigte seine fantastischen Kreationen in den Londoner Clubs und assistierte Rick Owens bei der Nobel-Pelzmarke Revillon, bevor er die Einladung erhielt, während der London Fashion Week bei Fashion East zu präsentieren, wo Casey Spooner den finalen Look präsentierte, was Kreischen und donnernden Applaus beim Publikum auslöste. Die Leute waren offenbar beglückt, Augenzeugen der Geburt einer neuen und bedeutenden Figur in der britischen Modeszene zu sein. Bald erhielt Pugh von Kylie Minogue den Auftrag, Kreationen für ihre Tour „Showgirls" zu entwerfen. Zudem arbeitete er mit Judy Blame, Nick Knight, Fischerspooner, Moët, MTV, machte einen Werbespot für HSBC und i-D. BoomBox schmiss ihm zu Ehren eine Party, Elle krönte ihn zum Young Designer of the Year, er modelte für Arena Homme Plus, fertigte Maßkleidung für Beth Ditto, stylte für alle

nennenswerten Magazine, präsentierte sich in Ausstellungen, u.a. im Victoria & Albert Museum und im Metropolitan Museum of Art, wurde von Bruce Weber und Mario Testino fotografiert, gestaltete einen Weihnachtsbaum für Topshop, war Gast-Herausgeber von Time Out und entwarf seine eigene Ken-Puppe. Abgesehen von alldem ist es ihm aber gelungen, seine raue und doch elegante, angriffs-lustige und zugleich luxuriöse, überaus eigenwillige Vision von Kleidung in einer modernen Welt herauszuarbeiten. Außerdem widmet sich Pugh Saison für Saison der Erforschung wiederkehrender Themen wie Aufblasbares, Pelz, Leder, Drei-ecke, PVC, Schwarz, Schwarz und noch einmal Schwarz. Dabei verschaffte er sich mit starker, durchdringender Stimme rasch Gehör. Seit September 2008 präsen-tierte er in Paris. Im Januar 2009 zeigte er bei seiner ersten Herrenkollektion – Spiegel und Pendant seiner Damenmode – mit Nägeln durchlöcherte Kleidung.

Originaire de Sunderland, le créateur Gareth Pugh est en train de planter le dernier clou dans le cercueil de la mode conventionnelle. Après l'obtention de son diplôme de Central Saint Martins en 2003, son costume en ballons gonflables à rayures rouges et blanches est pris en photo par Nicola Formichetti pour la couverture de Dazed & Confused en février 2004. Gareth Pugh présente alors ses créations fantasques dans les clubs londoniens. Il devient assistant de Rick Owens chez le fourreur de luxe Revillon, puis est invité à défiler dans le cadre de Fashion East pendant la London Fashion Week : le chanteur Casey Spooner clôture le défilé dans une tenue qui s'illumine soudain, déclenchant un tonnerre d'applaudissements de la part d'un public en délire qui se félicite d'être au bon endroit au bon moment pour assister à la naissance d'une importante nouvelle voix de la mode britannique. Peu de temps après, Kylie Minogue lui commande plusieurs costumes pour sa tournée Showgirls. Pugh a aussi collaboré avec Judy Blame, Nick Knight, Fischerspooner, Moët et MTV, ainsi que sur un spot publicitaire pour HSBC et i-D. BoomBox a donné une soirée en son honneur et le magazine Elle l'a couronné Young Designer of the Year. Pugh a posé dans Arena Homme Plus, créé des vêtements sur mesure pour Beth Ditto, collaboré en tant que styliste avec tous les magazines qui comptent, a vu ses créations exposées plusieurs fois, notamment au Victoria & Albert Museum et au Metropolitan Museum of Art, a été photographié par Bruce Weber et Mario Testino, a conçu un arbre de Noël pour Topshop, dirigé un numéro de Time Out et créé sa propre poupée Ken. Pour couronner le tableau, il a imprimé son infaillible vision de la mode d'aujourd'hui, à la fois austère et élégante, agressive mais luxueuse. Chaque saison, Gareth Pugh explore des thèmes récurrents tels les objets gonflables, la fourrure, le cuir, les triangles, le PVC, le noir, le noir et encore le noir, imposant à toute vitesse son style fort et rigoureux. Rendez-vous des défilés parisiens depuis septembre 2008, Gareth Pugh a présenté en janvier 2009 une première collection pour homme qui reflète et complète sa mode pour femme, avec des vêtements piqués de clous.   BEN REARDON

What are your signature designs? I've got my favourites, but I'm still trying to figure out what it is that I want to be known for **What is your favourite piece from any of your collections?** The Stealth Bomber I made for Nick Knight to shoot for British Vogue to celebrate him being chosen for the Moet Fashion Tribute **How would you describe your work?** A labour of love **What's your ultimate goal?** To own my own house **What inspires you?** Everything and anything, its a very abstract and personal thing **Can fashion still have a political ambition?** I have never considered what I do in any context other than what it is – clothes **Who do you have in mind when you design?** It's more important to imagine how something will look in movement, that's something very integral to what I do **Is the idea of creative collaboration important to you?** Definitely, it helps to see things from a different perspective. I work with a lot of very talented people on my shows and they all have their say in the final look and feel of the show **Who has been the greatest influence on your career?** My parents. I think I'm still trying to prove to them that I can make a living by doing something creative **How have your own experiences affected your work as a designer?** Outside influences have little affect on what I do. I just do what feels right, and sometimes it fits and makes sense, other times it doesn't, and you learn from that and move on **Which is more important in your work: the process or the product?** The process, but that's an ever changing quandary for me **Is designing difficult for you? If so, what drives you to continue?** I don't find designing difficult, it's everything else that goes with it that's hard **Have you ever been influenced or moved by the reaction to your designs?** To constantly try and better what I do, I think it is very important for me to remain in a constant state of dissatisfaction **What's your definition of beauty?** A gloss black cube **What is the most important lesson you've learned?** Nothing is ever as easy or as straight-forward as you might first think.

"I never get bored! I often think how lucky I am just for being able to do all the things I wanted to do"
JOHN RICHMOND

'Destroy, Disorientate, Disorder' and Debenhams, the British department store: John Richmond is equal parts raring-to-rock and ready-to-wear. The music-loving Mancunian has a singular talent for reconciling anarchic punk aesthetics with elegant tailoring. Born in 1961, Richmond graduated from Kingston Polytechnic in 1982 and worked as a freelance designer for Emporio Armani, Fiorucci and Joseph Tricot before forming his first label, Richmond-Cornejo, a collaboration with designer Maria Cornejo, in 1984. In 1987, he struck out on his own. During his career, Richmond has dressed pop icons such as Bryan Adams, David Bowie, Madonna and Mick Jagger; George Michael wore Richmond's Destroy jacket in the video for 'Faith'. John Richmond designs are synonymous with the spirit of rock and the smell of leather. Today, his label comprises three clothing lines: John Richmond, Richmond X and Richmond Denim, with eyewear and underwear collections also recently launched. A business partnership with Saverio Moschillo has provided Richmond with a worldwide network of showrooms, from Naples, Rome and Paris to Munich, Düsseldorf and New York. They house his leather biker jackets, oil-printed T-shirts, acid-orange pleated skirts and long-line sweaters. Richmond's flagship store in London's Conduit Street joins two Italian shops in Milan and Bari. Then there's the Designers at Debenhams collection, the John Richmond Smart Roadster car – needless to say, a John Richmond fragrance, childrenswear collection, watches and jewellery line are also in the pipeline. Other projects include the expansion of his stores, showcasing the younger diffusion ranges – X and Denim lines – to the global market. This project will mark the opening of 100 stores in the world's main markets by 2011.

„Destroy, Disorientate, Disorder" und das britische Kaufhaus Debenhams: John Richmond ist zu gleichen Teilen Rock'n'Roll und Prêt-à-porter. Der Musikliebhaber aus Manchester besitzt ein einzigartiges Talent für die Versöhnung von anarchischer Punk-Ästhetik mit eleganter Schneiderkunst. 1961 geboren, beendete Richmond 1982 das Kingston Polytechnikum und designte danach zunächst als Freelancer für Emporio Armani, Fiorucci und Joseph Tricot, bevor er 1984 in Kooperation mit der Designerin Maria Cornejo sein erstes Label Richmond-Cornejo gründete. Ab 1987 versuchte er sein Glück dann wieder allein. Im bisherigen Verlauf seiner Karriere kleidete er Popikonen wie Bryan Adams, David Bowie, Madonna und Mick Jagger ein. George Michael trug in seinem Video zu „Faith" die Destroy-Jacke von Richmond. Seine Entwürfe sind Synonyme für den Spirit of Rock und den Geruch von Leder. Heute umfasst sein Label drei verschiedene Linien: John Richmond, Richmond X und Richmond Denim; kürzlich kamen noch Brillen- und Dessouskollektionen dazu. Die geschäftliche Verbindung mit Saverio Moschillo ermöglicht Richmond den Zugang zu einem weltweiten Netz von Showrooms, sei es in Neapel oder Rom, in Paris oder München, Düsseldorf oder New York. Dort führt man seine Biker-Jacken, ölbedruckten T-Shirts, seine Faltenröcke in Neonorange und die lang geschnittenen Sweater. Richmonds neuester Flagship-Store in der Londoner Conduit Street steht in Verbindung mit zwei Läden in Italien – genauer gesagt: in Mailand und Bari. Außerdem wären da noch die Kollektion Designers at Debenhams und das Auto namens John Richmond Smart Roadster. Dass ein eigener Duft, eine Kinderkollektion sowie Uhren und Schmuck bereits in Planung sind, versteht sich da fast von selbst. Weitere Projekte umfassen die Expansion seiner Läden zur Präsentation der jüngeren Nebenlinien – X und Denim – auf dem weltweiten Markt. Im Rahmen dieses Projekts sind bis zum Jahr 2011 hundert Läden an den wichtigsten Plätzen der Welt avisiert.

Entre son slogan « Destroy, Disorientate, Disorder » et le grand magasin anglais Debenhams, on peut dire que John Richmond est à la fois rock'n'roll et prêt-à-porter. Originaire de Manchester, ce fan de musique possède un talent unique pour réconcilier esthétique anarchique punk et coupes élégantes. Né en 1961, Richmond sort diplômé de l'école polytechnique de Kingston en 1982 et travaille comme créateur free-lance pour Emporio Armani, Fiorucci et Joseph Tricot. En 1984, il fonde sa première griffe, Richmond-Cornejo, en collaboration avec la créatrice Maria Cornejo, mais décide de se lancer en solo dès 1987. Au cours de sa carrière, Richmond a habillé des icônes pop telles que Bryan Adams, David Bowie, Madonna et Mick Jagger ; George Michael a même porté son blouson Destroy dans son clip « Faith ». Les créations de John Richmond fusionnent l'esprit du rock et l'odeur du cuir. Aujourd'hui, sa griffe comprend trois lignes de mode : John Richmond, Richmond X et Richmond Denim, sans oublier le récent lancement de collections de lunettes et de sous-vêtements. Grâce à son partenariat commercial avec Saverio Moschillo, Richmond dispose d'un réseau mondial de showrooms installés à Naples, Rome, Paris, Munich, Düsseldorf et New York. Tous accueillent ses blousons de motard en cuir, ses T-shirts imprimés à l'huile, ses jupes plissées orange fluo et ses pulls aux lignes allongées. La boutique londonienne flambant neuve de Richmond dans Conduit Street vient s'ajouter aux deux boutiques italiennes de Milan et de Bari. Sans compter la collection Designers at Debenhams et la voiture John Richmond Smart Roadster. Logiquement, un parfum, une ligne pour enfant, une collection de montres et de bijoux John Richmond ne devraient plus tarder à voir le jour. Le créateur compte également étendre son réseau mondial d'enseignes pour présenter ses lignes de diffusion, X et Denim, qui ciblent une clientèle plus jeune. En effet, la marque compte ouvrir 100 boutiques sur les principaux marchés internationaux d'ici 2011.

NANCY WATERS

What are your signature designs? Observers decide what your signature is. Yes, I'm well known for leather jackets or 'RICH' jeans – in my head I change radically every season. Others see the signature of my work with a slight seasonal change **What are your favourite pieces from any of your collections?** I do not have a favourite piece. I just see the mistakes and changes that I want to make. I am never satisfied – I just enjoy creating the next piece **How would you describe your work?** Eclectic. It draws upon the past, present and future **What's your ultimate goal?** With a career of 20 years, including two children, one's goals change. I wake up every day and do something different from the day before. One day menswear, the next women's;

maybe a meeting with the sunglasses or childrenswear licensee or to Como to do the underwear or to the shoe factory! Is it men's or women's shoes today or childrenswear? I never get bored! I often think how lucky I am just to be able to do all the things I wanted to do **What inspires you?** Waking up thinking what am I going to do today? Another blank sheet of paper and I can do what I want **Can fashion still have a political ambition?** No. In its very nature it can't be taken seriously. Tomorrow we are going to change our mind **What do you have in mind when you design?** I get many images in my head of different people. Musicians, personalities, people I've seen on the street, the people around me **Is the idea of creative collaboration important to**

you? Yeah. It's fun working with other people, but sometimes it's difficult to be democratic **Who has been the greatest influence on your career?** Different periods have seen different people and circumstances. All have been important; it possibly started with David Bowie and Mick Ronson on Top of the Pops singing Starman around '72 **Which is more important in your work: the process or the product?** The process is much more enjoyable. The product is for other people's enjoyment **Is designing difficult for you?** Designing is fun and easy. There are days when you are on top of the world and others where you can't even draw a straight line **Have you ever been influenced or moved by the reaction to your designs?** Of course. If you get a positive

reaction, it's great for your confidence; and when it's negative, you feel like shit – but it makes me want to prove them wrong, and to work harder. But that is probably the Capricorn in me **What's your definition of beauty?** I hate this question, maybe because I can't articulate the answer. When it is in front of us, it's a bit like trying to put into words what a hiccup is. We all know, but we cannot write it down in a satisfying way **What's your philosophy?** You only get out what you put in **What is the most important lesson you've learned?** Try and be honest to others, but especially yourself. Only you can be you. What's the the point in trying to be something else?

"As hard and painful as designing can be, it is the thing I have always been most passionate about"
NARCISO RODRIGUEZ

Narciso Rodriguez designs clothes that are sliced, cut and put together with apparently effortless finesse. They are fluid and simple, architectural and modern, easy to wear but not casual, dressed-up but not too over-the-top. Rodriguez has an impeccable list of credentials. He graduated from Parsons School of Design in 1982, and after a brief period freelancing, joined Donna Karan at Anne Klein in 1985. He worked there for six years before moving to Calvin Klein as womenswear designer. In 1995, he relocated to Paris, where he stayed for two years with Cerruti, first as women's and men's design director, and then as creative director for the entire womenswear division. Never one to slow down the pace, in 1997 Rodriguez not only showed his debut signature line in Milan, but also became the womenswear design director at leather goods brand Loewe, a position he retained until 2001. In 2003, he received the CFDA's womenswear Designer of the Year Award and in 2004 was the recipient of the Hispanic Heritage Vision Award. Since 2001, he has concentrated on his eponymous line, which is produced and distributed by Aeffe SpA and shown at New York Fashion Week. Rodriguez's Latin roots (he was born in 1961 in New Jersey to Cuban-American parents) inspire the slick, glamorous side of his work while his experience in Europe has honed his fashion craftsmanship and tailoring expertise. This perfectly stylish balance has seduced some of the world's loveliest ladies, including Salma Hayek, Julianna Margulies and the late Carolyn Bessette, who married John F. Kennedy Jr in a Rodriguez creation. In May 2007, Rodriguez was announced winner of the Pratt Institute's Fashion Icon Award.

Narciso Rodriguez entwirft Kleider, die mit scheinbar müheloser Finesse zugeschnitten und zusammengefügt sind. Sie sind fließend und schlicht, skulptural und modern, tragbar, aber nicht alltäglich, schick, jedoch nicht überkandidelt. Die Referenzen, die der Designer vorzuweisen hat, sind tadellos. 1982 machte er seinen Abschluss an der Parsons School of Design, darauf folgte eine kurze Phase als freischaffender Designer. 1985 fing er unter Donna Karan beim Label Anne Klein an. Nach sechs Jahren wechselte er als Damenmodedesigner zu Calvin Klein. Im Jahr 1995 zog er nach Paris, wo er zwei Jahre für Cerruti tätig war, zunächst als Design Director für Damen wie für Herren und schließlich als Creative Director der gesamten Damenmode. In diesem Tempo ging es weiter – 1997 präsentierte Rodriguez nicht nur in Mailand die erste Kollektion seiner eigenen Linie, sondern wurde auch Design Director der Damenmode beim Lederwarenhersteller Loewe, was er bis 2001 bleiben sollte. 2003 wurde er von

der CFDA zum Designer of the Year für den Bereich Damenmode gewählt; 2004 zeichnete man ihn mit dem Hispanic Heritage Vision Award aus. Seit 2001 konzentriert sich der Designer ausschließlich auf seine eigene Linie, die von Aeffe SpA produziert und vertrieben und bei der New York Fashion Week vorgestellt wird. Seine Wurzeln (er wurde 1961 als Kind kubanisch-amerikanischer Eltern in New Jersey geboren) inspirieren Rodriguez zu den schicken glamourösen Aspekten seiner Arbeit, während die in Europa gesammelten Erfahrungen ihm im handwerklich-technischen Bereich zugute kommen. Wie perfekt sich beides ergänzt, konnte man schon an einigen der schönsten Frauen der Welt bewundern, etwa an Salma Hayek, Julianna Margulies und der inzwischen verstorbenen Carolyn Bessette, die John F. Kennedy Junior in einer Rodriguez-Kreation geheiratet hat. Im Mai 2007 wurde Rodriguez vom Pratt Institute mit dem Fashion Icon Award ausgezeichnet.

Narciso Rodriguez dessine des vêtements taillés, coupés et assemblés avec une grande finesse et une apparente facilité. Ses créations sont simples et fluides, architecturales et modernes, faciles à porter mais pas trop informelles, chic mais jamais surchargées. Rodriguez revendique une liste de références idéales : diplômé de la Parsons School of Design en 1982, il travaille en free-lance pendant une brève période avant de rejoindre Donna Karan chez Anne Klein en 1985. Il y reste six ans, puis part travailler chez Calvin Klein en tant que styliste pour femme. En 1995, il s'installe à Paris où il passe deux ans chez Cerruti, d'abord comme directeur des lignes pour femme et pour homme, puis comme directeur de la création de toutes les collections féminines. N'étant pas du genre à ralentir le rythme, en 1997 Rodriguez présente non seulement sa première collection signature à Milan, mais devient également directeur de la création féminine du maroquinier Loewe, un poste qu'il occupe jusqu'en 2001. En 2003, le CFDA le couronne Womenswear Designer of the Year, puis il reçoit en 2004 le Vision Award de la fondation Hispanic Heritage. Depuis 2001, il se consacre à sa ligne éponyme, produite et distribuée par Aeffe SpA et présentée à la New York Fashion Week. Ses racines latines (il est né en 1961 dans le New Jersey de parents d'origine cubaine) inspirent le côté brillant et glamour de son travail, tandis que son expérience européenne aiguise son savoir-faire et son expertise de la coupe : un savant équilibre stylistique qui séduit certaines des plus belles femmes du monde telles que Salma Hayek, Julianna Margulies et feue Carolyn Bessette, qui avait épousé John F. Kennedy Junior dans une robe dessinée par Rodriguez. En mai 2007, le Pratt Institute lui a décerné son Fashion Icon Award. TERRY NEWMAN

What are your signature designs? A dress **What's your favourite piece from any of your collections?** Autumn/winter 2000 black look on Carmen Kass opening the show **How would you describe your work?** Clean, tailored, feminine **What inspires you?** Life on the streets **Can fashion still have a political ambition?** Anything is possible **Who do you have in mind when you design?** A modern woman **Who has been the greatest influence on your career?** Cristobal Balenciaga **Which is more important in your work: the process or the product?** Both **Is designing difficult for you? If so, what drives you to continue?** As hard and painful as it can be, it is the thing I have always been most passionate about **Have you ever been influenced or moved by a reaction to your designs?** Whether you're slammed or applauded, you're always moved **What's your definition of beauty?** Grace **What's your philosophy?** Keep it simple! **What is the most important lesson you've learned?** To appreciate every day what life has to offer.

"I hope that my creations can give a little bit of joy"
SONIA RYKIEL

Sonia Rykiel is synonymous with Paris. Born in the city in 1930, she went on to encapsulate Parisian style with her chic fashion line. As an expectant mother, she had discovered that there were no sweaters available that were soft and flexible enough for her to wear through her pregnancy, so, in 1962, she created her own line of knitwear. This was so successful that she opened her first boutique in that momentous Parisian year, 1968. And, in their own way, Rykiel's designs were revolutionary. Her flattering knits – often in what was to become her trademark stripes – symbolised liberation for women's bodies from the stiff silhouette of the previous decade. She also increased the sex appeal of knits: freed from linings and hems, her dresses and sweaters were like second skins for the women who wore them. Rykiel has continued to build her very own French Empire since the 1970s. She recognised the wisdom of establishing a beauty line early on, launching a perfume in 1978 and cosmetics in 1987. Completely independent, Rykiel's business is very much a family affair. Husband Simon Bernstein is her business partner and daughter Nathalie Rykiel has been involved in the company since 1975. With such support, Sonia Rykiel has the freedom to do other things. Today, Madame Rykiel is something of a French institution. She has written novels, decorated hotels, sung a duet with Malcolm McLaren and even had a rose named after her. And the accolades keep on coming. Rykiel has been awarded an Oscar by the Fashion Group International and in December 2001, the French government named her Commander of l'Ordre National du Mérite. Now in her seventies, the grande dame of French fashion shows no signs of giving up. Her creations are impossibly sexy, impossibly shiny and impossibly decadent, and in spring/summer 2009, Sonia celebrated 40 years in the fashion game with a surprise tribute catwalk show organised by daughter Nathalie. Out came a procession of 30 girls rocking out 'Tribute' dresses designed by Rykiel's friends, peers and fashion designers including Martin Margiela, Jean Paul Gaultier, Karl Lagerfeld and Alber Elbaz in a breathless ode to the brilliant flame-haired queen of knits. Long may she reign.

Sonia Rykiel gilt inzwischen als Synonym für Paris. Dort wurde sie auch 1930 geboren, und später gelang es ihr, die Pariser Eleganz in ihrer schicken Modelinie auf den Punkt zu bringen. Als werdende Mutter hatte sie 1962 feststellen müssen, dass es keine Pullover gab, die für eine Schwangerschaft weich und elastisch genug waren, also entwarf sie kurzerhand ihre eigene Strickkollektion. Der Erfolg war so groß, dass Rykiel im für Paris so bedeutsamen Jahr 1968 ihre erste Boutique in der Stadt eröffnete. Und auf ihre Weise waren auch die damaligen Kreationen von Sonia Rykiel revolutionär. Ihre schmeichelnden Stricksachen – oft mit Streifen, die ihr Markenzeichen werden sollten – symbolisierten die Befreiung des weiblichen Körpers von der starren Silhouette des vorangegangenen Jahrzehnts. Sie steigerte auch den Sexappeal von Strick: frei von Futter und Säumen, wirkten ihre Kleider und Pullover wie eine zweite Haut ihrer Trägerin. Seit den 1970er-Jahren baut Rykiel kontinuierlich an ihrem ganz privaten französischen Imperium. Früh erkannte sie den Wert eigener Beautyprodukte und brachte 1978 ihren ersten Duft, 1987 die ersten Kosmetika unter ihrem Namen heraus. Das völlig autarke Unternehmen ist im Prinzip ein Familienbetrieb. Ehemann Simon Bernstein ist ihr Geschäftspartner, Tochter Nathalie Rykiel seit 1975 in die Firma inte-

griert. Dieser Rückhalt gibt Rykiel die Freiheit, auch andere Dinge als Mode zu machen. Inzwischen gilt Madame Rykiel als eine Art Institution. Sie hat Romane veröffentlicht, Hotels eingerichtet, ein Duett mit Malcolm McLaren gesungen, ja sogar eine Rose ist nach ihr benannt. Und die Reihe der Auszeichnungen reißt nicht ab: So erhielt Rykiel von der Fashion Group International einen Oscar; im Dezember 2001 ehrte die französische Regierung sie mit dem Titel Commandeur de l'Ordre National du Mérite. Auch wenn sie inzwischen in den Siebzigern ist, macht die Grande Dame der französischen Mode keine Anstalten, sich zur Ruhe zu setzen. Ihre Kreationen sind ungemein sexy, ungemein schön und ungemein dekadent. Anlässlich von Frühjahr/Sommer 2009 feierte Sonia Rykiel ihre 40 Jahre im Modezirkus mit einer Überraschungs-Catwalk-Show, die Tochter Nathalie ihr zu Ehren organisiert hatte. Heraus kam eine Prozession von 30 Mädchen, die „Tribute"-Kleider präsentierten, die Rykiels Freunde, Weggefährten und Modedesigner wie Martin Margiela, Jean Paul Gaultier, Karl Lagerfeld und Alber Elbaz kreiert hatten. Das Ganze war eine atemlose Ode an die Königin des Strick mit ihren flammend roten Haaren. Möge sie noch lange regieren.

Sonia Rykiel est devenue synonyme de Paris. Née en 1930 dans la capitale française, elle saisit la quintessence du style parisien dans ses collections de mode très chic. Pendant sa grossesse, elle n'arrive pas à trouver de pulls assez souples pour son ventre de femme enceinte, ce qui l'incite à créer sa propre ligne de maille en 1962. Elle remporte un tel succès qu'elle ouvre sa première boutique dès 1968, une année de bouleversement pour les Parisiens. A leur façon, les créations Rykiel sont tout aussi révolutionnaires : ses tricots flatteurs, souvent déclinés dans ce qui deviendra ses rayures signature, symbolisent alors l'émancipation des femmes, libérant leurs corps de la silhouette rigide imposée par la décennie précédente. Elle rehausse également le sex-appeal de la maille ; dépourvus de doublures et d'ourlets, ses robes et ses pulls enveloppent celles qui les portent comme une seconde peau. Depuis les années 70, Sonia Rykiel ne cesse de développer son propre empire français. Elle comprend très tôt l'intérêt de créer une ligne de beauté et lance un parfum en 1978, puis une gamme de maquillage en 1987. Entièrement indépendante, l'entreprise de Sonia Rykiel reste avant tout familiale. Son mari Simon Bernstein y est associé et sa fille Nathalie Rykiel y travaille depuis 1975. Forte d'un tel soutien, Sonia trouve le temps de se consacrer à d'autres passions. Aujourd'hui, Madame Rykiel est devenue une sorte d'institution française. Elle a écrit des romans, décoré des hôtels, chanté un duo avec Malcolm McLaren et revendique même une rose à son nom. Et les distinctions ne cessent de pleuvoir. Sonia Rykiel a reçu un Oscar du Fashion Group International, et le gouvernement français l'a adoubée Commandeur de l'Ordre National du Mérite en décembre 2001. A soixante-dix ans passés, la grande dame de la mode française n'a aucune envie d'abandonner. Ses créations sont incroyablement sexy, voyantes et décadentes. Pour le printemps/été 2009, un défilé surprise organisé par sa fille Nathalie rendait hommage aux 40 ans de carrière de Sonia : 30 filles ont paradé dans des robes « Tribute » conçues par les amis et pairs de Sonia Rykiel, des créateurs de mode parmi lesquels Martin Margiela, Jean Paul Gaultier, Karl Lagerfeld et Alber Elbaz, dans une ode époustouflante à la reine de la maille aux cheveux de feu. Longue vie à la reine ! LAUREN COCHRANE

What are your signature designs? I took away hems, discovered inside-out steams, abolished lining **What is your favourite piece from any of your collections?** A pullover. Very tight, sensuous. Black. My famous 'Poor Boy' sweater **How would you describe your work?** It's a philosophy of fashion. I have called it the 'Demode'. Which means that every women must consider what's beautiful and also not perfect in her figure **What's your ultimate goal?** To be happy. To create. To be a happy creator! I design clothes, I write and I am involved in all sorts of creations **What inspires you?** My daughter Nathalie, my three granddaughters, women in the street. I am also influenced by the books I read, the movies and all the arts. I am a sort of 'thief': my eyes and ears are always open **Can fashion still have a political ambition?** Everything that happens in the world matters to me. I am often scared. I hope that my creations can give a little bit of joy and happiness **Who do you have in mind when you design?** Most of the time, nobody in particular and all the women I can meet in the same time **Is the idea of creative collaboration important to you?** My team is very important to me. A creator is, in a certain way, always alone, but I need to be surrounded **Who has been the greatest influence on your career?** My daughter Nathalie **How have your own experiences affected your work as a designer?** Joy and pain are linked to my work. My creations are an expression of my feelings **Which is more important in your work: the process or the product?** Both are very important. The process is exciting, full of work and passion, full of doubts and tiredness, too. The product is like a gift, a smile, something concrete and gratifying **Is designing difficult for you? If so, what drives you to continue?** It's the purpose of my life **Have you ever been influenced or moved by the reaction to your designs?** Yes, of course! I am always open to reactions. It is necessary to be open-minded **What's your definition of beauty?** There isn't one definition of beauty. Beauty can be inside and outside. Beauty can be classical, eccentric, unusual, unexpected, intellectual... **What's your philosophy?** To love and to be loved **What is the most important lesson you've learned?** Everything that can hurt you can also make you stronger and make you learn something about yourself.

"The simpler the better"
JONATHAN SAUNDERS + POLLINI

His exuberant prints shown in his graduate collection were an instant hit and took many a fashion critic's breath away. Using traditional silk-screening techniques, Jonathan Saunders is now synonymous with geometric patterns and colour. Within a year of graduating from Central Saint Martins (MA with distinction in printed textiles) in 2002, Scottish-born Jonathan Saunders – the son of two ministers from Rutherglen – made his runway debut at London Fashion Week. Since then, Saunders' brilliant fusion of print and silhouette have been in great demand and he has gone on to consult for other major fashion houses such as Alexander McQueen, Chloé and Pucci. His namesake line has at the same time been growing in stature, stocked by prestigious stores such as Harrods and Harvey Nichols in London and Neiman Marcus in America. He showed for the first time in New York in February 2008, joining a string of British fashion designers like Matthew Williamson and Preen on the New York schedule, to build on his international business. Most recently, in 2008, he was named creative director of the fashion house Pollini.

Die überbordenden Print-Muster seiner Abschlusskollektion waren ein unmittelbarer Erfolg und nahmen vielen Modejournalisten den Atem. Durch seine Anwendung traditioneller Siebdrucktechnik gilt Jonathan Saunders' Name heute als Synonym für geometrische Muster und Farbe. Nur ein Jahr nach seinem Abschluss am Central Saint Martins (MA mit Prädikat im Fach Bedruckte Textilien) 2002 gab der in Schottland geborene Jonathan Saunders – Sohn einer Pfarrersfamilie aus Rutherglen – sein Laufsteg-Debüt bei der London Fashion Week. Seit damals ist Saunders' brillante Verbindung von Muster und Silhouette extrem gefragt, und er hat sich einen Namen als Berater großer Modehäuser wie Alexander McQueen, Chloé und Pucci gemacht. Parallel dazu hat die nach ihm selbst benannte Linie an Ansehen gewonnen und ist inzwischen in Nobelkaufhäusern wie Harrods und Harvey Nichols in London und Neiman Marcus in den USA vorrätig. In New York präsentierte er erstmals im Februar 2008 und trat damit einer Riege britischer Designer wie Matthew Williamson und Preen im New Yorker Kalender bei, um seine internationalen Geschäfte auszubauen. Zuletzt wurde er 2008 zum Creative Director des Modehauses Pollini ernannt.

Les imprimés exubérants que présente Jonathan Saunders dans sa collection de fin d'études remportent un succès immédiat et époustouflent plus d'un critique de mode. Fan des techniques de sérigraphie traditionnelles, son nom est aujourd'hui synonyme de couleur et de motifs géométriques. Un an après avoir décroché son diplôme à Central Saint Martins (un MA en textiles imprimés obtenu avec mention en 2002), cet Ecossais élevé par des parents pasteurs à Rutherglen défile déjà à la London Fashion Week. Depuis, sa fusion extrêmement brillante entre imprimé et silhouette est très demandée. Saunders a aussi travaillé comme consultant auprès de grandes maisons de mode telles Alexander McQueen, Chloé et Pucci. Parallèlement, sa collection éponyme prend de plus en plus d'ampleur, désormais distribuée par des détaillants aussi prestigieux qu'Harrods et Harvey Nichols à Londres, et Neiman Marcus aux Etats-Unis. Son premier défilé new-yorkais officiel a eu lieu en février 2008 aux côtés d'autres créateurs britanniques comme Matthew Williamson et Preen, ce qui lui a permis de développer son activité à l'international. Plus tard en 2008, il a été nommé directeur de la création de la maison Pollini. KAREN LEONG

What are your signature designs? Clothing that focuses on using colour, cut and print together. Graphic **What is your favourite piece from any of your collections?** Neoprene jacket (look no 22 autumn/winter 2008) on Dianne, ombre dress (look 37 autumn/winter 2008) on Alyona for my own collection for Pollini, the last look from the current autumn/winter collection **How would you describe your work?** It's more process driven than referenced. I start from both colour and fabric and how that relates to the person wearing it. I try to develop a textile design and image how that would work well when translated into a garment **What's your ultimate goal?** To have a sense of achievement. Both for me and for everyone I work with. For all of us to keep enjoying what we do **What inspires you?** When I see something new or see something that I am familiar with in a new way. I love artists such as Alan Jones, Richard Lindner, Rebecca Horn, Sophie Calle. Music – Pink Floyd (also their art direction). I have also met some great people who continue to give me inspiration **Who do you have in mind when you design?** I suppose it depends on the collection. I've never been very good at finding a 'muse'. I think I draw more on my friends **Is the idea of creative collaboration important to you?** I think it is vital. I've learned so much from the people that I've worked with. There are always so many people involved in getting a collection together, both on a practical and a creative level. All of these people are as necessary as a designer **Who has been the greatest influence on your career?** My best friend, Yvie. I've been so lucky to have known her since I was young in Scotland. She now works with me and I really trust her opinion and know she will always have my best interests at heart **How have your own experiences affected your work as a designer?** Coming from a textiles/product-design background has, of course, molded the direction I have taken as a designer. It was hard at the beginning to have the confidence to translate what I had learned into clothing, but it is also what helped me have a customer for my designs. Going to Saint Martins was definitely the experience that, through the guidance of Louise Wilson and Fleet Bigwood, made me learn how to focus on my point of view, despite the sometimes harrowing process. Working on Pollini has been a great experience for me. What I do for my own line is so specific and although it is carried through to a certain extent, it's good work in a different way. I am able to draw on aspects of the traditional image of the brand and have learned a lot about the development of accessories **Which is more important in your work: the process or the product?** Both are as important as the other, as both rely on each other **Is designing difficult for you? If so, what drives you to continue?** At times, yes. Fashion is so specific as it requires such a fast turn around and for decisions to be made quickly and confidently, which is sometimes difficult when it is a creative process. I generally feel an element of disappointment after finishing a collection and find myself wishing I had done certain things better, but it is this very thing that pushes you to try again. Balancing business management with being a creative person is also a challenge but having the people that I work with makes it achievable. I don't think I would carry on doing my own collection without my team **Have you ever been influenced or moved by the reaction to your designs?** There are opinions that are good to listen to and thee are others that are not. It's important to be convinced of your own work first as so much of fashion is taste. I have found people such as Sarah Mower really helpful as she is someone who tends to critique the execution on an idea as opposed to the idea itself **What's your definition of beauty?** Individuality **What's your philosophy?** To keep learning from my mistakes **What is the most important lesson you've learned?** The simpler the better.

"I like to look at fashion from a scientific way, that still remains true to its purpose"
MARIOS SCHWAB

Marios Schwab is the embodiment of a cosmopolitan. The 30-year-old half-Greek half-Austrian designer lived in Athens and Berlin before moving to London. At the renowned German fashion institution ESMOD, Schwab graduated with distinction and Best Student Award, after which he moved to London and graduated with an MA in womenswear fashion from Central Saint Martins in 2003. By this time his childhood ambition to be a ballet dancer was far behind him. His label was launched in 2005 and after showing for two seasons with Fashion East, Schwab debuted on schedule at London Fashion Week for spring/summer 2007 to high critical acclaim. Describing the little black dress as his design signature, his dresses have been worn by Kate Moss, Hilary Duff, Kylie Minogue and Clemence Poesy. Awarded Best New Designer at the British Fashion Awards in 2006, Schwab won the Swiss Textiles Award the next year. In 2008, Schwab collaborated with Swarovski for the Runway Rocks show, and continues to show in London.

Marios Schwab ist die Verkörperung eines Kosmopoliten. Der 30-Jährige ist zur Hälfte Grieche, zur Hälfte Österreicher und lebte in Athen und Berlin, bevor er seinen Wohnsitz nach London verlegte. Er absolvierte die renommierte deutsche Modeschule ESMOD mit Auszeichnung und dem Best Student Award. Anschließend ging er nach London, wo er am Central Saint Martins einen Master in Womenswear Fashion erwarb. Seinen Kindheitstraum, Tänzer zu werden, hatte er zu diesem Zeitpunkt schon weit hinter sich gelassen. 2005 gründete er sein eigenes Label, und nachdem er zwei Saisons lang bei der Fashion East vertreten gewesen war, gab er ein vielbeachtetes Debüt im offiziellen Kalender der London Fashion Week mit seiner Kollektion für Frühling/Sommer 2007. Das kleine Schwarze gilt als sein Markenzeichen, und so sieht man seine Kleider unter anderem an Kate Moss, Hilary Duff, Kylie Minogue und Clemence Poesy. Bei den British Fashion Awards 2006 wurde er als Best New Designer ausgezeichnet. Im Jahr darauf gewann Schwab den Swiss Textiles Award. 2008 arbeitete er gemeinsam mit Swarovski an der Show „Runway Rocks". Darüber hinaus präsentiert Schwab weiterhin in London.

Marios Schwab est le cosmopolite par excellence. Mi-grec, mi-autrichien, ce styliste de 30 ans a vécu à Athènes et à Berlin avant de venir s'installer à Londres. De la célèbre école de mode allemande ESMOD, Schwab sort diplômé avec les honneurs du jury et le prix de meilleur étudiant. C'est à ce moment-là qu'il part vivre à Londres, où il décroche en 2003 un MA en mode féminine de Central Saint Martins. S'il rêvait de devenir danseur classique quand il était petit, ces ambitions sont désormais loin derrière lui. Schwab lance sa griffe en 2005, puis, après deux saisons dans le cadre des défilés Fashion East, il fait ses débuts officiels aux collections printemps/été 2007 de la London Fashion Week devant une critique enthousiasmée. Avec la petite robe noire comme signature créative, ses modèles ont été portés par Kate Moss, Hilary Duff, Kylie Minogue et Clemence Poesy. Couronné Best New Designer aux British Fashion Awards en 2006, Schwab remporte le Swiss Textiles Award l'année suivante. En 2008, il collabore avec Swarovski pour le défilé Runway Rocks et continue à présenter ses collections à Londres.

KAREN LEONG

What are your signature designs? The little black dress, tactile fashion, garments that become personal **What is your favourite piece from any of your collections?** A bra covered in silver, which later formed part of a shoot in i-D **How would you describe your work?** Complex yet simple to read… conceptual yet sexy… I like to look at fashion in a scientific way, that still remains true to its purpose. I like looking at it always from a different angle **What's your ultimate goal?** To build a brand, to create against time, to perfect my vision and use it in different ways, not just in fashion **What inspires you?** The complexity of the human body **Can fashion still have a political ambition?** Should fashion have a political ambition? **Who do you have in mind when you design?** An enigmatic but still approachable woman **Is the idea of creative collaboration important to you?** I like challenging someone from a different creative backround to step into my vision, whether that is a musician or an artist. The same applies to whenever I design for someone else (for another house or non-related fashion Project) **Who has been the greatest influence on your career?** I can not just name one, but a few, my dad and mother, Louise Wilson, Nicola Formichetti, Tal Brenner, my first stylist. Each one of them in a different way and time **How have your own experiences affected your work as a designer?** I remember when I first left Athens at 15, I went to Austria to learn tailoring, one thought was in my mind, fashion. Four years later, living in Berlin, fashion was still a passion but not the same. Once I came to London, this became my expression **Which is more important in your work: the process or the product?** Both are equally important. The process is a journey, an adventure. Through this you're going to understand the product. Once the product is perfected, seeing it on the pages of a magazine, this becomes another journey from another perspective and equally pleasing **Is designing difficult for you? If so, what drives you to continue?** Designing is a small part of what I do and probably the easiest. It comes naturally in the long run. Depending on the concept, the research and complexity of making is what drives me. Controlling the business part is the hardest and most time-consuming, which is a kick in itself **Have you ever been influenced or moved by the reaction to your designs?** Take every opinion with a pinch of salt… sometimes, later I realised the point of me being a creator is to do what comes naturaly and instinctivly **What's your philosophy?** To live is to leave traces **What's the most important lesson you've learned?** Stay humble and be yourself.

"I love creating and I hate the empty feeling when it's done"
JEREMY SCOTT

Jeremy Scott's story is the stuff of fairy tales and syndicated game shows. Born in 1974 and raised in Kansas City, Missouri, Scott was the boy who read Italian 'Vogue' between classes and wrote about fashion in French essays. After graduating from New York's Pratt Institute, the 21-year-old made a pilgrimage to Paris, where his collection, made out of paper hospital gowns and inspired by the body-modifying artist Orlan, went down in fashion folklore. His first formal runway presentation in October 1997, 'Rich White Women', presenting asymmetrically cut trousers and multifunctional T-shirts, established Scott as a substantial Parisian presence. But controversy clings to the designer like a Pierre Cardin teddy bear brooch. Later collections, such as March 1998's infamous 'Contrapied' show, have met with a mixture of incredulity and derision, all the while establishing key details of the Scott aesthetic: attention to volume, obsession with logos (including bestselling back-to-front Paris print), a hard-edged Mugler-esque glamour and a wicked way with fur. In autumn 2001, Scott relocated to Los Angeles, a city that has welcomed his über-trash style with open arms, to such an extent that in January 2002 he achieved one of his long-term ambitions, appearing as a celebrity contestant on Wheel of Fortune. Scott continues to show in New York and LA. Scott's colourful, optimistic vision has developed into strong collaborations. In 2006, he designed bags for Longchamp with his telephone print and "this is not your bag" graphics. In 2008, Adidas launched a Jeremy Scott collection of clothing and shoes. His artistic energy continues to inspire his many celebrity fans, from Madonna and Beth Ditto to Asia Argento and Uffie. As Scott himself might say, vive l'avant-garde!

Jeremy Scotts Biografie klingt wie der Stoff, aus dem Märchen sind. Oder Fernsehshows. Der 1974 geborene und in Kansas City, Missouri, aufgewachsene Scott las tatsächlich schon als Schüler in der Pause die italienische Vogue und schrieb in Französisch Aufsätze über Mode. Nach einem Abschluss am New Yorker Pratt Institute pilgerte der damals 21-Jährige nach Paris, wo seine Kollektion aus papierenen Krankenhaushemden in die Modegeschichte einging. Dazu inspiriert hatte ihn die Künstlerin Orlan, die ihren Körper u. a. durch Schönheitsoperationen zum Kunstobjekt gemacht hat. Scotts erste offizielle Laufsteg-Schau präsentierte im Oktober 1997 unter dem Titel „Rich White Women" asymmetrisch geschnittene Hosen und multifunktionale T-shirts, mit denen der Designer sich in der Pariser Szene etablierte. Doch haftet ihm Widersprüchlichkeit wie eine Teddybär-Brosche von Pierre Cardin an. So wurden spätere Kollektionen, etwa die berüchtigte Show „Contrapied" vom März 1998, zwar mit einer Mischung aus Skepsis und Spott aufgenommen, setzten aber dennoch Maßstäbe für Scotts Ästhetik: Volumen, eine Passion für Logos (inklusive des Bestsellers in Gestalt eines umlaufenden Parisdrucks), kantiger, an Mugler erinnernder Glamour und ein verrücktes Faible für Pelz. Im Herbst 2001 verlegte Scott seinen Wohnsitz nach Los Angeles – in die Stadt, die seinen extrem kitschigen Stil mit solcher Begeisterung aufgenommen hatte. Die Resonanz war so groß, dass im Januar 2002 ein lang gehegter Wunsch Scotts in Erfüllung ging: Er war Stargast in der TV-Show „Wheel of Fortune". Seine Kollektionen zeigt Scott weiterhin in New York und LA. Aus seiner farbenfroh optimistischen Vision haben sich intensive Kooperationen entwickelt. 2006 entwarf er Taschen mit seinem Telefonmuster und den Schriftzügen „this is not your bag" für Longchamp. 2008 brachte Adidas eine Jeremy-Scott-Kollektion mit Kleidung und Schuhen heraus. Seine künstlerische Energie dient weiterhin vielen prominenten Fans als Inspiration, von Madonna über Beth Ditto bis hin zu Asia Argento und Uffie. Getreu Scotts Motto: Vive l'avant-garde!

L'histoire de Jeremy Scott est une affaire de contes de fées et de jeux télévisés. Né en 1974, il grandit à Kansas City dans le Missouri, où il est bien le seul à lire le Vogue italien entre les cours et à disserter sur la mode dans ses rédactions de français. Une fois diplômé du Pratt Institute de New York à 21 ans, Scott part en pèlerinage à Paris. La collection qu'il y présente marque un véritable tournant dans l'histoire de la mode, avec ses robes d'hôpitaux en papier inspirées par l'œuvre de l'artiste plasticienne Orlan. En octobre 1997, lors de son premier défilé officiel intitulé « Rich White Women », il présente des pantalons asymétriques et des T-shirts multifonctions qui assoient définitivement sa présence sur la scène parisienne. Mais la controverse s'accroche à lui comme une broche-nounours de Pierre Cardin. Les collections suivantes, par exemple le terrible défilé « Contrepied » de mars 1998, sont accueillies dans un mélange d'incrédulité et de dérision, bien que certains détails-clés parviennent à imposer l'esthétique de Scott : l'attention portée au volume, l'obsession des logos (notamment l'imprimé intégral « Paris » qui s'est très bien vendu), un glamour « mugleresque » aux lignes acérées et une utilisation scandaleuse de la fourrure. A l'automne 2001, Scott s'installe à Los Angeles, une ville qui accueille son style ultra-trash à bras ouverts. A tel point qu'en janvier 2002, il réalise l'un de ses plus vieux rêves : il participe à l'emission « Wheel of Fortune » en tant que candidat de marque. Scott continue à présenter ses collections à New York et L. A. Son optimisme multicolore s'exprime aussi à travers d'importantes collaborations. En 2006, il conçoit pour Longchamp une collection de sacs baptisée « This is not your bag » qui reprend ses imprimés de téléphone. En 2008, Adidas lance une collection de vêtements et de chaussures signée Jeremy Scott. Son énergie artistique continue d'inspirer ses nombreuses et célèbres admiratrices, qu'il s'agisse de Madonna, Beth Ditto, Asia Argento ou Uffie. Comme le dirait Scott lui-même, « vive l'avant-garde » !

GLENN WALDRON

What are your signature designs? Avant-garde high fashion streetwear with a touch of humour **What is your favourite piece from any of your collections?** They are all like children to me. It would be a sin to pick a favourite! **How would you describe your work?** Thought-provoking and defining of the times **What's your ultimate goal?** I want to touch people's lives **What inspires you?** Looking back at where I've come from, and thinking about where I want to go **Can**

fashion still have a political ambition? You bet! The slippery side to all this is that fashion can play both sides of the fence **Who do you have in mind when you design?** Myself, my friends, the kids in Harajuku **Is the idea of creative collaboration important to you?** No, not really – after working in film, which is reliant upon collaboration, I realised how spoilt I am to do what I want and how I want – not having to be accountable to anyone

else **Who has been the greatest influence on your career?** Myself, as I'm a self-made man **How have your own experiences affected your work as a designer?** I can't separate the two – what's my own and what's my work? There is no differentiation **Which is more important in your work: the process or the product?** More and more it's the process – I love creating and I hate the empty feeling when it's done **Is designing difficult for you? If so, what drives you to**

continue? Easy breezy – I do this stuff in my sleep now **Have you ever been influenced or moved by the reaction to your designs?** Of course, I've felt many emotions linked to people's reaction to my work. I've been flattered, touched and mind-blown by what my work has meant to others **What's your definition of beauty?** Ever-changing **What's your philosophy?** Leap first, look later **What is the most important lesson you've learned?** Get while the getting's good!

"The collections have been part of the process of growing up"
RAF SIMONS · JIL SANDER

Although he is now one of the indisputable kings of menswear, Raf Simons (born 1968) never took a single fashion course. Instead, he studied industrial design in Genk, Belgium, close to his hometown Neerpelt. Nevertheless, he took an internship at the Walter van Beirendonck Antwerp office while still at school, citing fashion as a major point of interest. Afterwards, Simons started working as a furniture designer, but gradually grew unhappy with this direction. In 1995, after moving to Antwerp and meeting up with Linda Loppa, head of the fashion department at the city's Royal Academy, he decided to switch career. Obsessed both by traditional, formal menswear and the rebellious dress codes of present and past youth cultures, Simons distilled a groundbreaking new style from these inspirations. From his first collection for autumn/winter 1995 on, he drew a tight, linear silhouette executed in classical materials that encapsulated references like English schoolboys, gothic music, punk, Kraftwerk and Bauhaus architecture. Despite international acclaim, Raf Simons surprisingly shut down his company after presenting his autumn/winter 1999 collection, in order to take a sabbatical and rearrange the internal structure of his business. After sealing a close co-operation with Belgian manufacturer CIG, Simons returned for autumn/winter 2000 with a new, multilayered and radical look, worn as ever by non-professional models scouted on the streets of Antwerp. These teenage boys were the subject of a collaboration with David Sims, resulting in photographs compiled in a book ('Isolated Heroes', 1999). Raf Simons designed the Ruffo Research men's collections for two seasons in 1999. Since October 2000, he has taught fashion at the University of Applied Arts in Vienna, and in February 2001, he guest edited an issue of i-D. In 2003, Simons curated two exhibitions ('The Fourth Sex' at Pitti Immagine, Florence, and 'Guided by Heroes' in Hasselt, Belgium) and collaborated with Peter Saville on his autumn/winter 2003 collection, 'Closer'. In May 2005, it was announced that Simons would take over as creative director at Jil Sander – Simons dedicated the autumn/winter 2009 collection to Sander.

Auch wenn er heute zu den unumstrittenen Königen der Herrenmode zählt, hat der 1968 geborene Raf Simons nie auch nur ein einziges Seminar zum Thema Mode besucht. Stattdessen studierte er im belgischen Genk nahe seiner Heimatstadt Neerpelt Industriedesign. Allerdings absolvierte er noch als Schüler ein Praktikum im Antwerpener Atelier von Walter van Beirendonck und interessierte sich bereits damals sehr für Mode. Zunächst arbeitete Simons als Möbeldesigner. Nachdem er nach Antwerpen gezogen war und dort Linda Loppa, die Leiterin der Modefakultät an der Königlichen Akademie, kennengelernt hatte, beschloss er 1995 umzusatteln. Fasziniert sowohl von der traditionellen klassischen Herrenmode als auch von den rebellischen Dresscodes der Jugendlichen verschiedenster Generationen, destillierte Simons aus diesen Inspirationen einen bahnbrechenden neuen Stil. Schon in seiner ersten Kollektion, Herbst/Winter 1995, entschied er sich für eine schmale, lineare Silhouette aus klassischen Materialien. Dazu kamen Bezüge zu englischen Schuluniformen, Gothic Music, Punk, Kraftwerk und Bauhausarchitektur. Trotz internationaler Anerkennung schloss Simons seine Firma überraschenderweise nach der Präsentation seiner Kollektion für Herbst/Winter 1999, um sich eine Auszeit zu gönnen und sein Geschäft international neu zu strukturieren. Nachdem die enge Zusammenarbeit mit dem belgischen Hersteller CIG besiegelt war, kehrte Simons für die Saison Herbst/Winter 2000 mit einem neuen, radikalen Look aus vielen Lagen zurück. Den präsentierten wie immer Amateur-Models, die man auf den Straßen von Antwerpen angeworben hatte. Um eben diese Teenager-Jungs ging es auch bei einem Projekt mit David Sims, das in dem Fotoband „Isolated Heroes" (1999) dokumentiert ist. Im Jahr 1999 entwarf Simons bei Ruffo Research die Herrenkollektionen für zwei Saisons. Seit Oktober 2000 lehrt er Mode an der Universität für Angewandte Kunst in Wien. Als Gastredakteur wirkte er im Februar 2001 an einer Ausgabe von i-D mit. 2003 war Simons Kurator von zwei Ausstellungen („The Fourth Sex" in der Fondazione Pitti Immagine in Florenz und „Guided by Heroes" im belgischen Hasselt) und erarbeitete zusammen mit Peter Saville seine Kollektion „Closer" für Herbst/Winter 2003. Im Mai 2005 gab Jil Sander bekannt, dass Raf Simons Creative Director würde. Seine Kollektion für Herbst/Winter 2009 widmete der Designer Jil Sander.

Bien qu'il soit sans conteste devenu l'un des rois de la mode pour homme, Raf Simons (né en 1968) n'a jamais suivi la moindre formation en mode. En fait, il a étudié le design industriel à Genk, près de sa ville natale de Neerpelt en Belgique. Pendant ses études, il fait toutefois un stage au bureau anversois de Walter van Beirendonck, car la mode figure parmi ses principaux centres d'intérêt. Ensuite, Simons commence à travailler comme designer de meubles. En 1995, après avoir emménagé à Anvers et rencontré Linda Loppa, directrice du département mode de l'Académie Royale de la ville, il décide de changer de carrière. Obsédé à la fois par la mode masculine classique et les codes vestimentaires de la jeunesse rebelle d'hier et d'aujourd'hui, Simons puise dans ces inspirations et invente un nouveau style révolutionnaire. Dès sa première collection à l'automne/hiver 1995, il définit une silhouette étroite et linéaire, façonnée dans des matières classiques pleines de références aux collégiens anglais, à la musique gothique, au punk, à Kraftwerk ou encore à l'architecture Bauhaus. Malgré un succès international, contre toute attente, Raf Simons ferme sa maison après avoir présenté sa collection automne/hiver 1999, décidant de prendre un congé sabbatique et de revoir la structure interne de son entreprise. Il signe ensuite un accord d'étroite coopération avec le fabricant belge CIG, puis revient à l'automne/hiver 2000 avec un nouveau look radical aux multiples facettes, présenté comme toujours sur des mannequins non professionnels recrutés dans les rues d'Anvers. Ces adolescents font d'ailleurs l'objet d'une collaboration avec David Sims, qui sort un livre de photographies (« Isolated Heroes », 1999). Par ailleurs, Raf Simons a conçu deux collections masculines pour Ruffo Research en 1999. Depuis octobre 2000, il enseigne la mode à l'Université des Arts Appliqués de Vienne et a été invité au comité de rédaction du numéro de février 2001 du magazine i-D. En 2003, il a organisé deux expositions (« The Fourth Sex » au Pitti Immagine de Florence et « Guided by Heroes » à Hasselt en Belgique) et a collaboré avec Peter Saville sur « Closer », sa collection automne/hiver 2003. En mai 2005, la maison Jil Sander annonce le recrutement de Raf Simons au poste de directeur de la création. Il dédie la collection automne/hiver 2009 à la créatrice dont la maison porte le nom.

PETER DE POTTER

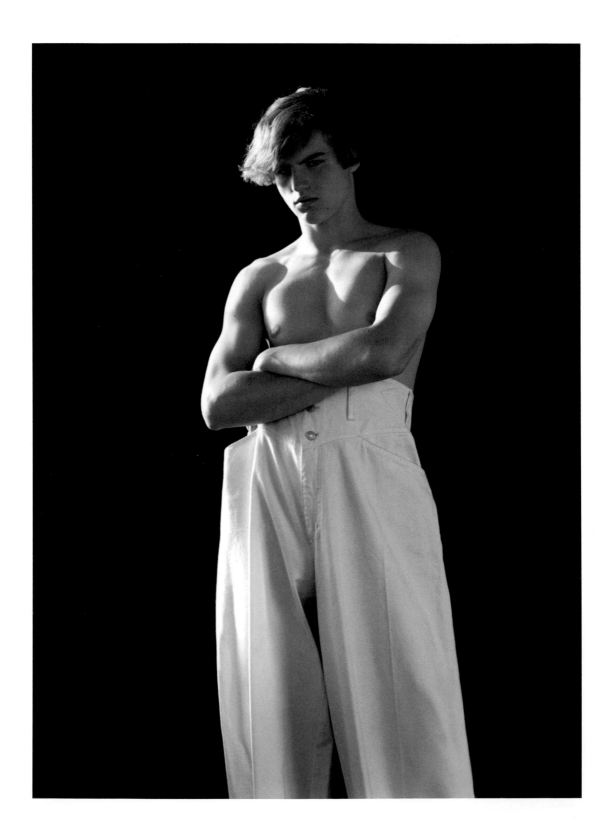

RAF SIMONS

PHOTOGRAPHY TIERNEY GEARON. STYLING VICTORIA BARTLETT. JUNE/JULY 2002.

What is your favourite piece from any of your collections? I really like the work for the hippy summer collection. I think that more than ever it was the moment that we concentrated on what we believed in. We moved away from all the other things that you think about, like the industry and everything. Of course it was a very uncommercial collection; it was a very difficult collection. It was a very special procedure to work on it. It was very unindustrial. For example, there were about 50 people involved in the hand painting for it **How would you describe your work?** I think that, more and more, all the collections have been part of the process of growing up. It is connected with casting. In the show, I used

all the boys that I was using eight years ago, that are now all 30 years old. Alexander, who was doing the last show, just became a father. You know, five or six years ago, all they were interested in was a T-shirt with a print and baggy pants. But now they have graduated and are starting to find jobs. They go out looking for jobs and they come back to me, and you know it's that suit from five years ago. So that makes me think, and look at the form that I am bringing out now. The second thing is that in fashion in general people will look to the piece itself. They concentrate on, 'How can I make this seam look special?' or 'What am I going to do with that button so it looks interesting?' I am not interested in that. At the moment,

I am more interested in the shape and the form. I have a big desire to make clothes without defining them, because we don't know what it means to make it right for the 21st century, to make it for the future **Who do you have in mind when you design?** I think there was a certain period when the show was an instrument to stay young. I was making these young, teenage collections, while I myself was already 30. And now I don't feel like that. Now, I am interested in making clothes for all audiences **Which is more important in your work: the process or the product?** In the past, the process was more important than the result. Now I am also focusing on the product **What is the most important lesson**

you've learned? To protect your 'baby'. I know that my business is not big. My business and my image are very out of balance with each other. I know that the business could have been bigger, but I would have had to make sacrifices and compromises. But now it is time to concentrate on the product – that's for sure. I am happy to do that. I used to have a real love-hate relationship with fashion, but at the moment I love it. I really love it. I love the fashion, I love the product and I love people who are really interested in buying clothes. It is not a new reaction; I have been feeling like this for a couple of years now.

"The perpetual 'restart' of fashion is very interesting and this permanent evolution is what pushes me to stay in this profession"
MARTINE SITBON · RUE DU MAIL

Martine Sitbon is a designer whose eye roves the globe for inspiration, referencing and subverting an eclectic mix of cultures while never exploiting her exotic upbringing. The child of an Italian mother and French father, Sitbon was born in Casablanca in 1951. At the age of ten, she moved to Paris, where she experienced firsthand the social transformations the city went through in the late '60s. She studied at the famed Studio Berçot, graduating in 1974 before travelling. After spending seven years rummaging through Hong Kong, Mexico, India, New York and Milan, she later fed this blend of the exotic and urban into her designs. In 1985, Sitbon launched her own label and presented her first show in Paris with a collection that famously gathered together monks' hoods, pastel colours, bloomers and a Velvet Underground soundtrack. Black may be key to the palette of the artistic intelligentsia, but Sitbon has enticed them with combinations of sober shades that threaten to clash head-on, but swerve just at the last minute. Her coolly dishevelled clothing often uses elements of leather and masculine tailoring to juxtapose the flea-market femininity of velvets, silks and satins. These contrasting combinations saw her recruited by Chloé in 1988 to design the label's womenswear line, a collaboration that lasted for nine seasons. In 1996, Sitbon opened her first boutique, in Paris. From 2001 to 2002, Sitbon was head designer for womenswear at Byblos. Now concentrating on her own-label menswear and womenswear, Sitbon remains the choice for those who love fashion's more eclectic side. Sitbon stopped showing in Paris from 2004 to 2007, when she presented her first edition of Rue du Mail together with her partner, Marc Ascoli. Within three seasons, the collection – comprising Sitbon's signature of beautifully sculpted asymmetric silhouettes, intelligent mix of muted colours and contrasting textures from satin to canvas – thrilled her fans as well as her young Hong Kong backer.

Martine Sitbon ist eine Designerin, die rund um den Globus nach Inspiration, Bezugspunkten und Subversion für einen eklektischen Mix der Kulturen sucht, ohne dafür ihre exotische Herkunft auszuschlachten. Sie wurde 1951 als Kind einer italienischen Mutter und eines französischen Vaters in Casablanca geboren. Als sie zehn Jahre alt war, zog sie mit ihrer Familie nach Paris, wo sie die gesellschaftlichen Umwälzungen Ende der 1960er aus unmittelbarer Nähe miterlebte. Sie studierte bis 1974 am berühmten Studio Berçot, um danach auf Reisen zu gehen. Nach sieben Jahren, die sie in Hongkong, Mexiko, Indien, New York und Mailand verbracht hatte, ließ sie diese Melange aus exotischen und urbanen Eindrücken in ihre Kreationen einfließen. 1985 präsentierte Sitbon ihr eigenes Label und ihre erste Schau in Paris mit einer denkwürdigen Kollektion aus Mönchskutten, Pastellfarben, Pumphosen und einem Soundtrack von Velvet Underground. Schwarz mag die dominierende Farbe der Künstler-Intelligenzia sein, doch Sitbon lockte sie mit Kombinationen sachlicher Farbtöne, die sich zu beißen scheinen, im letzten Augenblick aber doch noch harmonieren. Für ihre auf eine coole Art wirren Kleider benutzt sie oft Elemente aus der Leder- und Herrenschneiderei, die sie mit der Weiblichkeit von Flohmarktfunden aus Samt, Seide und Satin konfrontiert. Diese gegensätzlichen Kombinationen brachten

sie 1988 zu Chloé, wo sie die Damenlinie des Labels entwarf. Eine Partnerschaft, die neun Saisons lang hielt. 1996 eröffnete Sitbon ihre erste Pariser Boutique. Als Chefdesignerin der Damenmode war sie von 2001 bis 2002 für Byblos tätig. Heute konzentriert sich Sitbon ausschließlich auf die Damen- und Herrenmode ihres eigenen Labels und empfiehlt sich damit allen, die die eklektische Seite der Mode lieben. Von 2004 bis 2007 präsentierte Sitbon nicht in Paris. Erst mit ihrer ersten Kollektion für Rue du Mail gemeinsam mit ihrem Partner Marc Ascoli kehrte sie zurück. Innerhalb von drei Saisons begeisterte die Kollektion – mit den für Sitbon so typischen wunderbar skulpturalen asymmetrischen Silhouetten, einer intelligenten Mischung gedämpfter Farben und kontrastierenden Materialien von Satin bis Segeltuch – ihre Fans ebenso wie ihren jungen Sponsor aus Hongkong.

La créatrice Martine Sitbon parcourt le monde en quête d'inspiration, faisant référence de façon subversive à un mélange éclectique de cultures sans jamais exploiter ses propres origines exotiques. Martine Sitbon naît en 1951 à Casablanca d'une mère italienne et d'un père français. Elle arrive à Paris à l'âge de dix ans, où elle assiste aux premières loges aux transformations sociales que subit la capitale française jusqu'à la fin des années 60. Elle sort diplômée du célèbre Studio Berçot en 1974, puis part en voyage pour enrichir les compétences techniques qu'elle a déjà acquises d'un aspect multiculturel et de sa passion des tissus luxueux. Après sept années de découvertes entre Hong Kong, le Mexique, l'Inde, New York et Milan, elle insufflera plus tard ce mix exotique et urbain à ses créations. En 1985, Martine Sitbon lance sa propre griffe et présente son premier défilé à Paris avec une collection restée dans les annales qui mêle capuches monastiques, couleurs pastel, salopettes et musique du Velvet Underground. Le noir a beau être essentiel aux yeux de l'intelligentsia artistique, Martine Sitbon la convertit à d'autres couleurs sobres dans des combinaisons pas nécessairement harmonieuses, mais qui évitent toutefois le chaos chromatique. Ses vêtements tranquillement désordonnés conjuguent souvent des éléments du cuir et des costumes pour homme avec la féminité vintage des velours, des soies et des satins. Ces combinaisons contrastées attirent l'attention de la maison Chloé, qui embauche Martine Sitbon en 1988 pour dessiner sa ligne pour femme, une collaboration qui durera neuf saisons. En 1996, la créatrice ouvre sa première boutique à Paris. En 2001 et 2002, elle travaille comme styliste principale de la collection pour femme de Byblos. Aujourd'hui, Martine Sitbon se consacre à sa propre griffe pour homme et pour femme. Elle reste une créatrice de choix pour tous ceux qui privilégient le côté plus éclectique de la mode. Elle cesse de présenter ses collections à Paris entre 2004 et 2007, une année qui voit le lancement de la première édition Rue du Mail en partenariat avec Marc Ascoli. En l'espace de trois saisons, cette collection qui reprend les signatures de Martine Sitbon – silhouettes asymétriques magnifiquement sculptées, mélange intelligent de couleurs sourdes, textures contrastées du satin à la toile – suscite l'enthousiasme de ses fans comme celui de son jeune financier de Hong Kong.

LIZ HANCOCK

What are your signature designs? The mix of opposites – femininity and androgyny, fragility and rock, reality and dream – defines my style. I work with contrasts; I try in each collection to distance myself from obvious references. Mix up. Confuse **What is your favourite piece from any of your collections?** This question is difficult for me to answer… In a way, my favourite piece is always the next to come! **How would you describe your work?** Always a dichotomy between old clothes from the military and tailoring to flowing bias and draping. A mix of ordinary clothes with extraordinary pieces, respecting reality **What inspires you?** I accumulate extremely diverse emotions that may come from films, rock concerts, ballet, exhibitions **Can fashion still have a political ambition?** I hope so. Everything shouldn't come down solely to commercialism **Who do you have in mind when you design?** A girl who is lively, off-beat, original… **Is the idea of creative collaboration important to you?** Definitely. I love to work as a team; there is a synergetic effect, stimulation and an exchange of ideas invaluable in creative work **Who has been the greatest influence on your career?** When I was young, David Bowie, the Rolling Stones and Syd Barrett gave me the desire to do fashion **How have your own experiences affected your work as a designer?** Music has brought a lot to me and going to second-hand markets was the fundamental starting-point of my research. Later, modern dance and art left an impression on me. I have the impression that everything I have experienced has affected my work **Which is more important in your work: the process or the product?** With the product, history becomes real, but the most interesting part is the process. **Is designing difficult for you? If so, what drives you to continue?** The perpetual 'restart' of fashion is very interesting and this permanent evolution is what pushes me to stay in this profession. We can never sleep, we cannot count on anything and there is a real idea of a game **Have you ever been influenced or moved by the reaction to your designs?** Success, like failure, pushes you to do your work better **What's your philosophy?** Keep your feet on the ground and your head in the clouds.

"The thing I'm most interested in is continuity. I've always worked hard at not being today's flavour"
PAUL SMITH

A serious accident while riding his bike put paid to Paul Smith's dream of becoming a professional racing cyclist. However, this mishap propelled him to pursue a career involving his other passion: fashion. In 1970, Smith (born Nottingham, 1946) opened a store in his native city, selling his own early designs that reflected the types of clothing he loved but was unable to buy anywhere else. Studying fashion design at evening classes, and working closely with his wife, Pauline Denyer, a graduate of the Royal College of Art, by 1976 he was showing a full range of menswear in Paris. Carving out a distinctive look that combined the best of traditional English attire often with unusual or witty prints, Smith blazed a trail throughout the late '70s. His progress continued into the '80s – when he put boxer shorts back on the fashion map – and beyond, with stores opened in New York (1987), and Paris (1993). The designer now has a staggering 200 shops in Japan, and also offers a range of womenswear (launched in 1994) and clothing for kids, in addition to accessories, books, jewellery, fragrances, pens, rugs and china. In 2001, Smith was knighted, and despite the success and breadth of his company – wholesaling to 35 countries around the globe – his hands-on involvement remains integral to its success. Commercial accomplishments aside, Smith's aesthetic has retained its idiosyncrasies. His autumn/winter 2005 womenswear collection, with its tartan tailoring and trilbies, was a sideways glance at the '60s; for his menswear, in the same season, Smith gave a lesson in clash and contrast, combining python trousers with checked jackets and floral shirts. Paul Smith's global expansion continues to reach the first decade of the 21st century. While established in Asia and Europe, his unique aesthetic has also grown in America from East Coast New York to West Coast LA and San Francisco. The P.S. is in his personal touch, as the perfect shopkeeper.

Ein schwerer Unfall beendete Paul Smiths Traum von einer Karriere als Radrennfahrer. Allerdings veranlasste ihn dieses Missgeschick, aus seiner zweiten Passion – der Mode – eine Karriere zu machen. Der 1946 in Nottingham geborene Smith eröffnete 1970 in seiner Heimatstadt einen Laden, wo er seine frühen eigenen Entwürfe verkaufte – lauter Dinge, die er selbst gern getragen hätte, aber nirgends auftreiben konnte. In Abendkursen studierte er Modedesign und arbeitete außerdem eng mit seiner Frau Pauline Denyer, einer Absolventin des Royal College of Art, zusammen. 1976 konnte Smith eine komplette Herrenkollektion in Paris präsentieren. Sein ausgeprägt individueller Look vereinte die Vorzüge der traditionellen englischen Schneiderkunst mit oft ungewöhnlichen oder witzigen Mustern und hinterließ in den 1970er-Jahren deutliche Spuren. Die positive Entwicklung hielt bis in die 1980er-Jahre an – als er die Boxershorts wieder ins allgemeine Modebewusstsein zurück brachte – und darüber hinaus, mit Neueröffnungen von Läden in New York (1987) und Paris (1993). Inzwischen besitzt der Designer unglaubliche 200 Shops in Japan, wo er auch eine Damenkollektion (seit 1994), Kindersachen sowie Accessoires, Bücher, Schmuck, Düfte, Schreibgeräte, Teppiche und Porzellan führt. Im Jahr 2001 wurde Smith zum Ritter geschlagen, und trotz des Erfolges und der großen Produktpalette seines

Unternehmens – man beliefert Großhändler in 35 Ländern rund um den Globus – ist nach wie vor sein ganz persönliches Engagement integraler Bestandteil des Gelingens. Abgesehen von seinen kommerziellen Talenten hat sich Smith in seiner Ästhetik auch Eigenheiten bewahrt, die zum Teil auf Ablehnung stoßen. So war etwa die Damenkollektion Herbst/Winter 2005 mit ihren Schottenkaros und weichen Filzhüten ein Blick zurück auf die 1960er-Jahre. Den Männern erteilte Smith in derselben Saison eine Lektion zum Thema Kollision und Kontraste, indem er beispielsweise Hosen mit Pythonmuster, karierte Jacken und Hemden mit floralem Muster kombinierte. Paul Smiths weltweite Expansion geht auch im 21. Jahrhundert weiter. Nachdem er sich in Asien und Europa bereits etabliert hat, setzt sich seine unverwechselbare Ästhetik nun auch in Amerika, von New York bis nach Los Angeles und San Francisco zunehmend durch. Sein Erfolgsrezept ist dabei wohl das persönliche Engagement des perfekten Geschäftsmannes.

Un grave accident de vélo met un terme aux premières ambitions du jeune Paul Smith, qui rêvait de devenir cycliste professionnel, mais cette mésaventure le conduit à se consacrer à son autre passion : la mode. En 1970, Smith (né en 1946) ouvre une boutique dans sa ville natale de Nottingham où il vend ses premières créations, qui reflètent le type de vêtements qu'il adore mais qu'il n'arrive à trouver nulle part. Etudiant la mode en cours du soir tout en travaillant en étroite collaboration avec Pauline Denyer, son épouse diplômée du Royal College of Art, il développe si bien son entreprise qu'il finit par présenter une collection pour homme complète à Paris dès 1976. Forgeant un look original qui combine le meilleur du style anglais traditionnel à des imprimés souvent insolites ou pleins d'esprit, Paul Smith reste sur cette lancée jusqu'à la fin des années 70. Il poursuit son ascension pendant les années 80 et au-delà, époque à laquelle il remet les boxer shorts au goût du jour, avec l'ouverture de nouvelles boutiques à New York (1987) et à Paris (1993). Aujourd'hui, le créateur ne compte pas moins de 200 points de vente au Japon et propose également une ligne pour femme (lancée en 1994) ainsi qu'une collection pour enfant, sans mentionner les accessoires, les livres, les bijoux, les parfums, les stylos, les tapis et la porcelaine Paul Smith. En 2001, Paul Smith est fait Chevalier de Sa Majesté, et malgré l'immense succès et la diversification de son entreprise, qui vend dans 35 pays à travers le monde, son approche pratique reste un facteur essentiel de sa réussite. Outre ces exploits commerciaux, l'esthétique de Smith conserve ses traits distinctifs. Sa collection pour femme automne/hiver 2005, avec ses tailleurs et ses chapeaux mous en tartan, lorgne du côté des années 60, tandis que dans sa ligne masculine de la même saison, Smith nous donne une vraie leçon de choc et de contraste, juxtaposant pantalons en python, vestes à carreaux et chemises à fleurs. L'expansion mondiale de l'entreprise Paul Smith poursuit son cours pendant la première décennie du XXIe siècle. Bien établi en Asie et en Europe, son esthétique unique s'implante aussi aux Etats-Unis, de New York sur la côte est à L.A. et San Francisco sur la côte ouest. La touche personnelle de Paul Smith, c'est aussi de représenter le parfait commerçant. JAMES ANDERSON

What are your signature designs? Tradition mixed with the unexpected **What's your favourite piece from any of your collections?** I have no favourite piece, but the simplicity of my suits mixed with the eccentricity of special linings I like very much **How would you describe your work?** Curious **What's your ultimate goal?** Keeping things simple and having a business with a heart **What inspires you?** Observation and thinking **Can fashion still have a political ambition?** In my case, no **Who do you have in mind when you design?** People who want to show their own character **Is the idea of creative collaboration important to you?** A creative collaboration should be inspiring – if it is, then it is important **Who has been the greatest influence on your career?** My father and my wife **How have your own experiences affected your work** as a designer? They go hand in hand **Which is more important in your work: the process or the product?** Personally, the process, but the product pays my wages **Is designing difficult for you? If so, what drives you to continue?** I never think about design, the ideas seem to come naturally **Have you ever been influenced or moved by the reaction to your designs?** As my designs are not radical, this has never come to mind **What's your definition of beauty?** Something that is natural and not forced **What's your philosophy?** Making clothes for people from everyday walks of life **What is the most important lesson you've learned?** Always give yourself time to answer important requests.

"People who go to my fashion shows kinda go to a rock concert"
ANNA SUI

Anna Sui's singularity lies in her ability to weave her own passions into her work. Her creations are intricate pastiches of vintage eras and knowing nods to music and popular culture – from '60s Portobello to downtown rockers and B-Boys. Her love of fashion began early. Growing up in a sleepy suburb of Detroit, Sui (born 1955) spent her days styling her dolls and collating her 'genius files', a source book of magazine clippings that she continues to reference today. In 1972, she began studying at Parsons School of Design in New York, where she became a regular on the underground punk scene and where she met photographer Steven Meisel, a long-time friend and collaborator. Sui spent the remainder of the '70s designing for a string of sportswear companies. Then, in 1980, she presented a six-piece collection at the Boutique Show, receiving an immediate order from Macy's. Sui made her runway debut proper in 1991; the collection was a critically acclaimed homage to her heroine, Coco Chanel. And by the early '90s, her self-consciously maximalist look was helping to pave the way for designers like Marc Jacobs, sparking a revival in the New York fashion scene. In 1993, she won the CFDA Perry Ellis Award for New Fashion Talent. Sui encapsulated the grunge spirit of the times, with Smashing Pumpkins guitarist James Iha – a close friend – appearing in her winter 1995 'California Dreaming' show, and Courtney Love famously adopting Sui's classic baby-doll dresses. Sui now has stores in New York, LA, Taiwan, Hong Kong, Shanghai, Tokyo and Osaka, and has added denim, sportswear, shoes and accessories to her brand. Her kitsch cosmetics and best-selling fragrances, with distinctive rose-embossed packaging, have all helped to establish her as an important designer and shrewd businesswoman with an eccentric spirit and limitless sense of fun. In 2006, a limited-edition Anna Sui Boho Barbie was launched with Mattel.

Anna Suis Einzigartigkeit liegt darin begründet, dass sie spielerisch ihre eigenen Leidenschaften in ihre Arbeit hineinwebt. Ihre Kreationen sind aufwendige Imitationen von Vintage vergangener Epochen und Anspielungen auf Musik und Popkultur – vom Portobello der 1960er-Jahre bis zu den Vorstadtrockern und B-Boys. Ihre Liebe zur Mode entwickelte sich früh. Während ihrer Kindheit in einem verschlafenen Vorort von Detroit verbrachte die 1955 geborene Sui viel Zeit mit dem Stylen ihrer Puppen und dem Anlegen ihrer „Genius Files", einer Sammelmappe mit Zeitungsausschnitten, auf die sie bis heute zurückgreift. 1972 begann sie ihr Studium an der Parsons School of Design in New York, wo sie treues Mitglied der Underground-Punk-Szene wurde und den Fotografen Steven Meisel kennenlernte, der ihr langjähriger Freund und Kollege werden sollte. Den Rest der 1970er-Jahre verbrachte Sui mit dem Designen von Sportswear für diverse Firmen. 1980 präsentierte sie dann auf der Boutique Show eine sechsteilige Kollektion, die sofort von Macy's geordert wurde. Ihr offizielles Laufsteg-Debüt gab Sui schließlich 1991. Ihre damalige, von den Kritikern gefeierte Kollektion war eine Hommage an ihr Idol Coco Chanel. Ihr selbstbewusster maximalistischer Look bahnte Anfang der 1990er-Jahre Designern wie Marc Jacobs den Weg und sorgte für eine Neubelebung der New Yorker Modeszene.

1993 gewann sie den Perry Ellis Award for New Fashion Talent der CFDA. Sui griff den Grunge-Stil der damaligen Zeit auf, insbesondere als der Gitarrist der Smashing Pumpkins, James Iha – ein enger Freund der Designerin – in ihrer Schau „California Dreaming" im Winter 1995 auftrat und Courtney Love öffentlichkeitswirksam Suis klassische Babydoll-Kleider für sich entdeckte. Heute betreibt Sui eigene Läden in New York, LA, Taiwan, Hongkong, Shanghai, Tokio und Osaka und hat ihr Programm um Jeans, Sportswear, Schuhe sowie Accessoires erweitert. Nicht zuletzt haben ihre kitschig gestalteten Kosmetika und bestens verkäuflichen Düfte mit der typischen rosenverzierten Verpackung dazu beigetragen, sie als wichtige Designerin und kluge Geschäftsfrau mit exzentrischem Geschmack und grenzenlosem Sinn für Humor zu etablieren. 2006 brachte Mattel als limitierte Sonderedition eine Anna Sui Boho Barbie auf den Markt.

La singularité d'Anna Sui réside dans son talent ludique à intégrer ses propres passions dans son travail. Ses créations sont autant de pastiches élaborés des époques vintage que des clins d'œil entendus à la musique et à la culture pop, du Portobello des années 60 aux rockers et B-Boys d'aujourd'hui. Elle tombe amoureuse de la mode dès son plus jeune âge. Elevée dans une triste banlieue de Detroit, Anna Sui (née en 1955) passe ses journées à habiller ses poupées et à compiler ce qu'elle appelle ses «genius files», un album de photos découpées dans les magazines de mode dont elle se sert encore aujourd'hui. En 1972, elle entame des études à la Parsons School of Design de New York, où elle fraye avec la scène punk underground et rencontre le photographe Steven Meisel, qui deviendra son ami et collaborateur. Jusqu'à la fin des années 70, Anna Sui occupe plusieurs postes de styliste dans le sportswear. Puis, en 1980, elle présente au Boutique Show une petite collection de six pièces immédiatement achetée par Macy's. Anna Sui fait ses véritables débuts lors d'un premier défilé en 1991, avec une collection créée en hommage à son héroïne Coco Chanel et plébiscitée par la critique. Au début des années 90, son look délibérément maximaliste ouvre la voie à des créateurs tels que Marc Jacobs et déclenche le renouveau de la mode new-yorkaise. En 1993, elle remporte le prix Perry Ellis décerné aux nouveaux talents par le CFDA. Anna Sui saisit parfaitement l'esprit grunge de l'époque : son grand ami James Iha, guitariste des Smashing Pumpkins, défile pour sa collection «California Dreaming» de l'hiver 1995 et Courtney Love adopte ses petites robes de baby doll. Anna Sui possède actuellement des boutiques à New York, Los Angeles, Taiwan, Hong Kong, Shanghai, Tokyo et Osaka. Sa marque s'est enrichie d'une ligne de pièces en denim, d'une gamme sportswear, de chaussures et d'accessoires. Au-delà de leurs flacons roses originaux, ses produits de maquillage kitsch et ses parfums à succès ont contribué à faire d'elle une créatrice qui compte, une femme d'affaires avisée à l'esprit excentrique et au sens de l'humour illimité. En 2006, elle a sorti une poupée Barbie «bohemian chic» Anna Sui en édition limitée avec Mattel.

AIMEE FARRELL

What are your signature designs? When people think of my clothes, they think romantic and feminine with a lot of embellishment. I love folkloric and vintage, so there's all those elements thrown in. Then there's always rock'n'roll **What is your favourite piece from any of your collections?** A trompe l'œil print dress I did for spring 2001 **How would you describe your work?** My favourite thing is discovering something, absorbing it and then putting it into my collection and showing it off to everybody. People who go to my fashion shows kinda go to a rock concert, as I like to take them on a journey, an escapist journey. It's a fantasy, something that they are going to have fun with **What's your ultimate goal?** This is it! I like making beautiful clothes. I'm the ultimate consumer, so there's nothing better than to be able to do products that I love, plus cosmetics and perfumes **What inspires you?** I'm fortunate that I can find inspiration in anything I'm currently interested in and incorporate it into my work. Books I read, places I travel, exhibitions I see, music I listen to **Can fashion still have a political ambition?** I imagine it could – but that's not my intention. Perhaps I'm past the stage of being rebellious. It is possible to be really rebellious with fashion but usually it's a younger person who feels they need to make their statement that way. It's not an issue that I aspire to **Who do you have in mind when you design?** Again, there's always the selfish consumer in me **Is the idea of creative collaboration important to you?** Yes, naturally fashion involves collaboration. I collaborate with fabric houses and print companies. I'm proud of the beautiful knitwear I've developed with James Coviello for my show. Erickson Beamon and I think up fun ideas for jewellery. I'm lucky to have wonderful licensee products: perfume, cosmetics, shoes, hose, sunglasses **Who has been the greatest influence on your career?** My parents. I think I got my creative and artistic side from my mother and the practical and logical side from my father. If I didn't have that combination, I wouldn't be able to do what I'm doing **How have your own experiences affected your work as a designer?** Every experience I have could show up in my work **Which is more important in your work: the process or the product?** I learned a long time ago that designing is a process which doesn't come overnight – you have to develop it to get the end result that you want. The more you develop your craft, the more the product becomes the ideal product and the thing that you were aiming for **Is designing difficult for you? If so, what drives you to continue?** It's difficult and you are never happy. But that's part of the creative process **Have you ever been influenced or moved by the reaction to your designs?** The biggest compliment I've ever had was when a man who didn't really even know that much about fashion came up to me and said, "You know, my wife looks her most beautiful when she wears a dress she bought from you eight years ago." That really means something because it's heartfelt. An old dress that makes her feel happy every time she wears it. I mean, what more could you ask for? **What's your definition of beauty?** There are so many levels of beauty. There's the ideal beauty, but that's not always the most attractive thing. I think there's beauty in almost everything, if you look at it in a certain way **What's your philosophy?** Live your dream **What is the most important lesson you've learned?** That the world is a much bigger place than just fashion.

"I cannot deny the difficulty involved in creating designs. But I think I continue creating them because I enjoy it"
JUN TAKAHASHI • UNDERCOVER

Founded by Japanese designer Jun Takahashi in 1994, the Undercover label now includes some seriously discerning types among its fanbase, not least Rei Kawakubo, who in 2004 had Takahashi design a selection of blouses to sell in the Comme des Garçons store in Tokyo. Born in Kiryu, in 1969, and a graduate of the Bunka Academy, it was while studying that Takahashi began making clothes to wear himself, frustrated at not being able to find anything he liked in shops. His confidence and individuality sets him apart from many young Japanese designers, who are happy to rely on easily digestible, graphic-led T-shirts and slogans. Takahashi's approach is more complex and distinctive, and has been variously described as 'thrift-shop chic' or 'subversive couture'. Considering his belief that life is as much about pain as it is about beauty, it is not surprising that the resulting Undercover aesthetic makes for an anarchic collision of the violent (slashed, ripped and restitched fabrics) and the poetic (chiffon, lace and faded floral prints). Further clues to the designer's mindset are found in his fondness for defiant English punk bands – while still a student, he was a member of the Tokyo Sex Pistols. Having won prestigious Mainichi Fashion Grand Prize in 2001 and made his Paris catwalk debut with his spring/summer 2003 collection, Takahashi today continues to up the ante. Undercover is now split into five lines – Undercover, Undercoverism, Undakovit, Undakovrist and Undakovr, all of which are sold through a flagship store in Tokyo's fashionable Omotesando district. Further Undercover stores have opened in Paris and Milan, while global stockists continue to grow (in tandem with appreciative converts to the label). In 2008, Takahashi and Nigo (of A Bathing Ape) reconstructed their 'No Label' store within Dover Street Market, London. The following year, Undercover was invited to present their collection in the famous Boboli Gardens in Florence during Pitti Imagine.

Das 1994 vom japanischen Designer Jun Takahashi gegründete Label Undercover kann einige wirklich scharfsichtige Leute zu seinen Fans zählen. Etwa Rei Kawakubo, die Takahashi im Jahr 2004 eine Auswahl von Blusen entwerfen und anschließend im Laden von Comme des Garçons in Tokio verkaufen ließ. Der 1969 in Kiryu geborene Absolvent der Bunka-Akademie begann schon im College-Alter, seine Kleidung selbst zu entwerfen – aus Ärger darüber, dass er in keinem Laden etwas fand, das ihm zusagte. Sein Selbstvertrauen und seine Individualität unterscheiden ihn von vielen japanischen Jungdesignern, die sich nur zu gern auf eine leichte Kost aus grafisch gestalteten T-Shirts und Slogans verlassen. Takahashis Zugang ist komplexer und unverwechselbar, er wurde schon mit Begriffen wie „Thrift-shop Chic" oder „subversive Couture" versehen. Gemäß seiner Überzeugung, wonach Schmerz genauso Teil des Lebens ist wie Schönheit, kollidieren in der Ästhetik von Undercover folgerichtig gewalttätige Elemente (aufgeschlitzter, zerrissener und geflickter Stoff) mit poetischen (Chiffon, Spitze und verblichene Blumenmuster). Weiteren Aufschluss über die Denkweise des Designers gibt sein Faible für aufmüpfige englische Punkbands – in seiner Studentenzeit war er selbst Mitglied der Hommage-Band Tokyo Sex Pistols.

Nachdem er 2001 den Hauptpreis beim prestigeträchtigen Mainichi Fashion Grand Prize gewonnen und mit der Kollektion für Frühjahr/Sommer 2003 sein Debüt auf dem Pariser Catwalk gegeben hat, ist Takahashi heute dabei, seinen Marktwert weiter zu steigern. Undercover umfasst inzwischen fünf Linien – Undercover, Undercoverism, Undakovit, Undakovrist und Undakovr –, die allesamt im Flagship Store in Tokios Trendviertel Omotesando verkauft werden. Weitere Undercover-Läden wurden in Paris und Mailand eröffnet. Außerdem wächst parallel zur Zahl der dankbaren Anhänger des Labels auch die der interessierten Großhändler in aller Welt. 2008 gestalteten Takahashi und Nigo (von A Bathing Ape) ihren ‚No Label'-Laden im Londoner Dover Street Market um. Im darauf folgenden Jahr wurde Undercover eingeladen, seine Kollektion im Rahmen der Pitti Imagine in den berühmten Boboli-Gärten in Florenz zu präsentieren.

Fondée en 1994 par le créateur japonais Jun Takahashi, la griffe Undercover compte aujourd'hui parmi ses fans des personnages au goût très avisé, notamment Rei Kawakubo qui en 2004 a demandé au jeune styliste de lui dessiner une sélection de chemisiers pour les vendre dans la boutique Comme des Garçons de Tokyo. Né en 1969 à Kiryu et diplômé de la Bunka Academy, Jun Takahashi est encore étudiant quand il commence à confectionner ses propres vêtements, frustré de ne pas trouver ce qu'il aime dans les magasins. Son assurance et son individualité le distinguent de la plupart des autres jeunes créateurs japonais, qui se contentent souvent de proposer des T-shirts à l'esprit graphique et aux slogans facilement consommables. L'approche de Takahashi est bien plus complexe et originale, souvent décrite comme du « chic d'occasion » ou de la « couture subversive ». Comme Takahashi croit que la vie est autant faite de douleur que de beauté, rien de surprenant à ce que l'esthétique d'Undercover propose une collision anarchique entre violence (tissus tailladés, déchirés et recousus) et poésie (mousseline, dentelle et imprimés floraux passés). On trouve d'autres indices de l'état d'esprit du créateur dans sa prédilection pour les groupes punk anglais les plus provocants : encore étudiant, il était membre des Tokyo Sex Pistols, formés en hommage au groupe britannique. Après avoir remporté le prestigieux Mainichi Fashion Grand Prize en 2001 et fait ses débuts à Paris avec sa collection printemps/été 2003, aujourd'hui Jun Takahashi ne cesse de faire monter les enjeux. Undercover se divise désormais en cinq lignes : Undercover, Undercoverism, Undakovit, Undakovrist et Undakovr, toutes vendues par sa boutique indépendante à Omotesando, quartier branché de Tokyo. D'autres boutiques Undercover ont ouvert leurs portes à Paris et à Milan alors que les distributeurs internationaux continuent à se développer, en tandem avec les admirateurs convertis à la griffe. En 2008, Takahashi et Nigo (de A Bathing Ape) ont reconstruit leur boutique « No Label » au sein du Dover Street Market de Londres. L'année suivante, la marque Undercover a été invitée à présenter sa collection dans le fameux Jardin de Boboli pendant le salon Pitti Imagine de Florence.

JAMES ANDERSON

What is your favourite piece from any of your collections? The latest one (my collection for autumn/winter 2009) **What's your ultimate goal?** Peace **What inspires you?** All material things in the world, happenings and emotions **Can fashion still have a political ambition?** Yes **Who do you have in mind when you design?** No one in particular. If I really need to give you a more specific answer, my wife **Is the idea of creative collaboration important to you?** Yes, once in a while **Who has been the greatest influence on your career?** Rei Kawakubo **Which is more important in your work: the process or the product?** Both **Is designing difficult for you? If so, what drives you to continue?** I cannot deny the difficulty involved in creating designs. But I think I continue creating them because I enjoy it **Have you ever been influenced or moved by the reaction to your designs?** Yes, just for two minutes **What is the most important lesson you've learned?** A defiant spirit and positive thinking.

"I like to imagine being in the skin of women"
OLIVIER THEYSKENS

He lives in a 19th century brothel in Brussels, owns the head of a stuffed giraffe and makes macabre clothes riddled with sexual and religious connotations – but designer Olivier Theyskens is not as dark as he seems. He cried at 'E.T.', is David Attenborough's number one fan and would rather stay at home cooking than go out to some celeb-packed party. Theyskens fans include Smashing Pumpkins' Melissa Auf der Maur, who has catwalked for him, but the Belgian first made headline news when Madonna sent a personally faxed request on his 21st birthday. Born in Brussels in 1977, Theyskens dropped out of the city's Ecole Nationale Supérieure des Arts Visuels de la Cambre in January 1997 but presented his debut collection, 'Gloomy Trips', that August. Six months later, Madonna wore one of the dresses to the Oscars and a star was born. Theyskens' Gothic image was engendered on the catwalk: clothes were embroidered with real hair or decorated with dead skulls and stuffed birds, while his signature voluminous dresses, scarred with hook fasteners, made models look like beautiful Victorian governesses. In 2002, he joined the House of Rochas as artistic director – his first collection in March 2003 marked the return of Rochas as a fashion force. In 2005, Theyskens was given the Fashion Group's Star Honoree Award at the Night of Stars and, in the following year, he won Best International Designer at the CFDA Fashion Awards. Olivier Theyskens joined Nina Ricci in 2006, but left the design house in 2009.

Er lebt in einem ehemaligen Bordell aus dem 19. Jahrhundert in Brüssel, besitzt den ausgestopften Kopf einer Giraffe und macht makabre Mode voller sexueller und religiöser Anspielungen. Trotzdem ist der Designer Olivier Theyskens gar kein so düsterer Mensch, wie es vielleicht auf den ersten Blick scheint. Er weint bei „E.T.", ist der größte Bewunderer von David Attenborough und bleibt lieber zu Hause, um zu kochen, als auf irgendeine Promi-Party zu gehen. Zu Theyskens' Fans gehört unter anderem Melissa Auf der Maur. Die ehemalige Bassistin der Smashing Pumpkins hat für den Designer auch schon bei Schauen gemodelt. In die Schlagzeilen kam der Belgier jedoch erstmals, als Madonna ihm an seinem 21. Geburtstag höchstpersönlich eine Bestellung faxte. Der 1977 in Brüssel geborene Theyskens brach zwar im Januar 1997 sein Studium an der Ecole Nationale Supérieure des Arts Visuels de la Cambre in seiner Heimatstadt ab, präsentierte jedoch schon im August desselben Jahres seine Debütkollektion „Gloomy

Trips". Sechs Monate später trug Madonna eines dieser Kleider zur Oscar-Verleihung und machte dessen Designer damit über Nacht zum Star. Theyskens' Image als Gothic-Fan entstand auf dem Catwalk: durch Stoffe, die mit echten Haaren bestickt waren, Totenköpfe und ausgestopfte Vögel als Dekoration. Gleichzeitig ließen seine typisch voluminösen, mit zahllosen Häkchen versehenen Kleider die Models wie wunderschöne viktorianische Gouvernanten aussehen. 2002 wurde er Art Director im Hause Rochas. Seine erste Kollektion im März 2003 bedeutete die Rückkehr Rochas' als Marke von Rang. Im Jahr 2005 wurde Theyskens von der Fashion Group im Rahmen der Night of Stars als Star Honoree ausgezeichnet. Im darauf folgenden Jahr schnitt er bei den CFDA Fashion Awards als Best International Designer ab. Von 2006 bis 2009 war Theyskens für Nina Ricci tätig.

Certes, Olivier Theyskens vit dans un bordel bruxellois du XIXe siècle, possède une tête de girafe empaillée et crée des vêtements macabres aux connotations sexuelles et religieuses évidentes; pourtant, ce créateur n'est pas aussi sombre qu'il y paraît. En larmes devant « E.T. » et fan numéro un de David Attenborough, il préfère rester chez lui et faire la cuisine plutôt que de courir les soirées people. Theyskens compte des fans célèbres, tels que Melissa Auf der Maur, du groupe Smashing Pumpkins, qui a défilé pour lui. Le Belge a même fait la une des journaux lorsque Madonna lui a faxé une commande le jour de son XXIe anniversaire. Né à Bruxelles en 1977, Theyskens interrompt ses études à l'Ecole Nationale Supérieure des Arts Visuels de la Cambre en janvier 1997 et présente sa première collection, « Gloomy Trips », dès le mois d'août suivant. Six mois plus tard, Madonna porte l'une de ses robes à la cérémonie des Oscars: une étoile est née. L'image gothique de Theyskens trouve son origine sur les podiums de ses défilés: il présente des vêtements brodés de vrais poils ou décorés de crânes et d'oiseaux empaillés, tandis que ses robes volumineuses si caractéristiques, déformées par des crochets, donnent aux mannequins un air de gouvernantes de l'ère victorienne. En 2002, il devient directeur artistique de Rochas: sa première collection en mars 2003 marque le retour en force de cette vénérable maison de mode. En 2005, Theyskens reçoit le prix Star Honoree du Fashion Group lors de la Night of Stars, et l'année suivante, il remporte le titre de Best International Designer du CFDA. Olivier Theyskens rejoint ensuite la maison Nina Ricci au poste de directeur artistique, mais démissionne en 2009.

What are your signature designs? I'm looking for a sort of balance. My character is quite logical and mathematical, and in the construction of my collections sometimes I find a logic – of balance, of creativity and a love for fashion. I don't actually know what my signature piece would be. I think rather it's a whole, a spirit **What are your favourite pieces from any of your collections?** The ones that make the girls more beautiful. My favourite one season can be a pair of trousers; the next time it can be a skirt or a dress. I never like the same things. The important thing is the impact at that precise moment **How would you describe your work?** I have to be disciplined but I also have to consider letting myself go, allowing myself to take risks in innovation or creativity. My role is not totally artistic. You have to be really practical and you also

have to be a little bit anarchic **What's your ultimate goal?** I want to grow. Sometimes I think I also want to prove myself. But I love what I do, it gives me happiness, so my goal really is emotional **What inspires you?** I like to imagine being in the skin of women. In fact, the clothing sometimes doesn't express the real subject of the collection. Sometimes it's more a feeling – one of desperation or, at other times one of happiness. Behind the look and attitude, it's like something cinematic **Who do you have in mind when you design?** I give a lot of my time to rethinking woman and her body, because I love the body. Sometimes it's skinnier, sometimes it's more soft, sometimes it's a more muscular body. That's always the first step **What has been the greatest influence on your career?** My childhood. Everything I saw in my childhood I think,

unconsciously, I have inside me. I'm stimulated by TV, by the media, by the women around me, by me. But I think childhood is very, very important **Is designing difficult for you? If so, what drives you to continue?** What is difficult, in my case, is to put myself in the mood to design. Because when I'm good at designing, I draw very quickly, very precisely. The collections are done in just a few days. It's a situation where you are totally confident with yourself and totally okay to go in one direction and not another. That situation is difficult. Sometimes little things can break it completely: a fight with somebody, a stupid programme on TV can ruin your mood. Sometimes I feel like an opera singer – very complicated! **Have you ever been influenced or moved by the reaction to your designs?** I have been bothered by them sometimes **What's your**

definition of beauty? It has to move me. When I see something beautiful, it brings me so much happiness that I may cry. It doesn't happen often – I'm very critical and cynical about what I see **What's your philosophy?** My philosophy is to learn and to leave bad things behind; you don't have to keep them in your mind. You can learn and forget. What's interesting is to have lots of experiences, things that press you on to a higher level in your own humanity and in your own thinking. But things have to be good, not bad. And people, too **What is the most important lesson you've learned?** Not to trust good-looking people! I've been innocent and naïve about the motivations of some people. I've been very naïve. I'm still naïve…

"The starting point for each new collection is the previous collection"
JUSTIN THORNTON & THEA BREGAZZI · PREEN

Preen is Justin Thornton and Thea Bregazzi (both born in 1969). The pair grew up on the Isle of Man, meeting at the age of just 18 while both were studying for an art foundation course. However, the duo – and couple – did not start designing together until their island upbringing was in the past. Both attended fashion college on the mainland before setting out on their own after graduating. Thornton designed for Helen Storey's innovative 'Second Life' collection and Bregazzi started styling. It was Storey who brought them back together, asking them to jointly consult on her autumn/winter 1996 collection. The formation of Preen was the next logical step. The duo launched their first stand-alone collection in 1997, creating a buzz around individually crafted, deconstructed pieces that fused Victoriana with streetwear elements in a sharp, tailored silhouette. Construction and deconstruction have fascinated the couple ever since. Darlings of the style press during their formative years, Preen have developed their deconstruction tendencies, consistently providing alternatives to classic tailoring. Inspirations include circus performers, Pearly Kings and Queens and ballgowns. Such eccentricity had somewhat mystified fashion critics until their spring/summer 2003 collection. Shown at London Fashion Week, the duo softened their gritty, streetwear look for gentler shapes inspired by seminal fashion movie 'Belle de Jour' and even '70s rag doll Holly Hobby. They gained celebrity fans including 'American Vogue's' Anna Wintour, Claudia Schiffer and Gwyneth Paltrow. Their menswear line, launched in 2003, has been well received. Ewan McGregor and David Bowie are fans. Now a fixture on New York Fashion Week's calendar (since 2007), they also showed for the first time (Preen Line autumn/winter 2008) at Copenhagen Fashion Week.

Preen, das sind Justin Thornton und Thea Bregazzi, beide Jahrgang 1969. Das Paar wuchs auf der Isle of Man auf und lernte sich mit gerade mal 18 Jahren als Teilnehmer an einem Kunstseminar kennen. Mit den gemeinsamen Entwürfen begann das berufliche wie private Team jedoch erst, nachdem es die Insel verlassen hatte. Beide besuchten eine Modeschule auf dem Festland und gingen nach dem Abschluss erst einmal getrennte Wege. Thornton entwarf für Helen Storeys innovative Kollektion „Second Life", während Bregazzi zunächst als Stylistin arbeitete. Es war Storey, die die beiden wieder zusammenbrachte, als sie sie als Berater für ihre Kollektion Herbst/Winter 1996 engagierte. Die Gründung von Preen war dann nur noch der nächste logische Schritt. Die erste eigene Kollektion lancierte das Duo 1997. Ihre individuell gearbeiteten, dekonstruktiven Kreationen vereinten Aspekte viktorianischer Mode mit Streetwear-Elementen in klar umrissenen Silhouetten. Das Thema Konstruktion und Dekonstruktion fasziniert die beiden Designer seit jeher. Als Liebling der Modepresse in den Anfangsjahren hat Preen die Neigung zur Dekonstruktion inzwischen weiter ausgebaut und bietet konsequent Alternativen zu klassisch geschneiderter Klei-

dung an. Als Inspiration dienen dabei Zirkuskünstler, Pearly Kings and Queens sowie Ballroben. Diese Exzentrik bezauberte alle Kritiker. Seit seiner Kollektion für Frühjahr/Sommer 2003 hat das Designerpaar jedoch begonnen, den gewagten Streetwear-Look im Stil von „Belle de Jour" und der Lumpenpuppe Holly Hobby aus den 1970er-Jahren etwas abzuschwächen. Zu den prominenten Anhängern des Labels gehören Anna Wintour von der amerikanischen Vogue, Claudia Schiffer und Gwyneth Paltrow. Die 2003 vorgestellte Herrenlinie wurde ebenfalls wohlwollend aufgenommen. Hier zählen Ewan McGregor und David Bowie zu den Fans. Nachdem es fixer Bestandteil der New York Fashion Week geworden war (seit 2007), präsentierte sich das Label (mit Preen Line Herbst/Winter 2008) erstmal auch bei der Copenhagen Fashion Week.

Preen, c'est Justin Thornton et Thea Bregazzi (tous deux nés en 1969). Bien qu'ils aient tous deux grandi sur l'île de Man, ils se rencontrent seulement à l'âge de dix-huit ans dans une école d'art. Néanmoins, ce duo qui forme aussi un vrai couple dans la vie ne collaborera pas avant d'avoir laissé derrière lui son enfance passée sur l'île. Ils suivent des études de mode sur le continent et se lancent après l'obtention de leurs diplômes. Justin Thornton dessine pour la collection innovante « Second Life » de Helen Storey tandis que Thea Bregazzi travaille dans le stylisme. C'est justement Helen Storey qui les réunit lorsqu'elle leur demande de travailler ensemble en tant que consultants sur sa collection automne/hiver 1996. Logiquement, l'étape suivante voit la création de leur griffe Preen. Le duo lance sa première collection en 1997 et tout le monde ne parle plus que de leurs pièces déconstruites de production artisanale qui fusionnent l'époque victorienne à des éléments streetwear au sein d'une silhouette bien définie. Depuis, le couple reste fasciné par les questions de construction et de déconstruction. Chouchous de la presse spécialisée pendant leurs années de formation, ils développent à travers Preen leur tendance déconstructionniste et ne cessent de proposer des alternatives aux coupes classiques. Entre autres, ils s'inspirent des artistes de cirque, des « Pearly Kings and Queens » et des robes de bal, une excentricité qui laissera les critiques de mode dubitatifs jusqu'à leur collection printemps/été 2003 présentée à la London Fashion Week, où leur look streetwear dérangeant s'adoucit grâce à des formes plus faciles inspirées de « Belle de Jour » et même de la poupée en chiffon Holly Hobby des années 70. Ils séduisent des clientes célèbres telles qu'Anna Wintour du Vogue américain, Claudia Schiffer et Gwyneth Paltrow. Leur ligne pour homme lancée en 2003 a été bien accueillie : Ewan McGregor et David Bowie en sont fans. Désormais rendez-vous régulier du calendrier de la New York Fashion Week (depuis 2007), Preen a défilé pour la toute première fois à la Semaine de la mode de Copenhague (collection automne/hiver 2008).

LAUREN COCHRANE

What are your signature designs? A Preen signature design would be a garment which is craft-worked mixing opposing fabrics that would have an overall urban feel **What is your favourite piece from any collection?** Each season we have new favourites, but it's nice when we rediscover an old favourite in the back of our wardrobe **How would you describe your work?** We describe our work as an extension of how we are feeling at the time when we design a collection. The starting point for each new collection is the previous collection **What's your ultimate goal?** Independence and security in both work and life **What inspires you?** People and life experiences **Can fashion still have a political ambition?** No **Who do you have in mind when you design?** Not one particular person. Each season is an amalgamation of attitudes and feelings **Is the idea of creative collaboration important to you?** Yes, collaboration encourages the development of ideas **Who has been the greatest influence on your career?** No one person has been a major influence **How have your own experiences affected your work as a designer?** It's difficult to say, as every experience affects us in a new and different way **Which is more important in your work: the process or the product?** Both are important, but the product is what matters in the end **Is designing difficult for you? If so, what drives you to continue?** No, designing is not difficult. It is the fashion timetable and the pressure of business that are testing **Have you ever been influenced or moved by the reaction to your designs?** When people love what we do, it makes us very happy **What's your definition of beauty?** Individuality **What's your philosophy?** We don't have a philosophy as such, as long as we are true to our own ideas and thoughts and it doesn't matter what others think **What's the most important lesson you've learned?** To always trust our instincts.

"Sometimes I don't even design the product, I just invent a new process instead"
AITOR THROUP

Born in 1980 in Buenos Aires, Aitor Throup moved to Burnley, Lancashire, by way of Spain. A passion for technologically advanced garments (from labels such as Stone Island and C.P. Company), drawing and designing comic book characters led him to a BA in fashion design at Manchester Metropolitan University. The importance he places on narrative was apparent in his graduate collection from the RCA – entitled 'When Football Hooligans Become Hindu Gods', the collection comprised military elements and Hindu symbolism. Throup's design philosophy is one that is more organic than methodical, which always starts with the human form. Throup then allows his creations to evolve naturally, using a three-stage construction process of 'drawing, sculpture, garment' instead of a more conventional construction. At ITS#FIVE (International Talent Support) in 2006, Throup won the Collection of the Year Award and the i-D Styling Award, and went on to exhibit twice at London Fashion Week's MAN show. In 2008, Throup presented his first instalment of an ongoing seasonal 'Anatomy Series' collaboration with Stone Island at Milan Fashion Week and exhibited a special collaboration with C.P. Company. More recently, the football-obsessed Throup was appointed creative consultant for the British football brand Umbro. With Throup now working with his favourite brands from boyhood, he has come full circle.

1980 in Buenos Aires geboren, kam Aitor Throup über Spanien nach Burnley, Lancashire. Dank seines Faibles für High-Tech-Kleidung (von Labels wie Stone Island und C.P. Company) sowie für das Zeichnen und Entwerfen von Comic-figuren brachte er es zu einem Bachelor im Fach Modedesign an der Manchester Metropolitan University. Die Bedeutung, die er den Geschichten hinter seinen Kreationen beimisst, war an seiner Abschlusskollektion an der RCA ablesbar, die er „When Football Hooligans Become Hindu Gods" betitelte; folgerichtig waren darin militärische Elemente mit Hindu-Symbolismus kombiniert. Throups Design-Philosophie ist eher organisch als methodisch und hat ihren Ursprung stets in der menschlichen Gestalt. In der Folge gestattet er seinen Kreationen, sich im Verlauf eines dreistufigen Prozesses – Zeichnung, Plastik, Kleidungs-stück – quasi natürlich zu entwickeln. Bei ITS#FIVE (International Talent

Support) gewann Throup 2006 den Collection of The Year Award sowie den i-D Styling Award. Danach präsentierte er zweimal bei der Show MAN im Rahmen der London Fashion Week. 2008 zeigte Throup auf der Mailänder Modewoche seinen ersten Beitrag einer noch laufenden saisonalen Zusammenarbeit mit Stone Island unter dem Titel „Anatomy Series". Außerdem war dort das Ergebnis einer einmaligen Kooperation mit C.P. Company zu sehen. Erst kürzlich wurde der fußballversessene Throup zum kreativen Berater der britischen Fußball-Marke Umbro ernannt. Nachdem er nun für die Lieblingsmarken seiner Jugend tätig ist, hat sich für den Designer damit der Kreis geschlossen.

Né à Buenos Aires en 1980, Aitor Throup s'installe à Burnley dans le Lancashire après un détour par l'Espagne. Passionné par les vêtements technologiques (comme ceux des griffes Stone Island et C.P. Company), par le dessin et la création de personnages de bande dessinée, il suit un BA en création de mode à la Metropolitan University de Manchester. L'importance qu'il accorde au récit transparaît dans sa collection de fin d'études au Royal College of Arts : intitulée « When Football Hooligans Become Hindu Gods » elle présente des éléments militaires et des symboles hindouistes. La philosophie créative de Throup est plus organique que méthodique, puisque tout part toujours de la forme humaine. Il laisse ensuite ses créations évoluer naturellement à travers un processus de construction en trois étapes – « dessin, sculpture, vêtement » – au lieu d'adopter une structure plus conventionnelle. Au concours ITS#FIVE (International Talent Support), Throup remporte le Collection of The Year Award en 2006 et l'i-D Styling Award, puis présente deux collections aux défilés masculins de la London Fashion Week. En 2008, Throup expose une première installation issue de sa collaboration « Anatomy Series » permanente avec Stone Island à la Semaine de la mode de Milan, ainsi qu'un autre projet spécial conçu avec C.P. Company. Récemment, cet obsédé de football est devenu consultant en stylisme pour la griffe de sportswear anglaise Umbro. Maintenant qu'il travaille avec les marques qu'il adorait dans sa jeunesse, Throup revient à ses premières amours.

KAREN LEONG

What are your signature designs? The constant design feature in all my designs is what I call 'branding through construction'. This is an intricate system of blocking garments by creating a 'skin' around my own sculptures of the human body, from which I create all my garments. This results in a continuous signature system of seams and darts, which result in the construction of the garment itself being the primary tool to identify my work **What is your favourite piece from any of your collections?** Probably the sousaphone jacket from 'The Funeral of New Orleans: Part One', because of the amount of blood and tears it took my studio to create it. The shell is constructed around a life-size sculpture of a musician playing a sousaphone, and it has a completely detachable modular instrument case for a sousaphone (an exact three-dimensional rendition of the surface area of a sousaphone), which cannot only be used to protect and carry the instrument, but it can also be reconfigured and worn on the jacket itself to protect from adverse weather conditions **How would you describe your work?** New object research. Conceptual functionalism **What's your ultimate goal?** Fulfilment **What inspires you?** My daughter, Bramble Lily. The world around me and the challenge to interpret and document it. Other people's interpretations and documentations of it: Phil Hale, Chris Ware, Spring Hurlbut, Juan Muñoz, Leonardo da Vinci, Massimo Osti, Carlo Rivetti, Moreno Ferrari, Paul Harvey, Ian Brown **Can fashion still have a political ambition?** Of course **Who do you have in mind when you design?** Different versions of myself **Is the idea of creative collaboration important to you?** Definitely, if done at the right time. For me, collaborating has not only pushed me to learn new things, but more importantly, it has helped me to properly define my own work and philosophy **Who has been the greatest influence on your career?** Massimo Osti. His work pushed me to turn my drawings into designs **How have your own experiences affected your work as a designer?** Having grown up in Buenos Aires, Madrid and Burnley, I almost feel like I've lived three completely different lives, surrounded by different cultures. I enjoy knowing that whatever culture surrounds you at any specific time is not the way the rest of the world is thinking or behaving. In terms of my work though, Burnley is where my roots are **Which is more important in your work: the process or the product?** The process. Sometimes I don't even design the product, I just invent a new process instead, which dictates what the eventual product looks like **Is designing difficult for you? If so, what drives you to continue?** Designing can be very difficult at times, although it can also be instinctive and a design can be born when least expected. I believe in what I am attempting to define and communicate. I see it as a responsibility to complete my path, even if it's not easy at times **Have you ever been influenced or moved by the reaction to your designs?** Of course **What's your definition of beauty?** I'd like to think that beauty doesn't have a definition **What's your philosophy?** I always work from my justified design philosophy, which is centred around the idea of needing a reason, purpose or function behind every design decision. I have a fear of exposing my insecurities by making purely aesthetic or decorative decisions in my work **What is the most important lesson you've learned?** To have the confidence to take a break from my work.

"My definition of beauty is something between extremely ugly and extremely fantastic"
RICCARDO TISCI · GIVENCHY

In September 2004, Riccardo Tisci presented a show unconventional for high-gloss Milan Fashion Week: supermodels wearing intricately ruched and tiered black gowns moving around a smoky, atmospheric set littered with disused car parts and large black balls. Born in Italy (1975), Tisci moved to London at the age of 18 and graduated from Central Saint Martins in 1999. The following year, he moved back to Italy, where he developed a small collection of dresses and T-shirts for the London boutique Kokon To Zai. British 'Vogue' photographed them and Björk bought some, but production was a low-key affair with everything handmade by the designer's mother and eight sisters. In 2002, Tisci was appointed creative director of the Italian fashion house Coccapani, where he designed four well-received collections. During the same period, he designed the first 'Puma Rudolf Dassler Schuhfabrik' collection, injecting his sense of playful volume into women's sports pieces. 2004 was set to be his big breakthrough year – the designer won a contract with Ruffo Research, but after a few months, the company behind the brand put the project on hold, forcing Tisci to reconsider his plans. It was then that he launched his own label. The 12 outfits presented in September 2004 and modelled by the likes of Karen Elson and Mariacarla Boscono – the latter, his muse and best friend – were just a taste of things to come. In March 2005, Tisci was presented with his greatest challenge to date when he was named the new chief designer of womenswear at Givenchy. The Italian has since shelved his eponymous line in favour of concentrating all his energy on the grand Parisian couture house. Tisci is the fourth designer to head up the LVMH-owned brand since founder Hubert de Givenchy retired from fashion in 1995.

Im September 2004 präsentierte Riccardo Tisci eine für die ansonsten auf Hochglanz abonnierte Mailänder Modewoche reichlich ungewohnte Show: Supermodels in kompliziert gerüschten, aus mehreren Lagen bestehenden schwarzen Roben bewegten sich auf einem rauchigen, atmosphärisch dichten Set, auf dem alte Autoteile und große schwarze Bälle herumlagen. Der 1975 in Italien geborene Tisci zog mit 18 nach London und machte 1999 seinen Abschluss am Central Saint Martins. Im darauf folgenden Jahr ging er zurück nach Italien, wo er eine kleine Kollektion aus Kleidern und T-Shirts für die Londoner Boutique Kokon To Zai entwarf. Die britische Vogue fotografierte diese, und Björk kaufte ein paar Teile. Das Ganze war jedoch ein Low-Budget-Projekt – alles handgenäht von der Mutter des Designers und seinen acht Schwestern. 2002 ernannte das italienische Modehaus Coccapani Tisci zu seinem Chefdesigner. Er entwarf dort vier Kollektionen, die sehr gut aufgenommen wurden. Im selben Zeitraum designte Tisci auch die erste Kollektion „Puma Rudolf Dassler Schuhfabrik", bei der sein Gespür für verspielte Fülle sich in Sportmode für Damen niederschlug. 2004 war dann das Jahr des großen Durchbruchs – der Designer ergatterte

zunächst einen Vertrag mit Ruffo Research. Nach ein paar Monaten setzte das Unternehmen hinter der Marke das Projekt jedoch aus, was Tisci dazu zwang, seine Pläne zu überdenken. So kam es, dass er sein eigenes Label lancierte. Die zwölf Outfits, die im September 2004 von Models wie Karen Elson und Mariacarla Boscono – letztere ist die Muse und beste Freundin des Designers – präsentiert wurden, waren nur ein Vorgeschmack dessen, was noch kommen sollte. Denn im März 2005 stellte sich Tisci seiner bisher größten Herausforderung, als er zum neuen Chefdesigner der Damenmode bei Givenchy ernannt wurde. Die nach ihm benannte Linie lässt der Italiener im Moment ruhen, um all seine Energie für das große Pariser Modehaus aufzuwenden. Tisci ist der vierte Designer an der Spitze der Couture-Marke im Besitz von LVMH, seit sich ihr Gründer Hubert de Givenchy 1995 aus dem Modegeschäft zurückzog.

En septembre 2004, Riccardo Tisci présente un défilé tout à fait inattendu pour la très glamour Milan Fashion Week : des top models vêtues de robes noires décorées de volants et de ruchés complexes défilent autour d'un décor atmosphérique et enfumé, jonché de vieilles pièces détachées automobiles et de grands ballons noirs. Né en Italie (1975), Riccardo Tisci débarque à Londres à l'âge de 18 ans et sort diplômé de Central Saint Martins en 1999. L'année suivante, il revient en Italie pour développer une petite collection de robes et de T-shirts commandée par la boutique londonienne Kokon To Zai. Le Vogue anglais les photographie et Björk achète quelques pièces, mais la production reste modeste puisque tout est fait à la main par la mère et les huit sœurs du créateur. En 2002, Tisci est nommé directeur de la création de la maison italienne Coccapani, où il conçoit quatre collections plutôt bien accueillies. Au cours de cette période, il dessine également la première collection « Puma Rudolf Dassler Schuhfabrik », à laquelle il insuffle son sens ludique du volume dans des créations sport pour femme. C'est en 2004 qu'il perce enfin pour de bon : il remporte un contrat avec Ruffo Research mais au bout de quelques mois, l'entreprise qui possède la marque suspend le projet et contraint Tisci à revoir ses plans ; il décide alors de lancer sa propre griffe. Les 12 tenues présentées en septembre 2004 sur des mannequins telles que Karen Elson et Mariacarla Boscono, sa muse et meilleure amie, n'offrent qu'un avant-goût des collections à venir. En mars 2005, Riccardo Tisci doit relever son plus grand défi à ce jour lorsqu'il est nommé styliste principal des lignes pour femme de Givenchy. L'Italien met sa griffe éponyme en sommeil afin de consacrer toute son énergie à cette grande maison parisienne de haute couture. Depuis que son fondateur Hubert de Givenchy a pris sa retraite en 1995, Tisci est le quatrième créateur à superviser la marque de LVMH.

SIMON CHILVERS

What are your signature designs? The treatment of tulle by distorting it, by embroidering it. I love tulle because it is romantic but sexy. Also experimental jersey that's raw-cut and draped. Leather that's double layered and burnt to expose Swarovski crystals **What is your favourite piece from any of your collections?** The skirt with the leg holes with side drapes. That and the giant leather bomber with gathering on the shoulders that I featured in my most recent collection **How would you describe your work?** Conceptual, sensual and romantic raw **What's your ultimate goal?** Doing my own collection **What inspires you?** A lot of things: my eight sisters and my mum, Mariacarla, art, cinematography, especially old, cultural cinematography, music (going out to clubs) and the darkness when you go deep under the water **Can fashion still have a political ambition?** Yes it can, but it's not about taking sides, it's about giving emotion to the people who wear the clothes **Who do you have in mind when you design?** A woman who is confident in personality and body and understands my sexiness **Is the idea of creative collaboration important to you?** Yes, because a designer is the heart of a collection and of his own world but without a good pattern cutter, good production in the factory and a good presentation team he cannot express 100 per cent of himself **Who has been the greatest influence on your career?** The people who really believed in me right from the beginning, Central Saint Martins, Mariacarla, Diane Koutsis Hemmi, Seiko Matsuda and my family **How have your own experiences affected your work as a designer?** I come from a very poor family and I had to fight with life to get here without changing who I am and am always having to search for ways to express myself **Which is more important in your work: the process or the product?** Process is more important because I'm always trying to find something new and experimental. And it's more fun basically **Is designing difficult for you? If so, what drives you to continue?** No, it's not difficult. I am very shy. Designing is my way of communicating **Have you ever been influenced or moved by the reaction to your designs?** If it's well-meaning criticism it makes me happy, because I know it will make me grow. And when the criticism is good, it makes me emotional and drives me to give more **What's your definition of beauty?** Something between extremely ugly and extremely fantastic. I think skulls are beautiful, but most people find them horrifying **What's your philosophy?** Do good things and forget them, do bad things and remember them. That's the way my mamma taught me **What is the most important lesson you've learned?** The most important thing I learnt in life is that if someone does something bad to you, you must sit on the riverbank and watch the corpse float by. Which means never repay bad with bad, but wait for destiny to take care of it.

"What inspires me is whatever helps you to get away from mental pollution"
JEAN TOUITOU • APC

You'll never see an APC creation waltzing down a catwalk accessorised with a pair of horns. Instead, the subtle fashion brand has a coded elegance that attracts discerning customers drawn to its perfect jeans, shrunken blazers, sunglasses and radical T-shirts. In addition to clothing, there's the treasure trove of APC "things" on offer each season: guitar plectrums, books (such as their edition of Charles Anastase illustrations), shaving oil, candles, olive oil. And it's all the brainchild of Jean Touitou, who was born in Tunis in 1951 and graduated from the Sorbonne in Paris with a history degree and no intention whatsoever of becoming a fashion designer. It was entirely by accident that he landed his first job with Kenzo, which was followed by gigs at agnès b. and Irié before finally deciding to go his own way in 1987 with the launch of APC (Atelier de Production et de Création). Touitou began with menswear, and quickly followed with a womenswear collection debuting the year after. In 1991, the first APC shop opened in Japan and today the company has stores in Hong Kong, New York, Berlin and Paris, plus a comprehensive online service. Collaboration is important to Touitou, and over the years he has partnered Margiela, Martine Sitbon, Eley Kishimoto and Gimme 5 for innovative limited-edition projects. Jessica Ogden designs a childrenswear line and, since 2004, also the mini Madras collection of beachwear inspired by Indian textiles. The company also has a music division: Marc Jacobs and Sofia Coppola, among others, have put their names to compilations on the APC music label, and dance albums, punk-jazz and French-Arabic CDs have all been released to further express the brand's originality. In 2009, Touitou opened a boutique on London's Dover Street, a kindergarten in Paris' rue de Fleurus (designed by Laurent Daroo) and created a new classic jean with Supreme in New York. APC continues to infiltrate fashion with Touitou's personal political sensibility and catching the zeitgeist remains Touitou's driving force.

Sie werden nie eine Kreation von APC auf dem Laufsteg vorgeführt bekommen, die als Accessoire mit einem Paar Hörner versehen ist. Stattdessen propagiert diese feinsinnige Modemarke eine verschlüsselte Eleganz, die aufmerksame Kunden mit perfekten Jeans, kleinen Blazern, Sonnenbrillen und radikalen T-Shirts anzieht. Neben Kleidern gibt es bei APC in jeder Saison auch noch eine Art Schatzkiste mit den verschiedensten Dingen: Gitarrenplektren, Bücher (etwa die firmeneigene Edition von Charles Anastases Illustrationen), Rasieröl, Kerzen, Olivenöl. Das sind alles die Ideen von Jean Touitou, der 1951 in Tunis geboren wurde, an der Pariser Sorbonne einen Abschluss in Geschichte machte und nie vorhatte, Modedesigner zu werden. Sein erster Job bei Kenzo war ein absoluter Zufall. Danach folgten Engagements bei agnès b. und Irié, bevor er sich 1987 entschloss, eigene Wege zu gehen und APC (Atelier de Production et de Création) gründete. Touitou begann mit Herrenmode, gab aber schon ein Jahr später mit einer Kollektion sein Debüt in der Damenmode. 1991 eröffnete der erste APC-Laden in Japan. Inzwischen besitzt die Firma eigene Geschäfte in Hongkong, New York, Berlin und Paris sowie einen umfassenden Online-Shop. Kooperation

ist Touitou ungeheuer wichtig, und so hat er im Lauf der Jahre bereits mit Margiela, Martine Sitbon, Eley Kishimoto und Gimme 5 im Rahmen von innovativen Projekten mit limitierten Auflagen zusammengearbeitet. Jessica Ogden entwirft die Kinderkollektion und seit 2004 auch die von indischen Textilien inspirierte kleine Madras-Linie für Beachwear. Zum Unternehmen gehört auch eine Musikabteilung. Unter anderem haben Marc Jacobs und Sofia Coppola Compilations beim Musiklabel APC veröffentlicht. Dance-Alben, Punk-Jazz und CDs mit franco-arabischer Musik unterstreichen allesamt die Originalität der Marke. 2009 eröffnete Touitou in London einen Laden in der Dover Street, in Paris einen Kindergarten in der Rue de Fleurus (nach Entwürfen von Laurent Daroo),und er kreierte gemeinsam mit Supreme eine neue klassische Jeans in New York. APC beeinflusst die Mode weiterhin mit Touitous ganz persönlicher politischer Sensibilität, wobei die Reflexion des Zeitgeists nach wie vor Triebfeder dieses Designers ist.

On ne verra jamais une création APC valser toutes griffes dehors le long d'un podium. Au contraire, la mode subtile que propose cette marque se distingue par son élégance codée qui attire les clients les plus exigeants, séduits par ses jeans parfaitement coupés, ses petits blazers, ses lunettes de soleil et ses T-shirts à slogan. Outre les vêtements, APC propose chaque saison ses dernières «trouvailles»: plectres de guitare, livres (tels que l'édition APC des illustrations de Charles Anastase), huile de rasage, bougies ou huile d'olive. Des idées tout droit sorties du cerveau de Jean Touitou, né en 1951 à Tunis. Diplômé de la Sorbonne en histoire, il n'a jamais cherché à devenir styliste. C'est donc par pur hasard qu'il se retrouve chez Kenzo, avant de partir travailler chez agnès b. et Irié. Il finit par lancer sa propre griffe en 1987 et la baptise APC (Atelier de Production et de Création). Touitou propose d'abord une ligne pour homme, rapidement suivie d'une collection pour femme au début de l'année suivante. En 1991, la première boutique APC ouvre ses portes au Japon. Aujourd'hui, l'entreprise possède des points de vente à Hong Kong, New York, Berlin et Paris, sans oublier son service de vente sur Internet. La collaboration revêt beaucoup d'importance aux yeux de Jean Touitou, qui au fil des années s'est associé à Margiela, Martine Sitbon, Eley Kishimoto et Gimme 5 pour travailler sur des projets innovants en édition limitée. Jessica Ogden, qui dessine la ligne pour enfant d'APC, conçoit également depuis 2004 la collection de maillots de bain à mini-carreaux Madras, inspirée des textiles indiens. L'entreprise s'est également diversifiée dans la musique: Marc Jacobs et Sofia Coppola, entre autres, ont proposé leurs titres sur les compilations du label d'APC dont les albums électro, punk-jazz et franco-arabes expriment la grande originalité de la marque. En 2009, Jean Touitou a ouvert une boutique dans Dover Street à Londres, une crèche rue de Fleurus à Paris (conçue par Laurent Daroo) et créé un nouveau classique du jean avec Supreme à New York. APC continue à infiltrer la sensibilité politique de son créateur dans l'univers de la mode; saisir l'air du temps reste le grand moteur de Touitou.

TERRY NEWMAN

PHOTOGRAPHY JO METSON-SCOTT. STYLING MARCIA TAYLOR. DECEMBER 2004/JANUARY 2005.

What are your signature designs? My signature is to make the signature hard to see, but yet noticeable **What is your favourite piece from any of your collections?** This varies every day, otherwise fashion would not exist **How would you describe your work?** It's like putting a team together, be a bit of a guru/dictator/father/ entertainer in design and business **What's your ultimate goal?** Tee off at 2:00 p.m. on Fridays and read and write on Saturdays **What inspires you?** Not the Mercer Hotel lobby during fashion week, not dog shit in Paris streets, not French diplomacy asking for Hamas' help to release hostages, not being served by lumpen proletariat in any New York shop, what inspires me is whatever helps you to get away from mental pollution **Can fashion still have a political ambition?** Never had, never will. Sorry, but this question makes me laugh again **Who do you have in mind when you design?** Nobody **Is the idea of creative collaboration important to you?** Of course. C'est même vital **Who has been the greatest influence on your career?** Alvar Aalto **How have your own experiences affected your work as a designer?** I cannot be my own shrink. On top of that, I just fired mine **Which is more important in your work: the process or the product?** The product **Is designing difficult for you? If so, what drives you to continue?** Once you decide that suicide is not an option, you just keep going **Have you ever been influenced or moved by the reaction to your designs?** I am influenced by my own reactions, when I see actual products in actual shops **What's your definition of beauty?** I am no philosopher, I cannot develop a concept about that, please check on Hegel or Kant. I work on precepts, not on concepts **What's your philosophy?** No philosophy **What is the most important lesson you've learned?** I do not remember.

"I cannot live without design. I am design-addicted"
GIAMBATTISTA VALLI

In March 2005, Giambattista Valli showed his first eponymous collection in Paris. His debut emphasised polished pieces such as curvy tuxedos or tiny cocktail frocks in scarlet chiffon or black tulle. The Italian designer (born in Rome, 1966) already had an impressive CV by that time, however, with a role as artistic director of Emanuel Ungaro's ready-to-wear collections as his highest-profile appointment to date. Valli, who grew up in Rome, cites quintessential glamorous movie icons such as Claudia Cardinale, Marilyn Monroe and Rita Hayworth as early influences. His formal studies focused more squarely on fashion from 1980 when he studied at Rome's School of Art, followed by fashion training at the European Design Institute (1986) and an illustration degree at Central Saint Martins in London (1987). In 1988, Valli worked for seminal Roman designer Roberto Capucci, moving to Fendi as a senior designer of the Fendissime line in 1990; in 1995, he was appointed senior designer at Krizia. The following year, through a mutual friend, Valli met Emanuel Ungaro. The master couturier named Valli head designer of his ready-to-wear collections in 1997, eventually promoting him to the position of creative director of Ungaro ready-to-wear two years later. At Ungaro, Valli translated the established house codes of tumbling ruffles, tropical-flower colours and elegantly draped, ultra-feminine gowns for a younger generation of jet-setting glamour girls. His own line Giambattista Valli, today attracts an international, glamorous crowd, including Penelope Cruz, Sarah Jessica Parker, Natalie Portman and Tilda Swinton. Giambattista Valli has also become fashion's go-to label for head-turning accessories (in particular show-stopping high heels and bags). 2008 saw Valli sign a deal with top Italian fur manufacturer Ciwi Furs to design his own line of fur coats and jackets, and another one with skiwear label Moncler. Today there are more than 220 Giambattista Valli selling points in 45 countries worldwide.

Im März 2005 präsentierte Giambattista Valli in Paris seine erste Kollektion unter eigenem Namen. Im Mittelpunkt standen Hingucker wie figurbetonte Smokings oder winzige Cocktailkleidchen aus dunkelrotem Chiffon oder schwarzem Tüll. Der 1966 in Rom geborene und aufgewachsene Designer hatte zu diesem Zeitpunkt bereits eine eindrucksvolle Vita vorzuweisen. Die höchste Position, die er bisher innehatte, war die des künstlerischen Direktors der Prêt-à-porter-Kollektionen bei Emanuel Ungaro. Als früheste Einflüsse gibt der Designer glamouröse Filmdiven wie Claudia Cardinale, Marilyn Monroe und Rita Hayworth an. Seine offizielle Ausbildung konzentrierte sich jedoch auf die Mode ab 1980 als er an der Kunsthochschule in Rom studierte, dann am European Design Institute (1986) und schließlich noch einen Abschluss im Fach Illustration am Central Saint Martins in London (1987) machte. 1988 begann Valli für den aufstrebenden römischen Designer Roberto Capucci zu arbeiten, bis er 1990 als Senior Designer der Linie Fendissime zu Fendi wechselte. 1995 wurde er Senior Designer im Hause Krizia. Schon im folgenden Jahr lernte er über einen gemeinsamen Freund Emanuel Ungaro kennen. 1997 machte der Meister-Couturier Valli zunächst zum Chefdesigner seiner Prêt-à-porter-Kollek-

tionen und zwei Jahre später zum Creative Director desselben Bereichs. Bei Ungaro übersetzte der Designer den etablierten Stil des Hauses mit seinen Rüschenkaskaden, Farben tropischer Blumen und elegant drapierten, ultra-femininen Roben für eine jüngere Generation von Glamour-Girls des Jetset. Ein Thema, dem er auch bei seiner eigenen Marke Giambattista Valli treu geblieben ist, die heute internationale Stars wie Penelope Cruz, Sarah Jessica Parker, Natalie Portman und Tilda Swinton anspricht. Giambattista Valli hat sich außerdem zu einem Label entwickelt, an dem man nicht vorbeikommt, wenn man aufsehenerregende Accessoires sucht (insbesondere Highheels und Taschen). 2008 kam Valli zum einen mit der italienischen Nobel-Pelzmarke Ciwi Furs ins Geschäft, für die er eine eigene Linie mit Pelzmänteln und Jacken kreierte, zum anderen mit dem Skimoden-Hersteller Moncler. Weltweit gibt es heute mehr als 220 Läden in 45 Ländern, die Giambattista Valli verkaufen.

En mars 2005, Giambattista Valli présente sa première collection éponyme à Paris. Ses débuts mettent en scène des pièces telles que des smokings aux lignes arrondies et de minuscules robes de cocktail en mousseline écarlate ou en tulle noir. A ce stade, le créateur italien (né en 1966 à Rome) affiche déjà un CV impressionnant, dont la plus prestigieuse référence reste son poste de directeur artistique des collections de prêt-à-porter d'Emanuel Ungaro. Giambattista Valli, qui a grandi à Rome, dit avoir été largement influencé par les stars les plus glamour du grand écran comme Claudia Cardinale, Marilyn Monroe et Rita Hayworth. Il oriente plus sérieusement sa formation vers la mode dès 1980 en s'inscrivant d'abord à l'école d'art de sa ville, puis en suivant des études de mode à l'European Design Institute (1986) avant de sortir diplômé en illustration de Central Saint Martins à Londres (1987). En 1988, Valli travaille pour l'influent créateur romain Roberto Capucci, puis pour Fendi en tant que styliste senior de la ligne Fendissime en 1990 ; en 1995, il est nommé styliste senior chez Krizia. L'année suivante, Valli rencontre Emanuel Ungaro par le biais d'un ami commun. Le maître couturier le nomme styliste principal de ses collections de prêt-à-porter en 1997, puis le promeut au poste de directeur de la création du prêt-à-porter Ungaro deux ans plus tard. Chez Ungaro, Valli traduit les codes bien établis de la maison – cascades de volants, couleurs de fleurs tropicales et robes très féminines aux drapés élégants – à l'intention d'une plus jeune génération de filles chics et branchées. Il continue à exploiter ce thème dans sa griffe éponyme qui séduit désormais des clientes internationales aussi glamour que Penelope Cruz, Sarah Jessica Parker, Natalie Portman et Tilda Swinton. Les fashionistas privilégient aussi la marque Giambattista Valli quand elles cherchent des accessoires qui ne passent pas inaperçus (en particulier les talons aiguille et les sacs extravagants). En 2008, Valli signe un contrat avec le grand fabricant italien de fourrures Ciwi Furs pour dessiner sa propre ligne de manteaux et de vestes en fourrure, ainsi qu'un accord avec la marque de vêtements de ski Moncler. Aujourd'hui, on compte plus de 220 points de vente Giambattista Valli dans 45 pays à travers le monde.

SUSIE RUSHTON

What are your signature designs? Eclectic **What is your favourite piece from any of your collections?** Dresses, comfortable as a T-shirt but glamorous and for the red carpet **How would you describe your work?** I put fragments together to create an ageless image. It is not seasonal or trend driven. You can wear the dresses over and over again **What's your ultimate goal?** To find and interpret 100 per cent myself and invest it in my own work **What inspires you?** 1. Opposites, 2. Flashes of my personal life, 3. Art **Can fashion still have a political ambition?** Street fashion can have a political ambition, when it becomes a designer one, it is a moment after **Who do you have in mind when you design?** People I have come across who gave me an emotion. For example in the way they walk or smoke or their style of life. It is the opposite of a dream **Is the idea of creative collaboration important to you?** Yes – very important. Something interesting always comes out. I like working with assistants and artists like Marcus Tomlinson **Who has been the greatest influence on your career?** Vionnet, Halston, YSL, Loulou de la Falaise, Antonio Lopez, Andy Warhol and Studio 54, and disco music **How have your own experiences affected your work as a designer?** Growing up in Rome gave me eclecticism: the mix-up of styles, from Roman to Renaissance, to Baroque, to Fascist architecture, all living in harmony… **Which is more important in your work: the process or the product?** The process: project and style. Millions of women interpreting my style **Is designing difficult for you? If so, what drives you to continue?** I cannot live without design. I am design-addicted. Sometimes it would be nice to detox **Have you ever been influenced or moved by the reaction to your designs?** Friends and press people make critiques. I always listen to their suggestions. Sometimes a negative critique can confirm I was right or a good critique can encourage discussion. Critiques are very important because it means your style is still alive and it is always important to evolve **What's your definition of beauty?** Something hidden, not obvious, an unconscious beauty **What's your philosophy?** To share **What is the most important lesson you've learned?** To be open to the unexpected in life so that it is always surprising.

"Fashion is a language"
AN VANDEVORST & FILIP ARICKX · AF VANDEVORST

AF Vandevorst, the Belgian design duo of An Vandevorst (born 1968) and Filip Arickx (born 1971), view fashion as nothing less than a way to communicate the inner workings of the mind. The husband-and-wife design team met in 1987 at the Royal Academy in Antwerp. On graduating, Vandevorst worked as an assistant to Dries Van Noten. Meanwhile, Arickx, who worked for Dirk Bikkembergs for three years as a teenager, completed military service after leaving the Academy, and then worked as a freelance designer and stylist. Together, they established their own label in 1997, and presented their first collection in Paris for autumn/winter 1998. The label quickly came to the attention of both the fashion press and establishment; after only their second collection, they were awarded Paris Fashion Week's Venus de la Mode award for 'Le Futur Grand Créateur', a prestigious prize for newcomers. For the spring/summer and autumn/winter 2000 seasons, the pair were invited to design the Ruffo Research collection, an opportunity periodically offered to young designers by the Italian leather house Ruffo. AF Vandevorst clothes convey a slouchy confidence, and a version of femininity that evokes a sexy yet intellectual cool. Traditional clothing (horse riding equipment, kimonos, frock coats) is often referenced, reworked and refined until it sits slightly left-of-centre; a medical-style red cross is their enduring symbol. For collection themes, they often favour the unexpected, as for autumn/winter 2003, when honey bees provided inspiration. Following no set colour palette, AF Vandevorst stray from muted tones into brights. The label has expanded to encompass footwear, accessories and lingerie and the couple found time to curate an exhibition at MoMu (The Antwerp Fashion Museum) in 2005. In 2008, the duo celebrated their 10th anniversary.

Für AF Vandevorst, das belgische Designerduo An Vandevorst (Jahrgang 1968) und Filip Arickx (Jahrgang 1971), ist Mode nichts Geringeres als eine Möglichkeit, die Vorgänge des Geistes sichtbar zu machen. Das Ehepaar lernte sich 1987 an der Königlichen Akademie in Antwerpen kennen. Nach ihrem Abschluss arbeitete Vandevorst zunächst als Assistentin für Dries van Noten. Arickx hatte schon als Teenager drei Jahre lang bei Dirk Bikkembergs gejobbt und absolvierte nach der Akademie erst einmal seinen Wehrdienst. Anschließend arbeitete er als freischaffender Designer und Stylist. Das gemeinsame eigene Label gründeten die beiden 1997. Ihre erste Kollektion, Herbst/Winter 1998, präsentierten sie in Paris. Rasch gewannen sie die Aufmerksamkeit sowohl der Presse als auch des Fashion Establishments. So wurden sie bereits für ihre zweite Kollektion im Rahmen der Pariser Modewoche mit der Vénus de la Mode als Le Futur Grand Créateur ausgezeichnet, einem prestigeträchtigen Preis für Newcomer. Für Frühjahr/Sommer sowie Herbst/Winter 2000 erhielt das Paar den Auftrag, die Kollektion für Ruffo Research zu entwerfen. Der italienische Lederwarenhersteller Ruffo bietet jungen Designern regelmäßig diese Gelegenheit. Die Entwürfe von AF Vandevorst drücken lässiges Selbstvertrauen aus, zugleich wirken sie auf eine Weise feminin, die sexy, aber zugleich intellektuell und cool rüberkommt. Traditionelle Kleidung (Reitkleidung, Kimonos, Gehröcke) wird oft zitiert, umgearbeitet und leicht verfremdet. Symbol des Labels ist seit jeher ein rotes Kreuz wie im medizinischen Bereich. Als Themen ihrer Kollektionen wählen die Designer oft Ungewöhnliches, wie die Bienen im Herbst/Winter 2003. Was die Farben angeht, ist man bei AF Vandevorst völlig ungebunden und bedient sich mal bei den gedämpften und mal bei den kräftigen Tönen. Man erweiterte die Produktpalette des Labels um Schuhe, Accessoires und Dessous. Im Jahr 2005 kuratierte das Ehepaar zudem eine Ausstellung im MoMu (dem Antwerpener Mode-Museum). Sein zehnjähriges Bestehen feierte das Label 2008.

AF Vandevorst, le duo de créateurs belges formé par An Vandevorst (née en 1968) et Filip Arickx (né en 1971), considère la mode comme rien de moins qu'un moyen de révéler les rouages cachés de l'esprit. Aujourd'hui mariés, ils se sont rencontrés en 1987 à l'Académie Royale d'Anvers. Une fois diplômée, An Vandevorst travaille comme assistante pour Dries Van Noten, tandis que Filip Arickx, qui avait fait ses classes pendant trois ans auprès de Dirk Bikkembergs, effectue son service militaire après avoir quitté l'Académie et avant de travailler comme créateur et styliste en free-lance. Ensemble, ils fondent leur propre griffe en 1997 et présentent une première collection à Paris lors des défilés automne/hiver 1998. Leur travail attire rapidement l'attention de la presse et du monde de la mode; dès leur deuxième collection, le duo reçoit le prix du Futur Grand Créateur des Vénus de la Mode, récompense prestigieuse décernée aux nouveaux talents pendant la Semaine de la Mode de Paris. Pour les saisons printemps/été et automne/hiver 2000, ils sont invités à dessiner la collection Ruffo Research, une opportunité que le grand maroquinier italien Ruffo offre régulièrement aux jeunes créateurs. Des vêtements AF Vandevorst émanent une confiance désinvolte et une féminité originale témoignant d'une attitude cool, sexy mais néanmoins intello. Les collections font souvent référence aux costumes traditionnels (tenues d'équitation, kimonos, fracs), retravaillés et raffinés jusqu'à leur conférer une asymétrie légèrement décalée sur la gauche, avec une croix rouge d'inspiration médicale comme symbole récurrent. Pour les thèmes de leurs collections, ils privilégient souvent l'inattendu, comme pour la saison automne/hiver 2003 inspirée par les abeilles. Ne suivant aucune palette de couleurs prédéfinie, AF Vandevorst vagabonde des tons les plus neutres aux plus vifs. La griffe s'étoffe de collections de chaussures, d'accessoires et de lingerie, et en 2005, le couple trouve même le temps d'organiser une exposition au MoMu (le Musée de la Mode d'Anvers). Le duo a célébré son 10e anniversaire en 2008.

LIZ HANCOCK

What are your signature designs? Assembling by studding, classics with a twist, contrast, humour, leather applications **What is your favorite piece from any of your collections?** Every piece we've made has a specific meaning for us. Every garment we've designed was or is important for the evolution and development of the next one **How would you describe your work?** The research in the world of AF Vandevorst and the challenge of pushing back frontiers and opening new horizons **What's your ultimate goal?** The freedom to keep on exploring and expanding our universe and all of this in collaboration with people who are stimulated to work with the two of us **What inspires you?** Every emotion and situation. As long as it encourages us to take a decision or a certain position **Can fashion still have a political ambition?** Yes, fashion is a language **Who do you have in mind when you design?** Our own generation **Is the idea of creative collaboration important to you?** Yes, because it can lead to an energetic interchange **What has been the greatest influence of your career?** Our own attitude **How have your own experiences affected your work as a designer?** Our work is a reflection of our own experiences **Which is more important in your work: the process or the product?** The process, which leads, in the end, to satisfaction with the result **Is designing difficult for you? If so, what drives you to continue?** Designing is like writing a book: the words come out fluidly but to put them in the right context is not always that easy **Have you ever been influenced or moved by the reaction to your designs?** It's a valuable experience **What's your definition of beauty?** Beauty lies in the unexpected **What's your philosophy?** Open-mindedness **What is the most important lesson you've learned?** A rolling stone gathers no moss.

"I am always driven to push forward, searching for what is modern. That is what motivates me"
DONATELLA VERSACE

Donatella Versace (born 1959) is a goddess of fashion. The female figurehead of one of the few remaining family-run fashion houses, she presides over seven brands under the Versace name. Her flamboyant, party-girl image has become synonymous with Versace itself. Gianni (born 1946) and Donatella grew up in Reggio Calabria, southern Italy. While her much older brother moved to Milan to seek his fashion fortune, Donatella studied for a degree in languages at the University of Florence. While there, her brother's career took off. After working for Callaghan and Genny, he set up his solo label in 1978. Suggesting the family's love for bright colours, body-hugging shapes and a large dose of glamour, it was a great success. The two worked together for much of the '80s and '90s, with Donatella concentrating on the sumptuous advertising images for which Versace is known to this day. She also set up the children's line, Young Versace, in 1993 and worked as head designer on the diffusion label, Versus. When Gianni was tragically killed in 1997, his sister became chief designer. She met the challenge. Versace was brought into the 21st century by fusing Gianni's very Italian glamour with Donatella's own rock'n'roll instincts. Versace is continually in the public eye, not least because of its – and Donatella's – famous friends. Jon Bon Jovi, Courtney Love and Elizabeth Hurley are all devoted Versace fans. Madonna even posed as a sexy secretary in Versace's spring/summer 2005 ad campaign. Donatella is also responsible for extending the brand's range, setting up both a cosmetics line and Palazzo Versace, the first six-star Versace hotel, which opened on the Gold Coast of Australia in 2000. As well as clothing, accessories, fragrances, jewellery and timepieces, there is now a Versace home furnishings collection, as well as an interior design facility for private jets and helicopters, and even a limited-edition Versace Lamborghini sports car. Donatella Versace is 20 per cent owner of Gianni Versace SpA and holds the position of creative director and vice-president of the board, while her daughter, Allegra, is 50 per cent owner.

Die 1959 geborene Donatella Versace ist eine Modegöttin. Als weibliche Galionsfigur eines der wenigen noch in Familienbesitz befindlichen Modehäuser herrscht sie über sieben Marken mit dem Namen Versace. Ihr schillerndes Image als Party-Girl ist zum Synonym für Versace selbst geworden. Gianni (Jahrgang 1946) und Donatella wuchsen im süditalienischen Reggio Calabria auf. Während ihr deutlich älterer Bruder nach Mailand zog, um sein Glück in der Mode zu suchen, studierte Donatella an der Universität von Florenz Sprachen. In jener Zeit nahm die Karriere des Bruders ihren Anfang. Nachdem er zunächst für Callaghan und Genny gearbeitet hatte, gründete er 1978 sein eigenes Label. Gemäß der familiären Vorliebe für kräftige Farben, figurbetonte Schnitte und eine große Portion Glamour wurde es ein immenser Erfolg. Die beiden arbeiteten in den 1980er- und 1990er-Jahren über weite Strecken zusammen, wobei Donatella sich stark auf die prachtvollen Werbeauftritte konzentrierte, für die Versace bis heute bekannt ist. Sie gründete aber auch 1993 die Kinderlinie Young Versace und fungierte als Hauptdesignerin der Nebenlinie Versus. Nach Giannis tragischem Tod im Jahr 1997 wurde seine Schwester Chefdesignerin. Sie meisterte diese Herausforderung und führte Versace ins 21. Jahrhundert, indem sie Gian-

nis sehr italienischen Glamour mit ihren eigenen Rock'n'Roll-Instinkten verband. Das Haus Versace steht nach wie vor im Blickpunkt des öffentlichen Interesses, nicht zuletzt wegen seiner und ihrer prominenten Freunde. Jon Bon Jovi, Courtney Love und Elizabeth Hurley sind allesamt treue Versace-Fans. In der Werbekampagne für Frühjahr/Sommer 2005 spielt sogar Madonna eine sexy Sekretärin. Donatella verantwortet übrigens auch die Erweiterung des Spektrums von Versace, etwa mit eigenen Kosmetika und dem ersten Sechs-Sterne-Hotel der Marke, dem 2000 an der australischen Gold Coast eröffneten Palazzo Versace. Neben Kleidung, Accessoires, Düften, Schmuck und Uhren gibt es nun auch noch eine Wohnkollektion sowie eine Abteilung für die Inneneinrichtung von Privatjets und Helikoptern und mit Versace Lamborghini sogar eine Sonderedition von Sportwagen. Donatella Versace hält 20 % an der Gianni Versace SpA. Zudem ist sie Creative Director und stellvertretende Aufsichtsratschefin. Ihre Tocher Allegra besitzt 50 Prozent der Gianni Versace SpA.

Donatella Versace (née en 1959) est une déesse de la mode. Figure féminine de l'une des rares entreprises encore familiales, elle supervise les sept marques de la griffe Versace. Sa flamboyante image de fêtarde est même devenue synonyme de Versace. Gianni (né en 1946) et Donatella ont grandi à Reggio Calabria, une ville du sud de l'Italie. Lorsque son frère, de plus de vingt ans son aîné, s'installe à Milan pour faire carrière dans la mode, Donatella étudie les langues à l'université de Florence. C'est pendant cette période que la carrière de son frère décolle. Après avoir travaillé pour Callaghan et Genny, il crée sa propre griffe en 1978. Incarnant la passion de la famille pour les couleurs vives, les formes moulantes et une haute dose de glamour, il remporte un vif succès. Ils travaillent ensemble pendant la majeure partie des années 80 et 90, Donatella se concentrant sur les somptueuses images publicitaires qui feront la gloire de Versace. En 1993, elle lance également la ligne pour enfant Young Versace et travaille comme styliste principale sur la ligne Versus. Quand Gianni est tragiquement assassiné en 1997, sa sœur devient directrice de la création. Mais elle relève le défi. Versace entre dans le XXIe siècle en fusionnant le glamour très italien de Gianni avec les instincts rock'n'roll de Donatella. La marque Versace occupe constamment le devant de la scène, en partie grâce à ses amis célèbres : Jon Bon Jovi, Courtney Love et Elizabeth Hurley sont tous des fans dévoués de Versace. Madonna a même accepté de jouer le rôle d'une secrétaire sexy pour la campagne publicitaire printemps/été 2005. Donatella a également réussi à étendre l'offre de la marque, avec le lancement d'une ligne de maquillage et de Palazzo Versace, premier hôtel Versace six étoiles ouvert sur la Gold Coast australienne en l'an 2000. Outre les lignes de vêtements, d'accessoires, de parfums, de bijoux et de montres, Versace compte désormais une collection de meubles, un service de design d'intérieur pour jets privés et hélicoptères, et même une Lamborghini Versace en édition limitée. Donatella Versace assume les fonctions de directrice de la création et de vice-présidente du conseil d'administration de Gianni Versace SpA, dont elle détient 20 % des parts. Sa fille, Allegra, possède 50 % de Gianni Versace SpA.

LAUREN COCHRANE

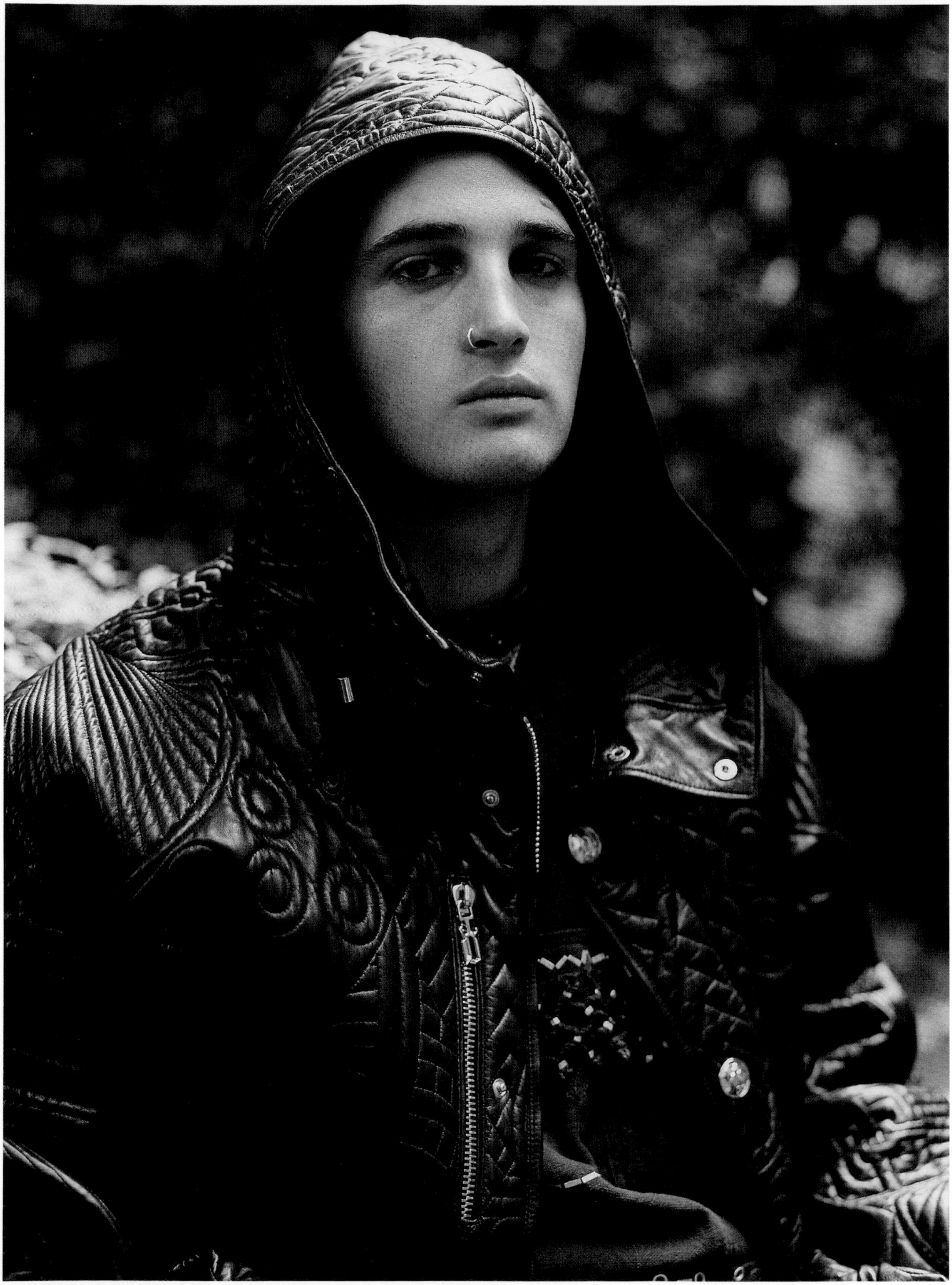

PHOTOGRAPHY ALICE HAWKINS. STYLING SAM WILLOUGHBY. MODEL MUTYA. MAY 2007.

What are your signature designs? The jungle print, the evening dress that Catherine Zeta Jones wore to the Oscars in 2001, the silk fringe dress that Sharon Stone wore to the Oscars in 2002, the leather pant suit with lace-up details and fringes **How would you describe your work?** The style and ideas behind the collection always come from the same thought channel: Versace, myself and my team. Everything that goes on the runway and every Versace item is something that I 'feel for' **What inspires you?** I am a very curious person and therefore get my inspiration from music, photographs, films, from meeting people, discovering new places, attitudes and new trends around the world **Who do you have in mind when you design?** Someone who has individuality, intelligence, with an inner confidence which reflects on the outside **Is the idea of creative collaboration important to you?** My design team is composed of 30 people from all over the world who are like family to me. I believe fashion derives from group work and I have a very open-minded team. Not everyone agrees with me, which is the way I prefer it – I don't like to surround myself with 'yes' people. I am a great believer in the fact that creativity comes from a conflict of ideas **Who has been the greatest influence on your career?** My brother has been the best maestro I could ever have. Everything I know I have learned from him, and everything that I do, and will do, will always have a touch of Gianni **How have your own experiences affected your work as a designer?** New ideas come from having an open mind. I live intensely all the moments of my life and, in each one of those moments, I try to find an interesting and stimulating aspect **Is designing difficult for you?** I adore the world of fashion. It's a passion for me, so I don't think I will ever get tired of it **What's your definition of beauty?** I am convinced that looking good can only come from the inside. It is how you feel about yourself **What's your philosophy?** I am always driven to push forward, searching for what is modern. That is what motivates me **What is the most important lesson you've learned?** To live every day to the full, as if it were the last.

"I'm always most productive when I'm around people I admire who inspire and challenge me"
STUART VEVERS · LOEWE

The career of Stuart Vevers (born in Carlisle, England) so far is one of hard graft rather than chance or luck. Citing that "fashion was about hard work" as the most useful thing he learned from his student days at University of Westminster, Vevers' first job after leaving college in 1996 was with Calvin Klein in New York. Milan beckoned two years later; at Bottega Veneta, Vevers was in charge of accessories. While still at Bottega Veneta, Vevers started working with Luella Bartley – Bartley is part of Vevers' fashion gang, which includes Giles Deacon and Katie Grand. The collaboration lasted eight years and Vevers is also godfather to Bartley's second child. Next came his appointment as Givenchy's accessory designer for both ready-to-wear and couture. From 2002, Vevers juggled Givenchy, Luella, a two-season stint on his own line and work as Louis Vuitton's accessories designer – as a member of Marc Jacobs's creative team, Vevers concentrated on bags. At the end of 2004, Vevers returned to London and became Mulberry's design director. Instrumental to the brand's turnaround, his handbag hits include the Emmy, Agyness and Mabel. He won the British Fashion Council's Accessory Designer of the Year Award in 2006. Then, in 2007, Vevers replaced Jose Enrique Ona Selfa to become Loewe's creative director. Now based in Madrid – he has Spanish lessons twice a week – all eyes are on Vevers to see where the 160-year-old Spanish luxury brand will be led under his guidance.

Die Karriere des im englischen Carlisle geborenen Stuart Vevers ist bislang eher von harter Arbeit als von Zufall oder Glück bestimmt gewesen. Nach eigener Aussage gilt ihm der Satz „Mode ist harte Arbeit" als das Nützlichste, was er als Student an der University of Westminster gelernt hat. Den ersten Job nach seinem Hochschulabschluss 1996 bekam Vevers bei Calvin Klein in New York. Zwei Jahre später lockte Mailand, wo er bei Bottega Veneta für die Accessoires verantwortlich war. Noch während dieser Zeit begann Vevers mit Luella Bartley zu arbeiten – Bartley gehört ebenso wie Giles Deacon und Katie Grand zu Vevers' Mode-Clique. Ihre Kooperation dauerte acht Jahre, in denen Vevers sogar Pate von Bartleys zweitem Kind wurde. Als nächstes folgte die Ernennung zum Accessoire-Designer bei Givenchy, sowohl für Prêt-à-porter wie für die Couture. Ab 2002 jonglierte Vevers Givenchy, Luella, eine zwei Saisons dauernde Schicht für seine eigene Linie und einen Job als Accessoire-Designer bei Louis Vuitton – als Mitglied von Marc Jacobs' Kreativteam konzentrierte er sich auf Taschen. Ende 2004 kehrte Vevers als Design Director von Mulberry nach London zurück. Mit seinen Handtaschen-Hits Emmy, Agyness und Mabel war er maßgeblich an der Kehrtwende der Marke beteiligt. 2006 gewann er die Auszeichnung Accessory Designer of the Year des British Fashion Council. 2007 folgte Vevers Jose Enrique Ona Selfa auf den Posten des Creative Director bei Loewe. Nun lebt er in Madrid – bekommt zweimal wöchentlich Spanischunterricht –, und alle sind gespannt darauf, wo er die 160 Jahre alte spanische Luxusmarke wohl hinführen wird.

A ce jour, la carrière de Stuart Vevers (né à Carlisle en Angleterre) tient plus du labeur que du hasard ou de la chance. «La mode, c'est du travail acharné », telle est la phrase qu'il cite comme la chose la plus utile qu'il ait apprise pendant ses études à l'Université de Westminster. Après avoir quitté la fac en 1996, il décroche son premier job chez Calvin Klein à New York, puis deux ans plus tard, part pour Milan où il est en charge des accessoires chez Bottega Veneta. C'est pendant cette période qu'il commence à travailler avec Luella Bartley, qui fait partie de sa bande aux côtés de Giles Deacon et Katie Grand. Leur collaboration durera huit ans ; Vevers est aussi le parrain du second fils de Luella Bartley. Il devient ensuite créateur d'accessoires chez Givenchy, pour le prêt-à-porter et la haute couture. A partir de 2002, Stuart Vevers jongle entre Givenchy, Luella, un travail de deux saisons sur sa propre collection et une collaboration comme créateur d'accessoires chez Louis Vuitton dans l'équipe créative de Marc Jacobs, où il se concentre sur les sacs. Fin 2004, Vevers revient à Londres et décroche la direction de la création de Mulberry. Ses sacs à main Emmy, Agyness et Mabel, entre autres, jouent un rôle crucial dans le renouveau de la marque et remportent un succès éclatant. En 2006, Vevers est élu Accessory Designer of the Year par le British Fashion Council. L'année suivante, il remplace Jose Enrique Ona Selfa à la direction de la création de Loewe et s'installe à Madrid, où il prend des cours d'espagnol deux fois par semaine. Tous les yeux sont tournés vers lui pour savoir quelle orientation il donnera à cette griffe de luxe espagnole fondée il y a 160 ans.

KAREN LEONG

PHOTOGRAPHY BEN DUNBAR-BRUNTON. STYLING ERIKA KURIHARA. MODEL DANIELA. APRIL 2009.

What are your signature designs? Investment pieces that combine heritage and iconic references with a tough attitude and youthful references **What is your favourite piece from any of your collections?** It's usually the most recent pieces. I'm really happy with some of the work that I've done at Loewe so far. I've challenged the way I was working and that's always good. The Loewe 'Calle' is my favourite piece so far. It is very Loewe, soft and slouchy. The inspiration is the everyday supermarket shopping bag: I wanted to reduce the idea of a bag to its purest functional level. Then refine it by adding luxurious leathers, rich constructions and a bold, oversized padlock, a Loewe signature. My aim was for it to feel rich and luxurious and at the same time youthful and fresh. Probably the most exciting was working with Marc on the Murakami bag collection at LV. There's been a few more over the years, the graffiti sprayed bags at Bottega Veneta, the Gisele bag at Luella, the Mulberry bags that all my friends suddenly asked for discounts on! I'm very fond of the Fraggle/Muppet pieces we did at Mulberry **How would you describe your work?** The combination of a house's heritage and dna with a progressive, bold approach. I enjoy working with the soul of a house and my challenge is to combine that with my personal taste and to make everything we do relevant for the time we live in **What's your ultimate goal?** Creativity for its own sake has little interest for me. Creativity that produces pieces that I see people wearing, that are functional things of beauty, that's my goal. Pieces that will be remembered and treasured **What inspires you?** People. I'm always most productive when I'm around people I admire, who inspire and challenge me **Can fashion still have a political ambition?** I believe so. It is a mirror of the times. You can't create in a vacuum. **Who do you have in mind when you design?** I often have a cinematic reference at the start of the season. I think it helps that it's a character and not a real person. It somehow frees you up. Then again I will reference people I know, even if it's just someone I've met just a few times, like a celebrity **Is the idea of creative collaboration important to you?** Yes, every day. Whether it's with other designers, artists, stylists, hair and make-up artists, photographers, print designers or the craftspeople who make it all come to life. Modern fashion is about working with dozens of other creative people to create the collections and the environment they are presented in **Who has been the greatest influence on your career?** Mr Arnault **How have your own experiences affected your work as a designer?** I've lived and worked in the four fashion capitals, plus Madrid now, and each has been a huge and very different learning experience. Travel, moving to a new city, meeting new people, I think this has had the biggest impact on my work **Which is more important in your work: the process or the product?** Product. Sometimes, when the stars are aligned, you just get lucky. If you end up with something beautiful, does it matter where it came from? **Is designing difficult for you? If so, what drives you to continue?** It has its moments. Especially when you start a brand-new season. But a collection is the combination of a clear idea at the start and hundreds of small decisions along the way. But, no, it's not difficult, sometimes it's hard to see what I do as a job, its what I love **Have you ever been influenced or moved by the reaction to your designs?** Yes, all the time. If someone I respect says something, I try to keep an open mind. The biggest feedback for me, though, comes when someone likes something you've created enough that they go into a store and buy it. That still surprises and drives me. I've gone up to people at parties and told them I designed something they are wearing and it's fascinating. I'm often surprised at what pieces are successful. I like being challenged by the customer and try never to underestimate them **What's your definition of beauty?** Real things. A wonky smile or stupid laugh. I'm not drawn to pure perfection in beauty **What's your philosophy?** Work hard and be nice to people **What is the most important lesson you've learned?** You've got to love what your working on, nothing replaces that. You've got to feel passionate about what you do. There are lots of long hours and hurdles to get over until a collection comes together. You've got to feel a certain amount of stress. It's what gets you up in the morning and makes you work late into the night.

"Creative collaboration makes you richer"
MILAN VUKMIROVIC · TRUSSARDI

In November 2006, Beatrice Trussardi appointed super stylist turned photographer and magazine editor Milan Vukmirovic as the creative director of Trussardi 1911. It marked an exciting new direction for the family-run Italian fashion house. In just over a year, the flagship store in Milan was restyled, the menswear line launched and the ethos of the whole brand re-alined. He is a handsome, trilingual, witty and well-travelled French man. Vukmirovic is six foot two with decades of experience in the fashion world. In 1997, he co-founded Parisian concept store Colette. On leaving Colette, he began working as design director of the Gucci Group next to Tom Ford, prior to joining Jil Sander, where he directed the house's style for a few years. Always moving forward, Vukmirovic then helped launch 'L'Officiel Hommes' in January 2005, where he currently presides as editor-in-chief, regularly shooting the beautiful main fashion stories. In 2008, he photographed advertising campaigns for luxury labels including Giorgio Armani, Hugo Boss, Neil Barrett, Azzaro Parfums and Trussardi Maison. Vukmirovic's design studio is inside the Palazzo Trussardi Alla Scala, where the 200-square-metre flagship store also opened in June 2008. Every week he travels between Milan, Paris (where he still runs 'L'Officiel') and Miami, where he's partnered with friends to open The Webster, a multi-brand store opening later this year. Trussardi began making leather gloves in 1910 and then expanded to leisure sports accessories for men but instead of emblazoning the Trussardi emblem across the new bags, Vukmirovic chose camouflage patterns on embossed leather as one theme on the huge man-bags, overnight trip bags and camouflage print weekend bags. Trussardi celebrates its centenary next year and Vukmirovic and Beatrice Trussardi have set their sights on a future collection for women. The line is beginning slowly with bags and shoes and, rather excitingly, some of the pieces from the current men's collection are being reproduced for women.

Im November 2006 ernannte Beatrice Trussardi den Fotografen, Zeitschriften-herausgeber und ehemaligen Superstylisten Milan Vukmirovic zum Creative Dircctor von Trussardi 1911. Das bedeutete einen aufregenden Richtungs-wechsel für das italienische Modehaus in Familienbesitz Nur ein gutes Jahr später war der Mailänder Flagship-Store umgestaltet, die Herrenlinie auf dem Markt und das Ethos der ganzen Marke neu ausgerichtet. Genauer gesagt handelt es sich um einen attraktiven, dreisprachigen, geistreichen und weitgereisten Franzosen. Vukmirovic ist knapp 1,90 Meter groß und besitzt jahrzehntelange Erfahrung in der Modebranche. 1997 war er Mitbegründer des Concept Store Colette. Und als er Colette verließ, begann er als Design Director neben Tom Ford bei der Gucci Gruppe, bevor er bei Jil Sander einstieg, wo er einige Jahre lang den Stil des Hauses bestimmte. Ständig nach vorn schauend half Vukmirovic auch beim Start von L'Officiel Hommes im Januar 2005, wo er bis heute als Herausgeber fungiert und regelmäßig die wichtigsten Modestrecken fotografiert. 2008 fotografierte er Werbekampagnen für Luxuslabels wie Giorgio Armani, Hugo Boss, Neil Barrett, Azzaro Parfums und Trussardi Maison. Vukmirovics Design-Atelier befindet sich im Palazzo Trussardi Alla Scala, wo im Juni 2008 auch der 200 m² große Flagship-Store eröffnet wurde. Allwöchentlich reist der Modemacher zwischen Mailand, Paris (dort leitet er nach wie vor L'Officiel) und Miami, wo er gemeinsam mit Freunden im Laufe dieses Jahres mit The Webster einen Laden für verschiedenste Marken eröffnen wird. Trussardi begann 1911 mit der Fertigung von Lederhandschuhen und entwickelte sich mit der Zeit zum Hersteller von Freizeitsport-Accessoires für Herren. Doch anstatt das Trussardi-Logo fett auf die neuen Taschen zu setzen, wählte Vukmirovic Camouflage-Muster auf geprägtem Leder als ein Thema für die riesigen Manbags, die Reisetaschen für eine Nacht und Wochend-Reisetaschen mit Camouflage-Druck. 2011 feiert Trussardi sein 100-jähriges Bestehen, und Vukmirovic und Beatrice Trussardi haben den Blick auf eine künftige Damenkollektion gerichtet. Die Linie startet langsam, mit Taschen und Schuhen und, ziemlich aufregend, mit einigen für Frauen reproduzierten Stücken aus der aktuellen Männerkollektion.

En novembre 2006, Beatrice Trussardi nomme Milan Vukmirovic, le supercréateur devenu photographe et rédacteur en chef, au poste de directeur de la création de Trussardi 1911, ce qui marque le début d'une ère nouvelle et fascinante pour cette entreprise familiale italienne. En l'espace d'un an, la boutique de Milan est entièrement relookée et la ligne pour homme lancée. Ce beau Français trilingue est un homme aguerri et plein d'esprit. Vukmirovic (il mesure 1,90 m) a déjà plusieurs décennies d'expérience dans le monde de la mode. Cofondateur de la boutique concept parisienne Colette en 1997, il travaille ensuite comme directeur du design du Groupe Gucci aux côtés de Tom Ford, avant de rejoindre Jil Sander pour superviser le style de la maison pendant plusieurs années. Sur sa lancée, Vukmirovic contribue au lancement du magazine L'Officiel Hommes en janvier 2005, dont il est toujours rédacteur en chef et pour lequel il signe régulièrement les magnifiques photos des grands dossiers de mode. En 2008, il photographie des campagnes publicitaires pour des marques de luxe telles Giorgio Armani, Hugo Boss, Neil Barrett, Azzaro Parfums et Trussardi Maison. Situé à l'intérieur du Palazzo Trussardi Alla Scala, le studio de création de Vukmirovic côtoie la boutique de 200 mètres carrés ouverte par la maison en juin 2008. Chaque semaine, il voyage entre Milan, Paris et Miami, où il s'est associé avec des amis pour ouvrir The Webster, une boutique multimarques qui sera inaugurée cette année. La maison Trussardi a commencé à fabriquer des gants en cuir en 1911 avant de se diversifier dans les accessoires de sport pour homme. Au lieu de sigler les nouveaux sacs avec l'emblème Trussardi, Vukmirovic préfère utiliser des motifs camouflage sur cuir gaufré comme déclinaison thématique pour les énormes sacoches masculines et autres sacs de voyage. Alors que Trussardi célèbrera son centenaire en 2011, Vukmirovic et Beatrice Trussardi prévoient de lancer une collection pour femme, d'abord avec des sacs et des chaussures. Ensuite, et c'est plutôt excitant, ils comptent reproduire certaines pièces de la collection pour homme actuelle à l'attention de ces dames.   BEN REARDON

What are your signature designs? I think that's something you know when you stop doing fashion because then you look back. It's too early in my career to say **What inspires you?** Mostly music and the young culture in the streets **Can fashion still have a political ambition?** I think it's always very dangerous to mix fashion and politics, because to many people fashion seems very futile. Fashion is not considered to be political, but when you are a fashion designer, I think you have a certain responsibility through your creations to leave a message. Actually, for me, our times are very violent. What's violent to me is the growing manipulation by the media and the constant pressure of a consumerism that tends to unify everything, and that's why I want to fight for diversity and help people to cultivate their differences **Who do you have in mind when you design?** I watch a lot of movies. But the reality is that I am more and more influenced by real people, actually my friends, my very close friends. I have some women around me from different ages that I really look at. They are very different. I like to look at them because each one has a different elegance, a different sense of style and way to seduce **Is the idea of creative collaboration important to you?** It's very easy to become a megalomaniac and think that you are the only one to be right. It's dangerous and you have to share opinions. Creative collaboration makes you richer **Who has been the greatest influence on your career?** Yves Saint Laurent, because I feel very close to the sense of elegance he always had in his collections. Whatever the trend was, he almost suffered physically to fight for his own idea of femininity, elegance and beauty, and he stuck to this all his life **Which is more important in your work: the process or the product?** I have to say both, because I really enjoy the process. I like working with people and having creative collaborations. The beginning of a collection is usually one of my favourite moments. But in the end, what you create has to be worn. So I think it's both **Is designing difficult for you?** Designing is not difficult at all. That is the moment when I enjoy myself the most **Have you ever been influenced or moved by the reaction to your designs?** Honestly, you have to read every critic; I'm always moved by them. You have to accept a different point of view and maybe sometimes it can help you to do better. A positive critic can be a great support. But I totally disagree when a negative review becomes too personal **What's your definition of beauty?** Beauty is like an emotion for me. I think emotion in life is very important. Life can be so difficult – it's beauty that makes it. Beauty also gives you a feeling of a certain eternity **What's your philosophy?** One of my biggest philosophies is that you have to fight for what you believe in. You have to believe in yourself; you have to stay true to yourself **What is the most important lesson you've learned?** You have to allow yourself and others to make mistakes, because you learn a lot from them.

"Create clothes that have a familiarity and wearability, but constantly push the limits of how people perceive the latter"
ALEXANDER WANG

Since his debut on the New York fashion scene in 2006, Alexander Wang has cemented his reputation as the go-to brand for cool, stylish clothes for cool, stylish girls. Born and raised in San Francisco, California, to a Chinese-American family, Wang moved to New York at the age of 18 to study fashion at Parsons School of Design. During this time, he undertook a number of internships, including placements at Marc Jacobs, 'Teen Vogue', 'American Vogue' and Derek Lam, before deciding to drop out of university in 2006 and launch himself as a fully independent fashion designer. Wang debuted his eponymous womenswear collection of cashmere knits one year later to instant critical acclaim, and by his sophomore collection, for autumn/winter 2007, the young designer had been touted as one of the most exciting designers of a new generation. Believing a T-shirt and jeans can be just as sexy as an evening gown, Wang has since cultivated a design signature of slouchy tees, layered dresses and trousers that perfectly merge his Californian upbringing with his current downtown New York living. His simple, yet chic clothes are widely acknowledged as the garments of choice for supermodels off-duty, and he counts many of the big-name girls as his best friends. This year sees Wang continue to cultivate his grunge-meets-glamour aesthetic by launching a slick accessories line of high heels and bags, and a diffusion line of T-shirts called T by Alexander Wang. Today Alexander Wang sells to over 150 boutiques and retail stores worldwide. While his accolades include a nomination for the 2008 CFDA Swarovski Womenswear Designer of the Year Award, a place amongst the top ten finalists for the Vogue/CFDA Fashion Fund and the prestigious Ecco Domani Emerging Designer Award. Long may his success continue.

Seit seinem Debüt in der New Yorker Modeszene 2006 hat Alexander Wang seinen Ruf gefestigt, das Label schlechthin zu sein, das coole Klamotten für coole Mädchen liefert. Als Spross einer chinesisch-amerikanischen Familie wurde Wang in San Francisco geboren, wo er auch aufwuchs. Mit 18 ging er zum Modestudium an der Parsons School of Design nach New York. Er absolvierte eine Reihe von Praktika, unter anderem bei Marc Jacobs, Teen Vogue, bei der amerikanischen Vogue und bei Derek Lam, bevor er sich 2006 entschied, die Universität zu verlassen, um sich als komplett unabhängiger Designer zu versuchen. Sein Debüt gab Wang im Jahr darauf mit einer Strickkollektion aus Kaschmir für Damen, die auf Anhieb begeistert aufgenommen wurde. Als seine zweite Kollektion, für Herbst/Winter 2007, herauskam, wurde der junge Modemacher bereits lautstark als einer der aufregendsten Designer einer neuen Generation gefeiert. Mit der Einstellung, dass ein T-Shirt und Jeans ebenso sexy sein können wie eine Abendrobe, hat Wang seither seine eigene Handschrift in Form von lässigen T-Shirts, Lagenkleidern und Hosen kultiviert, die allesamt auf perfekte Weise seine kalifornische Herkunft mit seinem gegenwärtigen Zuhause in Downtown New York in Einklang bringen. Sein schlichten, aber trotzdem schicken Sachen gelten weithin als Lieblingsfreizeitkleidung von Supermodels. Daher zählen viele der Mädchen mit großen Namen zu seinen besten Freundinnen. Auch in diesem Jahr bleibt Wang weiterhin seiner „Grunge meets glamour"-Ästhetik treu, und zwar in Gestalt einer kleinen Accessoirelinie mit High Heels und Taschen sowie einer T-Shirt-Nebenkollektion namens T by Alexander Wang. Inzwischen verkauft Alexander Wang seine Kreationen in mehr als 150 Boutiquen und Kaufhäusern weltweit. Zu seinen Auszeichnungen zählen die Nominierung bei der CFDA für den Swarovski Womenswear Designer of the Year Award 2008, ein Platz unter den zehn Finalisten für den Vogue/CFDA Fashion Fund und der renommierte Ecco Domani Emerging Designer Award. Möge sein Erfolg von langer Dauer sein.

Depuis ses débuts à New York en 2006, Alexander Wang a imposé sa marque de vêtements comme celle des filles cool et branchées. Né dans une famille sino-américaine à San Francisco en Californie, Wang s'installe à New York dès ses 18 ans pour étudier la mode à la Parsons School of Design. Pendant ses études, il effectue plusieurs stages, notamment chez Marc Jacobs, Teen Vogue, Vogue et Derek Lam. En 2006, il décide d'arrêter ses études pour se lancer à son compte. Un an plus tard, Wang présente une première collection éponyme de maille en cachemire pour femme qui enchante immédiatement la critique. L'année suivante, sa deuxième collection pour la saison automne-hiver 2007 incite la presse à le décrire comme l'un des créateurs les plus fascinants de la nouvelle génération. Convaincu qu'un T-shirt et un jean peuvent être aussi sexy qu'une robe du soir, Alexander Wang cultive depuis un style signature fait de T-shirts informes et de robes superposées sur des pantalons qui fusionne à la perfection ses origines californiennes avec sa vie actuelle dans le downtown new-yorkais. Quand elles ne sont pas de service, les top-modèles adorent porter ses vêtements simples mais chics, et Wang compte les plus célèbres d'entre elles parmi ses meilleures amies. Cette année, il continue à explorer son esthétique à la fois grunge et glamour en lançant une impeccable collection de sacs et de chaussures à talons, ainsi qu'une ligne de diffusion proposant des T-shirts, « T by Alexander Wang ». Aujourd'hui, sa marque est distribuée dans plus de 150 boutiques et grands magasins à travers le monde. Nommé pour le prix CFDA Swarovski Womenswear Designer Of The Year en 2008, il figurait aussi parmi les dix derniers finalistes du Vogue/CFDA Fashion Fund et du prestigieux Ecco Domani Emerging Designer Award. Et ce n'est qu'un début ! HOLLY SHACKLETON

What are your signature designs? To find a balance in creating clothes, and challenging what's wearable, accessible, dressed up, dressed down or what's not acceptable **What is your favourite piece from any of your collections?** The classic sweatshirt that we constantly try to evolve **How would you describe your work?** Labour of love **What's your ultimate goal?** To live a long and happy life **What inspires you?** People and personalities **Who do you have in mind when you design?** My customer, but pushing her into new territory **Is the idea of creative collaboration important to you?** YES. Without it, I would be drained **Who has been the greatest influence on your career?** My family and friends. Without them, I wouldn't be here **How have your own experiences affected your work as a designer?** Not having much experience has enabled me to create and build with much more freedom **Which is more important in your work: the process or the product?** Equally important. Without the process, you would not have the product **Is designing difficult for you? If so, what drives you to continue?** Sometimes inspiration is not always as forgiving **Have you ever been influenced or moved by the reaction to your designs?** Yes, constant critique and dialogue is what evolves me as a designer **What's your definition of beauty?** Anything you want it to be. Each person decides for themselves **What's your philosophy?** Create clothes that have a familiarity and wearability, but constantly push the limits of how people perceive the latter **What is the most important lesson you've learned?** To trust your own instinct.

"I do what I do and those who sympathise with my work will wear it"
JUNYA WATANABE

Junya Watanabe (born Tokyo, 1961) is the much-fêted protégé of Rei Kawakubo. Graduating from Bunka Fashion College in 1984, he immediately joined Comme des Garçons as a pattern-cutter. By 1987, he was designing their Tricot line. He presented his first solo collection in 1992 at the Tokyo collections; a year later, he showed at Paris Fashion Week. Although designing under his own name, he is still employed by Comme des Garçons, who fund and produce the collections. Despite an obvious debt to Rei Kawakubo in his work, Watanabe still stands apart from his mentor and friend with a vision that is indisputably his own. He has often used technical or functional fabrics, creating clothes that still retain a sense of calm and femininity. This was displayed most explicitly at his autumn/winter 1999 show, where the catwalk was under a constant shower of water: rain seemed to splash off the outfits, which were created in fabric by the Japanese company Toray, who develop materials for extreme conditions. Despite the wealth of creativity on display, Watanabe's clothes were a response to more fundamental issues: a practical answer to conditions and lifestyles. In contrast to this, Watanabe's designs are also an exercise in sensitivity and, through his remarkably complex pattern cutting, his sculptural clothing presents a virtually unrivalled delicacy. In 2001, Watanabe presented his first menswear collection in Paris. Today, he is one of the most celebrated designers in Paris fashion.

Der 1961 in Tokio geborene Junya Watanabe ist der viel gefeierte Protegé von Rei Kawakubo. Unmittelbar nach seinem Abschluss am Bunka Fashion College 1984 fing er als Zuschneider bei Comme des Garçons an. 1987 entwarf er bereits die Nebenlinie Tricot des japanischen Modehauses. Die erste Solokollektion präsentierte Watanabe dann 1992 in Tokio, ein Jahr später war er auf der Pariser Modewoche vertreten. Auch wenn er inzwischen unter eigenem Namen entwirft, ist der Japaner noch Angestellter des Unternehmens Comme des Garçons, das seine Kollektionen auch finanziert und produziert. Obwohl er in seiner Arbeit von Rei Kawakubo entscheidend beeinflusst wurde, unterscheidet sich Watanabe doch mit einer zweifellos eigenständigen Vision von seiner Mentorin und Freundin. Oft benutzt er Mikrofasern und andere funktionale Stoffe für seine Kreationen, die dennoch eine Aura von Gelassenheit und Weiblichkeit besitzen. Am deutlichsten wurde dies bisher bei seiner Schau für Herbst/Winter 1999, als er den Catwalk ununterbrochen beregnen ließ. Das Wasser schien von den Outfits

abzuperlen, die aus einem Material der japanischen Firma Toray gefertigt waren. Dieses Unternehmen ist auf die Herstellung von Geweben für Extrembedingungen spezialisiert. Doch trotz dieser originellen Präsentation waren die Kreationen von Watanabe eine Reaktion auf fundamentalere Herausforderungen, nämlich eine praktische Antwort auf verschiedene Lebensumstände und -stile. Zugleich ist die Mode des Japaners aber auch eine Art Sensitivitätstraining, und dank seiner bemerkenswert komplexen Schnitte sind die skulpturalen Entwürfe auch von einer unvergleichlichen Zartheit. 2001 präsentierte Watanabe seine erste Herrenkollektion in Paris. Heute ist er einer der meistgefeierten Designer der Pariser Modeszene.

Junya Watanabe (né en 1961 à Tokyo) est le célèbre protégé de Rei Kawakubo. Diplômé du Bunka Fashion College en 1984, il commence immédiatement à travailler chez Comme des Garçons en tant que traceur de patrons. En 1987, il dessine déjà pour la ligne Tricot. Il présente sa première collection « en solo » aux défilés de Tokyo ; un an plus tard, il est invité à la Semaine de la Mode de Paris (bien qu'il dessine sous son propre nom, Watanabe est toujours employé par Comme des Garçons, qui finance et produit ses collections). Très marqué par l'influence de Rei Kawakubo, le travail de Watanabe se distingue toutefois de celui de son amie et mentor grâce à une approche indiscutablement personnelle. Les vêtements qu'il taille souvent dans des tissus techno et fonctionnels n'en sont pas moins empreints de calme et de féminité. Son talent apparaît de façon explicite à l'occasion de son défilé automne/hiver 1999, où les mannequins défilent sur un podium constamment aspergé d'eau : les gouttes de pluie rebondissent sur les vêtements coupés dans un tissu produit par Toray, une entreprise japonaise qui développe des matériaux résistant aux conditions extrêmes. Bien qu'ils démontrent l'immense créativité de Watanabe, ses vêtements apportent avant tout une réponse à des problèmes plus fondamentaux, une solution pratique aux divers climats et modes de vie. Ils témoignent également de la grande sensibilité du créateur qui, grâce à des coupes d'une remarquable complexité, confère à ses pièces sculpturales une délicatesse incomparable. En 2001, Watanabe présente sa première collection pour homme à Paris. Il est aujourd'hui l'un des créateurs les plus en vue de la scène parisienne.

MARCUS ROSS

How would you describe your work?
Strength and tenderness that I try my best every time to express in the clothes, in a straightforward way **What's your ultimate goal?** I have the same attitude towards work and creativity that Rei Kawakubo and all of us at Comme des Garçons have **What inspires you?** To make strong clothes **Can fashion still have a political ambition?** While I respect the viewpoint that fashion reflects social and political issues, that is not the basis of my designs **Who do you have in mind when you design?** The ideal customer – that is, I do what I do, and those who sympathise with my work will wear it **Is the idea of creative collaboration important to you?** It is an inestimable experience and enrichment to work with companies such as Levi's, to come into contact with the depth of their technique and expertise and the weight of history **Who has been the greatest influence on your career?** I learned everything about creation at Comme des Garçons **Which is more important in your work: the process or the product?** Both. In my women's collection, each time I put all my energy into new challenges, searching for new patterns and innovative fabrics. But I'm also conscious that groping for new forms is not everything in clothes-making **Have you ever been influenced or moved by the reaction to your designs?** I have never thought about whether or not I am successful. My aim is only to create a good collection.

"Power is sexy. I like the men and women that I dress to look important"
VIVIENNE WESTWOOD

Vivienne Westwood is a legend in her own lifetime, a designer who inspires many other designers and who makes clothes that delight her loyal customers. Born in Derbyshire in 1941, she first became a household name when, in partnership with Malcolm McLaren, she invented the punk uniform. Let It Rock, SEX, Seditionaries, Pirates, and Buffalo Girls were all early collections they created together at their shop in World's End, Chelsea. All became classics and served to challenge common preconceptions of what fashion could be. Since severing business ties with McLaren, Westwood has gone on to become one of the most revered figures within the fashion industry. She has achieved all this without any formal training. In the '80s, she was hailed by 'Women's Wear Daily' as one of the six most influential designers of all time, and in 2004 the Victoria & Albert Museum launched a travelling retrospective exhibition defining her iconic status. There is an intellectual method to the madness of her creative energy. Historical references, techniques and fabrics are intrinsic to her approach to design. Her subversive shapes and constructions have consistently proved to be ahead of their time. Awarded an OBE 15 years after being arrested on the night of the Queen's Silver Jubilee, she has now become a part of the establishment she continues to oppose. Today she shows her ready-to-wear women's collection in Paris and a menswear collection, MAN, in Milan. While the interest in vintage Westwood has never been more intense, her diffusion line Anglomania regularly references pieces from her earlier collections. Westwood also has three best-selling perfumes – Libertine, Boudoir and Anglomania – and has shops all over the world. Westwood wrote a cultural Manifesto called Active Resistance to Propaganda as a call to arms for all intellectuals against passive acceptance of propaganda and obsessive consumption. In 2008, Westwood showed her Red Label in London after almost a decade of absence from London Fashion Week and called on other British brands that now only show abroad to follow her example.

Vivienne Westwood ist schon zu Lebzeiten eine Legende – eine Designerin, die viele andere Modeschöpfer inspiriert und mit ihren Entwürfen eine treue Kundschaft entzückt. Geboren wurde sie 1941 in Derbyshire. Erstmals machte sie sich einen Namen, als sie gemeinsam mit Malcolm McLaren die Punk-Uniform erfand. Let It Rock, SEX, Seditionaries, Pirates und Buffalo Girls sind frühe Kollektionen, die sie zusammen in ihrem Laden World's End in Chelsea entwarfen. Sie wurden allesamt zu Klassikern und stellten gängige Vorurteile darüber, was Mode sein könnte, in Frage. Nachdem sie die Geschäftsbeziehung mit McLaren beendet hatte, wurde Westwood zu einer der meistgeachteten Figuren der Branche. Erreicht hat sie all das ohne jegliche konventionelle Ausbildung. In den 1980er-Jahren erkor Women's Wear Daily sie zu einem der sechs einflussreichsten Designer aller Zeiten. 2004 präsentierte das Victoria & Albert Museum eine Retrospektive rund um ihren Status als Mode-Ikone. Westwoods kreative Arbeitswut hat intellektuelle Methode. So sind historische Bezüge, Techniken und Materialien wesentliche Elemente ihres Designkonzepts. Ihre subversiven Silhouetten und Konstruktionen sind, wie man immer wieder feststellen kann, ihrer Zeit voraus. 15 Jahre nachdem sie in der Nacht des silbernen Thronjubiläums der Queen verhaftet worden war, zeichnete man sie als Officer of the Order of the British Empire aus. Inzwischen ist sie selbst Teil des Establishments, gegen das sie aber nach wie vor ankämpft. Heute zeigt sie ihre Prêt-à-porter-Kollektion für Damen in Paris und eine Herrenkollektion namens MAN in Mailand. Während das Interesse an ihren Vintage-Teilen so groß ist wie noch nie, nimmt sie in ihrer Nebenlinie Anglomania selbst regelmäßig Bezug auf Entwürfe aus früheren Kollektionen. Westwood hat auch bereits drei Düfte auf den Markt gebracht, die sich als Bestseller erwiesen: Libertine, Boudoir und Anglomania. Ihre Läden findet man auf der ganzen Welt. Die Designerin hat ein gesellschaftskritisches Manifest namens „Active Residence to Propaganda" geschrieben. Darin ruft sie alle Intellektuellen gegen das passive Hinnehmen von Propaganda und obsessivem Konsum zu den Waffen. 2008 präsentierte sie nach fast einem Jahrzehnt Abwesenheit bei der London Fashion Week ihr Red Label in der Hauptstadt. Zugleich rief sie andere britische Marken, die ihre Kollektionen bis dato nur im Ausland zeigten, dazu auf, ihrem Beispiel zu folgen.

Vivienne Westwood est une légende vivante, une créatrice qui inspire de nombreux autres stylistes et dont les vêtements font le bonheur de ses fidèles clients. Née en 1941 dans le Derbyshire, elle devient d'abord célèbre dans toute l'Angleterre pour l'uniforme punk qu'elle invente avec Malcolm McLaren. Let It Rock, SEX, Seditionaries, Pirates et Buffalo Girls sont autant de collections qu'ils créent ensemble dans leur première boutique du World's End à Chelsea. Toutes sont devenues des classiques et ont servi à remettre en question les idées préconçues sur ce que la mode doit être. Depuis qu'elle a mis un terme à ses relations d'affaires avec McLaren, Vivienne Westwood est devenue l'un des personnages les plus révérés par le monde de la mode, et ce, sans la moindre formation. Dans les années 80, Women's Wear Daily la classe parmi les six créateurs les plus influents de l'époque. En 2004, le Victoria & Albert Museum lance une grande rétrospective itinérante qui assoie son statut d'icône. On distingue de la méthode et de l'intellect dans la folie de son énergie créative. Références, techniques et tissus historiques font partie intégrante de son approche de la mode. Ses formes et ses constructions subversives se sont toujours avérées très en avance sur leur temps. Décorée Officier de l'Empire britannique 15 ans après son arrestation, la nuit du jubilé d'argent de la reine, elle fait désormais partie de l'establishment auquel elle continue pourtant de s'opposer. Aujourd'hui, elle présente sa collection de prêt-à-porter pour femme à Paris et sa collection pour homme, MAN, à Milan. Alors que l'intérêt pour les pièces Westwood vintage n'a jamais été aussi intense, sa ligne secondaire Anglomania fait régulièrement référence aux vêtements de ses anciennes collections. Vivienne Westwood a également lancé trois parfums à succès, Libertine, Boudoir et Anglomania, et possède des boutiques dans le monde entier. Elle a rédigé un manifeste culturel intitulé « Active Residence to Propaganda », un appel aux armes lancé à tous les intellectuels pour combattre l'acceptation passive de la propagande et de la consommation obsessionnelle. En 2008, Vivienne Westwood a présenté sa collection Red Label dans la capitale britannique après presque dix ans d'absence de la London Fashion Week, montrant l'exemple à d'autres marques anglaises qui ne défilent désormais plus qu'à l'étranger.

TERRY NEWMAN

PHOTOGRAPHY MARIUS HANSEN. MODELS WORLD'S END STAFF. VIVIENNE WESTWOOD AND AGYNESS DEYN, MAY 2008

What are your signature designs? I think they're so well-known that you can fill this in yourself. One thing that people do forget is that I reintroduced the idea of fine knitwear into fashion. There's nothing more sexy than a twin set... more sexy still is the cardigan of the twin set, worn by itself with the buttons undone. You did not have this fine knitwear until I persevered, getting it from English companies when the machinery to make it didn't even exist in fashion knitwear companies. I'm just making the point that the things I do are very, very fundamental sometimes to what filters into the fashion world **What's your favourite piece from any of your collections?** My favourite garment of all time is my knitted dress, which I've been wearing for at least the last five years. You just look so stunning wearing this dress with very high heels. It uses the technique of hand-knitting to perfection. I will mention also that in my career, I've done three special trousers, which I think are just the greatest: bondage trousers, pirate trousers, alien trousers. I always like my latest collections the best of all **How would you describe your work?** Very simply, avant-garde **What's your ultimate goal?** It's a question of organisation, to make the clothes more easily available in order to satisfy the demand. I just want people, once they've got their money together, to go and buy something, to be able to see my things straight away in order to choose them **What inspires you?** I get my ideas from the work itself. When you start to do something, then you find another way to do it. It's only by doing something one way that you have an idea of how it could be done another way. Of course, I also get inspired by things I see, but I do not get inspired by the street these days **Can fashion still have a political ambition?** I look upon government as a one-way corridor, to facilitate the interests of business. At the same time, the government tries to convince everybody else that this is good for them. And so people are being trained by the media to be perfect consumers of mass-manufactured rubbish. The people who wear this stuff have bought the system, and their appearance demonstrates the fact that their brains have been removed. I think it's important to make great clothes so that people can look individual, and not a product of mass advertising **Who do you have in mind when you design?** The answer is nobody and everybody **What has been the greatest influence on your career?** I would say my World's End shop, which I've had since 1970. And that's because I was making clothes and selling them direct through the shop, so I always had access to the public and I always had customers. So I developed all my strengths without being frustrated in any way and I was always able to be the judge of my own work **How have your own experiences affected your work as a designer?** I had a cardinal change in my attitude after punk rock. I realised that my idea of attacking the establishment was naïve – if you try to attack the establishment, you actually feed the establishment. You give it all these ideas, it goes into mass manufacture and it has a big effect on the fashion world. So what I decided to do was go very fast and not care about attacking anything. Just to come up with the ideas and not be held back in any way. And since then, I've been miles down the road in front of anything **Is designing difficult for you? If so, what drives you to continue?** When I view my catwalk show, my thought each season is the same: "Six months ago that didn't exist; now it does exist. Nobody ever walked the planet wearing this before." And that's what drives me on **What's your definition of beauty?** Everybody knows if a woman is beautiful or not. It's something that you can't deny. But I'm not terribly interested in beauty. What touches me is someone who understands herself **What's your philosophy?** Power is sexy. I like the men and women that I dress to look important. When I see that, I'm happy **What is the most important lesson you've learned?** Keep a smile on your face.

"The most important lesson I've learned is, be kind"
BERNHARD WILLHELM

Since graduating from Antwerp's Royal Academy back in 1998, Bernhard Willhelm has created an original, beautiful and completely off-the-wall universe. During his time at college, Willhelm assisted the cream of fashion avant-garde, including Walter Van Beirendonck, Alexander McQueen, Vivienne Westwood and Dirk Bikkembergs and the lineage and experience passed on from working with these designers is more than evident in his designs. Willhelm launched his womenswear in 1999, followed in quick succession by menswear in 2000, before settling in Paris in 2002, a place this native German still calls home. Recurring themes include his twisted take on European tradition, with lederhosen and bratwurst appearing as clothing embellishments whilst Western themes like McDonald's and American football have provided inspiration at various points in his career. From 2002 to 2004, Willhelm directed the Italian house of Capucci, along with support from Tara Subkoff of Imitation of Christ and Sybilla, where he launched their first Prêt-à-Porter collection. Working across media, Willhelm has shown exhibitions, published books, designed school uniforms, launched a shoe line with Camper, a clothing line with Yoox, art directed record covers, starred on magazine covers and collaborated with tastemakers, including Björk and Nick Knight. His work challenges stereotypes and is characterised by storytelling, none more so than for his 'Bernhard Willhelm: Het Totaal Rappel' exhibition at the Antwerp Academy. The exhibition saw Willhelm create installations specific to each collection in collaboration with Swiss artists Taiyo Onorato and Nico Krebs, who worked with Willhelm on his brilliant look books and showroom presentations. The result was phenomenal. Glitter worlds, wooden mazes and computer graphics presented a complete and unflinching setting for his consistently brilliant designs, proving once again that Bernhard Willhelm will always be five steps ahead of the game.

Seit seinem Abschluss an der Antwerpener Royal Academy im Jahr 1998 hat Bernhard Willhelm ein originelles, wunderschönes und total verrücktes Universum erschaffen. Während des Studiums assistierte Willhelm bei der Creme de la Creme der Modeavantgarde, u.a. bei Walter Van Beirendonck, Alexander McQueen, Vivienne Westwood und Dirk Bikkembergs. Die Erfahrung, die er aus der Arbeit mit diesen Designern gewonnen hat, ist seinen Kreationen deutlich anzusehen. Damenmode präsentierte Willhelm erstmals 1999, rasch gefolgt von einer Herrenkollektion im Jahr 2000, bevor er sich schließlich 2002 in Paris niederließ, wo sich der gebürtige Deutsche nach wie vor zuhause fühlt. Wiederkehrende Themen bei ihm sind die eigenwillige Auseinandersetzung mit der europäischen Tradition. Da tauchen Lederhosen und Bratwürste als Zierrat auf, während an anderen Stellen seiner Karriere auch schon McDonalds und American Football als Inspiration dienten. Von 2002 bis 2004 war Willhelm Chef des italienischen Modehauses Capucci, und zwar gemeinsam mit Tara Subkoff von Imitation of Christ und Sybilla, wo er ihre erste Prêt-à-Porter-Kollektion herausbrachte. Bei seiner Arbeit quer durch alle Medien hat Willhelm bereits

Ausstellungen präsentiert, Bücher publiziert, Schuluniformen entworfen, eine Schuh-Linie bei Camper und Kleider für Yoox designt, als Art Director Plattencover entworfen, für Zeitschriftentitel posiert und mit Trendfiguren wie Björk und Nick Knight zusammengearbeitet. Seine Arbeit stellt Stereotypen in Frage und erzählt immer eine Geschichte, was nirgends deutlicher wurde als bei seiner Ausstellung „Bernhard Willhelm: Het Totaal Rappel" in der Antwerpener Akademie. Er schuf dafür Installationen für die jeweiligen Kollektionen, und zwar in Zusammenarbeit mit den Schweizer Künstlern Taiyo Onorato und Nico Krebs, die Willhelm schon bei seinen brillanten Look Books und Showroom-Präsentationen unterstützt haben. Das Resultat war phänomenal: Glitzerwelten, Holzlabyrinthe und Computergrafiken lieferten die Bühne für seine durchwegs überragenden Entwürfe. Womit wieder einmal der Beweis erbracht wäre, dass Willhelm allen anderen stets fünf Schritte voraus ist.

Depuis qu'il a décroché son diplôme de l'Académie Royale d'Anvers en 1998, Bernhard Willhelm s'est créé un univers original, magnifique et totalement désaxé. Pendant ses études, il travaille comme assistant pour la crème de l'avant-garde de la mode, notamment Walter Van Beirendonck, Alexander McQueen, Vivienne Westwood et Dirk Bikkembergs. Les valeurs et l'expérience qu'il acquiert auprès de ces couturiers transparaissent de façon tout à fait flagrante dans ses créations. En 1999, Willhelm lance sa ligne pour femme, rapidement suivie d'une collection pour homme en l'an 2000. Il s'installe à Paris en 2002, une ville où cet Allemand d'origine se sent encore aujourd'hui comme chez lui. Ses sujets de prédilection incluent une vision décalée de la tradition européenne, comme en témoigne l'utilisation de culottes tyroliennes en cuir et de saucisses grillées décoratives sur ses vêtements, et les thèmes occidentaux tels McDonald's et le football américain, qui l'ont inspiré à diverses reprises au cours de sa carrière. Entre 2002 et 2004, Willhelm dirige la maison italienne Capucci avec le soutien de Tara Subkoff d'Imitation of Christ et de Sybilla, et lance la première collection de prêt à porter de la marque. Artiste multidisciplinaire, il a fait l'objet de plusieurs expositions, publié des livres, conçu des uniformes scolaires, lancé une ligne de chaussures avec Camper, une collection de vêtements avec Yoox, créé des couvertures de disques, posé à la une de plusieurs magazines et collaboré avec des prescripteurs de tendances comme Björk et Nick Knight. Son travail remet en question les stéréotypes et repose principalement sur la narration, comme l'illustrait son exposition « Bernhard Willhelm: Het Totaal Rappel » à l'Académie d'Anvers : Willhelm y montrait des installations consacrées à chacune de ses collections, en collaboration avec les artistes suisses Taiyo Onorato et Nico Krebs qui avaient travaillé avec lui sur ses fabuleux look books et ses défilés. Le résultat était phénoménal: Mondes scintillants, dédales en bois et graphisme numérique formaient un décor total et implacable pour ses créations toujours réussies, et prouvaient une fois de plus que Bernhard Willhelm aura toujours cinq longueurs d'avance sur les autres.

BEN REARDON

What are your signature designs? You decide **What is your favourite piece from any of your collections?** The pieces I wear myself **How would you describe your work?** WUNDERSCHÖN **What's your ultimate goal?** The next collection **What inspires you?** Laziness **Can fashion still have a political ambition?** No. It's not ambitious enough **Who do you have in mind when you design?** An idea, never a person **Is the idea of creative collaboration important to you?** My team is everything **Who has been the greatest influence of your career?** My business partner, Jutta Kraus **How have your own experiences affected your work as a designer?** I keep on cooking **Which is more important to you: the process or the product?** Both, they have the same value **Is designing difficult for you? If so, what drives you to continue?** If the drive is not there, you should forget about this job **Have you ever been influenced or moved by the reaction to your designs?** Yes, my mother is still complaining **What's your definition of beauty?** Chaos (let's not be emotional about it) **What's your philosophy?** Forget about philosophy **What is the most important lesson you've learned?** Be kind.

"Colour is the thing I'm best known for. If people pigeonhole me, so what? Long live the pink dress!"
MATTHEW WILLIAMSON

Matthew Williamson uses colour in a way very few designers dare match. He routinely splashes ultra pinks, fluorescent yellows and acid greens with an energising flourish onto women's day and eveningwear. This has become his signature style since the debut of his first collection, 'Electric Angels', in 1997 – a combination of kaleidoscopic bias-cut dresses and separates, sometimes embroidered and fused with a bohemian edge. Modelled by friends Jade Jagger, Kate Moss and Helena Christensen, it was a presentation that affirmed the London-based designer's influences: fame, glamour and India (Williamson's garments often read like a travel diary, tracing his love of exotic destinations). Since that first collection, it's been the intricate detail, contemporary styling and sexy silhouettes that have kept the applause coming. Born in Chorlton, Manchester, in 1971, Williamson graduated from Central Saint Martins in 1994 and set up his own label in 1996 after spending two years as consultant at UK mass-market chain Monsoon. 2002 saw the launch of a homeware range and a move to show his womenswear collections at New York Fashion Week. A first foray into perfume and home fragrance – a collaboration with perfumer and friend Lyn Harris – saw the creation of the limited-edition perfume Incense. The first Matthew Williamson flagship store opened in 2004 on London's Bruton Street. Williamson took over as creative director at the Italian house Emilio Pucci in 2005. But in September 2008, he returned to London full-time in order to focus on his own label's ventures and expansion. In September 2007, Williamson celebrated his label's 10th year anniversary with a one-off show at London Fashion Week and an exhibition dedicated to his retrospective titled "Matthew Williamson – 10 Years in Fashion" at the Design Museum (London). Williamson was awarded the Möet & Chandon Fashion Tribute (2005) and the Red Carpet Designer of the Year at the British Fashion Awards (2008).

Matthew Williamson kombiniert Farben mit einem Wagemut, den nur sehr wenige Designer aufbringen. Mit kräftigem Schwung verteilt er knallige Pinktöne, Neongelb und -grün auf Alltags- und Abendmode für Damen. Das ist sein Markenzeichen seit dem Debüt 1997 mit seiner ersten Kollektion „Electric Angels" – einer Kombination von diagonal geschnittenen kaleidoskopischen Kleidern und Einzelteilen, die teilweise bestickt oder mit einem Touch Bohème versehen waren. Die Models damals waren seine Freundinnen Jade Jagger, Kate Moss und Helena Christensen, und die Schau bestätigte die Einflüsse auf den in London lebenden Designer: Prominenz, Glamour und Indien (so lesen sich Williamsons Kleider oft wie ein Reisetagebuch, das seine Vorliebe für exotische Ziele dokumentiert). Nach jener ersten Kollektion waren jedoch raffinierte Details, zeitgemäßes Styling und sexy Silhouetten für den anhaltenden Applaus verantwortlich. Der 1971 in Manchester geborene Williamson machte 1994 seinen Abschluss am Central Saint Martins und gründete 1996 sein eigenes Label, nachdem er zwei Jahre lang als Berater für die britische Modekette Monsoon gearbeitet hatte. 2002 kam noch eine Homeware-Kollektion dazu. Außerdem zog es den Designer nach New York, wo er im Rahmen der Modewoche seine Damenkollektionen prä-

sentierte. Ein erstes Hineinschnuppern in den Markt der Düfte und Home Fragrances war die Zusammenarbeit mit der Parfümeurin und Freundin Lyn Harris bei der Kreation des in limitierter Auflage auf den Markt gebrachten Parfums Incense. Den ersten nach ihm benannten Flagship-Store eröffnete Williamson 2004 in der Londoner Bruton Street. 2005 übernahm er die Position des Creative Director beim italienischen Modehaus Emilio Pucci. Im September 2008 kehrte er jedoch nach London zurück, um sich voll auf die Projekte und die Expansion seines eigenen Labels zu konzentrieren. Exakt ein Jahr zuvor hatte Williamson das 10-jährige Bestehen seiner Marke mit einer einzigartigen Show bei der London Fashion Week sowie der Ausstellung „Matthew Williamson – 10 Years in Fashion" im Londoner Design Museum gefeiert. An Auszeichnungen kann der Designer den Möet & Chandon Fashion Tribute (2005) und den Titel Red Carpet Designer of the Year im Rahmen der British Fashion Awards (2008) vorweisen.

Matthew Williamson utilise la couleur comme peu d'autres créateurs oseraient le faire. Régulièrement, il éclabousse avec panache et énergie ses tenues féminines de jour et de soir de roses flashy, de jaunes fluorescents et de verts acidulés. Depuis sa première collection « Electric Angels » en 1997, ce style s'est imposé comme sa signature : une combinaison de robes et de séparés kaléidoscopiques coupés en biais, parfois brodés et au look un peu bohème. Grâce à ses amies mannequins Jade Jagger, Kate Moss et Helena Christensen, ce défilé confirme les influences du créateur londonien : la gloire, le glamour et l'Inde (les vêtements de Williamson se lisent souvent comme des carnets de voyage qui témoignent de sa passion pour les destinations exotiques). Depuis cette première collection, il remporte un succès croissant grâce aux détails complexes, au style contemporain et à la silhouette sexy de ses vêtements. Né en 1971 dans le quartier Chorlton de Manchester, Williamson sort diplômé de Central Saint Martins en 1994. Après avoir travaillé pendant deux ans comme consultant pour la chaîne de distribution britannique Monsoon, il crée sa propre griffe en 1996. En 2002, il lance une gamme d'articles pour la maison et décide de présenter ses collections pour femme à la New York Fashion Week. Une première incursion dans les domaines du parfum et du parfum d'intérieur, fruit d'une collaboration avec son amie parfumeuse Lyn Harris, voit la création d'une fragrance en édition limitée, « Incense ». La première boutique indépendante Matthew Williamson a ouvert ses portes en 2004 dans Bruton Street à Londres. En 2005, le créateur britannique devient directeur de la création de la maison italienne Emilio Pucci, qu'il quitte en septembre 2008 pour revenir à Londres et se concentrer à temps plein sur les projets et l'expansion de sa propre griffe. En septembre 2007, Williamson célèbre le 10e anniversaire de sa marque lors d'un défilé exceptionnel pendant la London Fashion Week et à travers une rétrospective intitulée « Matthew Williamson – 10 Years in Fashion » au Design Museum (Londres). Matthew Williamson est lauréat du Moët & Chandon Fashion Tribute (2005) et du titre de Red Carpet Designer of the Year des British Fashion Awards (2008). TERRY NEWMAN

PHOTOGRAPHY JESSE SHADOAN. STYLING TIFFANY PENTZ. MODEL ANGELA LINDVALL. NOVEMBER 2003.

What are your signature designs? My style is all about creating very feminine, sexy clothes that women really desire **What's your favourite piece from any of your collections?** I love the first dress that I ever did. It's pink with a turquoise cowl at the neck, so simple. But I love it most because of what it did for my career **What's your ultimate goal?** To be bought by an Italian or French house very quickly. You start out in London and it's great in the beginning because everyone is so hungry for new designers. But when you get to my stage, you're not new anymore. It's very difficult in this country because we don't take fashion seriously as a business **What inspires you?** Ultimately, I'm most inspired by travel, by the places that I visit. I try to fuse Western style with a very Eastern, exotic feel. I pick up all of the colour and texture when I'm abroad, particularly in India, Thailand and Bali **Who do you have in mind when you design?** It's a combination of women **Is designing difficult for you ? If so, what drives you to continue?** If it was easy, it wouldn't be interesting **What's your definition of beauty?** I think people are most attractive when they appear confident and happy in themselves **What's your philosophy?** Everything in moderation **What is the most important lesson you've learned?** How to work for myself and be responsible. If shit goes wrong, I'm much more comfortable blaming myself.

"You can say that designing is quite easy; the difficulty lies in finding a new way to explore beauty"
YOHJI YAMAMOTO

Famed for his abstract silhouettes, flat shoes and unswerving loyalty to the colour black, Yohji Yamamoto is one of the most influential fashion designers working today. Yamamoto's clothing combines intellectual rigour with breathtaking romance; in his hands, stark and often extremely challenging modernity segues with references to Parisian haute couture. Born in Japan in 1943, Yamamoto was brought up by his seamstress mother, following his father's death in the Second World War. It was in an attempt to please his mother that he initially studied law at Tokyo's Keio University, later switching to fashion at the Bunka school, where he graduated in 1969. Yamamoto established his own label in 1971, holding his first show in Tokyo in 1977. By the time he had made his Paris debut in 1981, along with his girlfriend at the time, Rei Kawakubo of Comme des Garçons, his label was already a commercial success back in Japan. Yamamoto sent out models wearing white make-up and asymmetric black clothing, and the establishment dubbed his look 'Hiroshima Chic'. His womenswear and menswear – the latter shown in Paris for the first time in 1984 – became a status symbol for urban creative types. He now has over 223 retail outlets worldwide, a groundbreaking collaboration with Adidas (Y-3), five fragrances, casual collections, Y's For Women (established 1972) and Y's For Men (1971). His first major solo exhibition, was held in 2005 at the Musée de la Mode in Paris. Yamamoto is also a karate black belt and chief organiser of the Worldwide Karate Association. Yamamoto opened two new flagship boutiques in Paris and New York, and a concept store in Antwerp. He also received the rank of Officer in the National Order of Merit from the president of the French Republic.

Yohji Yamamoto ist berühmt für seine abstrakten Silhouetten, flachen Schuhe und die unverbrüchliche Treue zur Farbe Schwarz. Zudem ist er einer der einflussreichsten Modedesigner der Gegenwart. Seine Kleider verbinden intellektuelle Schärfe mit atemberaubender Romantik. Unter seinen Meisterhänden verträgt sich absolute und oft extrem anspruchsvolle Modernität mit Bezügen zur Pariser Haute Couture. Yamamoto wurde 1943 in Japan geboren, und nachdem sein Vater im Zweiten Weltkrieg umgekommen war, sorgte seine Mutter als Näherin für den Lebensunterhalt. Auf Wunsch seiner Mutter studierte er zunächst Jura an der Tokioter Keio-Universität, wechselte dann aber zum Modestudium an die Bunka School, wo er 1969 seinen Abschluss machte. 1971 gründete Yamamoto sein eigenes Label. Die erste Schau fand 1977 in Tokio statt. Als er 1981 gemeinsam mit seiner damaligen Freundin Rei Kawakubo von Comme des Garçons sein Debüt in Paris gab, war seine Marke zu Hause in Japan bereits ein kommerzieller Erfolg. Yamamoto schickte die Models mit weißem Make-up und asymmetrischen schwarzen Kleidern auf den Laufsteg, woraufhin das Mode-

Establishment diesen Look mit dem Etikett „Hiroshima Chic" versah. Bald waren sowohl seine Damen- wie seine Herrenmode – letztere wurde erstmal 1984 in Paris präsentiert – Statussymbole kreativer Stadtmenschen. Inzwischen verfügt er über 223 Einzelhandelsgeschäfte weltweit, dazu kommen noch eine wegweisende Kooperation mit Adidas (Y-3), fünf verschiedene Parfüms, sowie die Casual-Kollektionen Y's For Women (1972 gegründet) und Y's For Men (seit 1971). Seine erste große Einzelausstellung war 2005 im Pariser Musée de la Mode zu sehen. Yamamoto ist auch Träger des schwarzen Karategürtels und Chef-Organisator der Worldwide Karate Association. Er eröffnete zwei neue Flagship-Boutiquen in Paris und New York sowie einen Concept Store in Antwerpen. Für seine Verdienste ernannte der französische Präsident Yamamoto zum Offizier der Ehrenlegion.

Réputé pour ses silhouettes abstraites, ses chaussures plates et son inébranlable loyauté envers la couleur noire, Yohji Yamamoto est l'un des créateurs de mode les plus influents actuellement en exercice. La mode de Yamamoto combine rigueur intellectuelle et romantisme échevelé ; dans ses mains expertes, une modernité austère et souvent extrêmement provocatrice s'adoucit de références à la haute couture parisienne. Né en 1943 au Japon, Yamamoto grandit seul auprès de sa mère couturière, son père étant mort pendant la Seconde Guerre mondiale. C'est en cherchant à faire plaisir à sa mère qu'il entre à l'université Keio de Tokyo pour étudier le droit, qu'il abandonnera plus tard au profit d'un cours de mode à l'école Bunka, dont il sort diplômé en 1969. Yamamoto fonde sa propre griffe en 1971 et présente son premier défilé à Tokyo en 1977. Lorsqu'il fait ses débuts parisiens en 1981 aux côtés de sa petite amie de l'époque, Rei Kawakubo de Comme des Garçons, sa griffe remporte déjà un grand succès commercial au Japon. Il fait défiler des mannequins au visage entièrement peint en blanc et portant d'étranges vêtements noirs asymétriques, ce qui incite l'establishment à qualifier son look de « Hiroshima Chic ». Ses collections pour homme comme pour femme (sa ligne féminine étant présentée pour la première fois à Paris en 1984) deviennent un symbole de statut pour les jeunes urbains créatifs. Il compte aujourd'hui à son actif plus de 223 points de vente à travers le monde, une collaboration révolutionnaire avec Adidas (Y-3), cinq parfums et deux collections plus faciles à porter, Y's For Women (créée en 1972) et Y's For Men (1971). Sa première grande expo y solo, a été organisée en 2005 au musée de la Mode de Paris. Yamamoto est également ceinture noire de karaté et organisateur en chef de l'Association Mondiale de Karaté. Il a ouvert deux nouvelles boutiques à Paris et New York, ainsi qu'un concept store à Anvers. De plus, il a été décoré du titre d'Officier de l'Ordre National du Mérite par le Président de la République Française. SUSIE RUSHTON

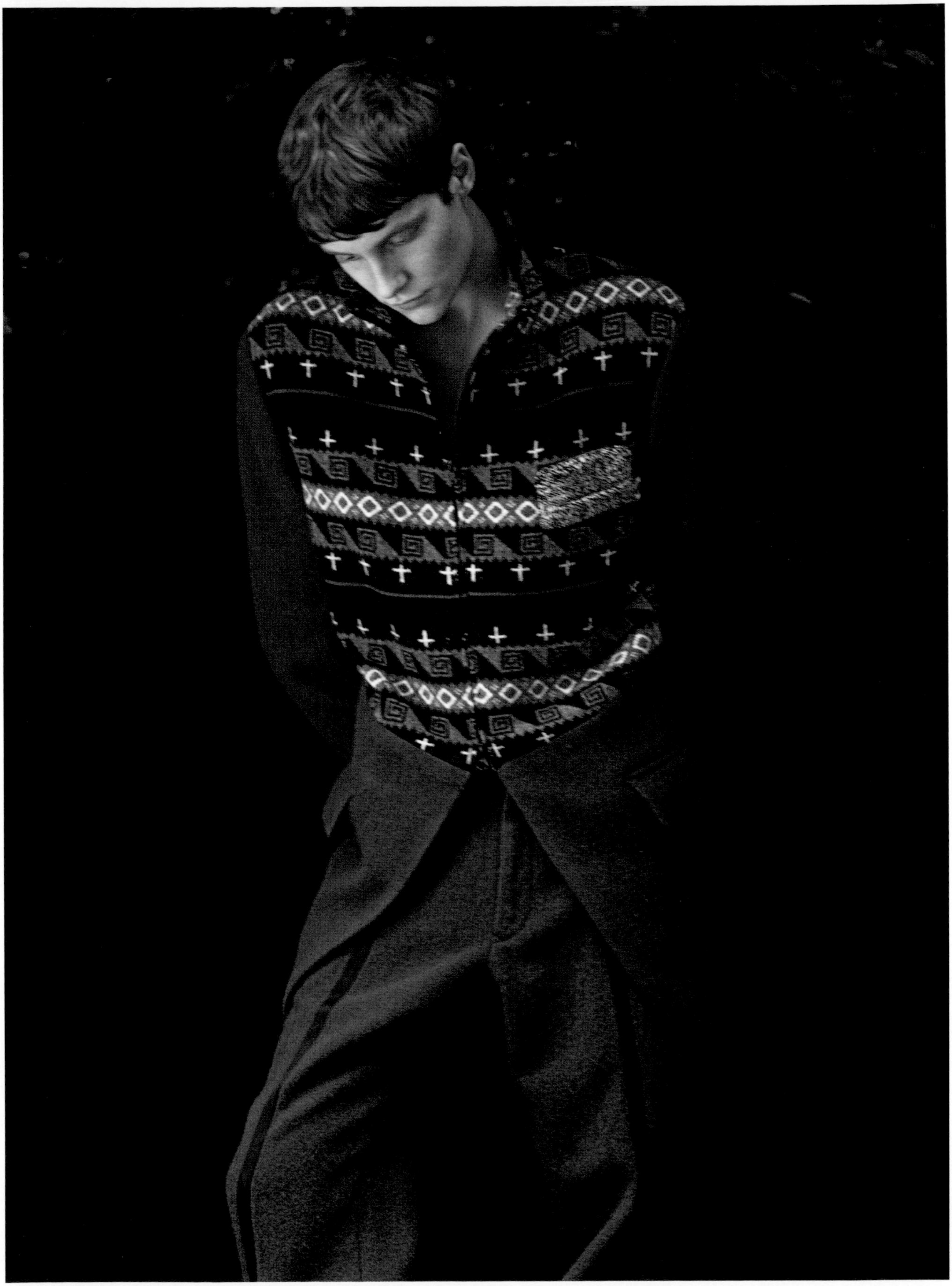

What are your signature designs? Oversized coats, over-sized shirts, over-sized jackets... anything over-sized **What's your favourite piece from any of your collections?** In terms of 'piece', I don't have a favourite. Psychologically, to be human is to forget about sadness or bitterness, so I have few memories of those emotions. I've always thought that I want to forget about the things which have already passed. I always think that it might have been done in a better way. In terms of the show collections, some of them are still quite impressive in my opinion, I guess **How would you describe your work?** I've played all of my cards **What's your ultimate goal?** I've already reached a goal. I'm enjoying the rest of my life. Now it's time to enjoy time, time to spend time **What inspires you?** Inspire... the word which has been thrown at me a thousand times, and to which every time I've replied in a different way. I guess it's every phenomenon that inspires us every moment **Can fashion still have a political ambition?** If fashion has a role, it's to be immoral. A role to transfer the weak, humiliating and deplorable aspects of human nature into something charming. Art is always used or consumed by the authority of the time. Art cooperates by resistance. In this sense, fashion could have something to do with social ambition. But political ambition? I don't see it in fashion. But, if fashion does have such ambition, I would describe it as 'freedom'! **Who do you have in mind when you design?** The Sozzani sisters, Madonna, Jodie Foster, and Pina Bausch **Is the idea of creative collaboration important to you?** Important is not the right word. Creative collaboration can be used in a technological way; that is to combine technology with craftsmanship. But when we talk about creativity there must be ego, and when there are two egos, we cannot help but compromise. So I don't find collaboration important in terms of creativity. I could find one collaboration in ten in which both sides influence each other in a good way. Conflict is expected from the beginning, so in a way you should go into collaboration with reason and intelligence **Who has been the greatest influence on your career?** Sigh-sigh-sigh. Mother... oh... Mother... again and forever. **How have your own experiences affected your work as a designer?** This is a matter which people should never speak about and which people never do speak about; this question is getting too close to it. It is trying to reach it. You could write a novel about it, I guess. Everyone has his own private stories, which he never speaks about, which he could never speak about, and it's a bit impertinent to ask. It's difficult, isn't it? **Which is more important in your work: the process or the product?** This is the best of all questions! I cannot be happier than when I'm in the process. Then the product is a reality – and reality hits. In a season which has done well, I feel 'Ah, I've compromised...,' and in a season which did not work as much, I think 'It was the wrong time, I have not done enough.' I feel the responsibility as a result. My heart is beating whilst in the process... but daybreak always comes **Is designing difficult for you? If so, what drives you to continue?** It should be said in this way: I can keep on designing just because of its difficulty. You can say that designing is quite easy; the difficulty lies in finding a new way to explore beauty **Have you ever been influenced or moved by the reaction to your designs?** I have opposite feelings: one is feeling a bit embarrassed and saying "It's not such good work." The other is such a strong feeling that it can't be expressed with the words 'influenced' or 'moved' but the words 'I'll kill everyone!' would fit better. Sometimes, I find a smart critic who analyses the unconscious phase which lies in my work. It teaches me a lesson **What's your definition of beauty?** Condition; coincidence and chance. A beautiful flower does not exist. There's only one moment when a flower looks beautiful **What's your philosophy?** Oh, come on **What is the most important lesson you've learned?** I am what I am due to four or five women. Please give me compensation!

"It's really amazing when you see your designs on the streets"
ITALO ZUCCHELLI · CALVIN KLEIN

When Calvin Klein stepped down in 2003, Italo Zucchelli assumed the role of design director of the brand's menswear collections, following four seasons of working directly with Klein. The spring/summer 2004 collection, shown in 2003, was Zucchelli's first. Zucchelli is a graduate of the Polimoda School of Fashion Design in Florence (1988), although he previously attended courses for two years at the Architecture University, also in Florence. Prior to being recruited by Calvin Klein, he spent two years as menswear designer for Jil Sander; then a spell as designer at Romeo Gigli. Born on 6 April 1965, he grew up near the Italian coastal town of La Spezia. Zucchelli recalls that his first glimpse into the world of Calvin Klein was provided in 1982, with a men's underwear advertisement that starred Olympic pole-vault athlete Tom Hintnaus. Zucchelli's designs encapsulate the spirit of Calvin Klein's sexy, American philosophy, an aesthetic inspired by the human form and the idea of designing clothes that relate directly to the body in a sophisticated and effortless manner. The simplicity and purity of the brand's design roots is a discipline in itself, one that Zucchelli deploys with a certain European panache, and inherent sense of sophisticated cool that has not only met with critical acclaim, but is an honest continuation of the Calvin Klein brand philosophy. Zucchelli lives and works in New York City.

Als Calvin Klein sich 2003 zurückzog, übernahm Italo Zucchelli den Posten des Design Director für die Herrenkollektionen, nachdem er vier Saisons lang eng mit Klein persönlich zusammengearbeitet hatte. Zucchellis Debüt war die 2003 präsentierte Kollektion Frühjahr/Sommer 2004. Zucchelli ist Absolvent der Polimoda Schule für Modedesign in Florenz (1988), studierte zuvor jedoch ebenfalls in Florenz zwei Jahre lang Architektur. Bevor er von Calvin Klein engagiert wurde, hatte er zwei Jahre lang Herrenmode für Jil Sander entworfen und anschließend als Designer bei Romeo Gigli gearbeitet. Geboren wurde er am 6. April 1965, aufgewachsen ist er in der Nähe der italienischen Hafenstadt La Spezia. Zucchelli erinnert sich, dass er den ersten Eindruck von der Welt Calvin Kleins einer Werbung für Herrenunterwäsche von 1982 verdankte, die den olympischen Stabhochspringer Tom Hintnaus zeigte. Zucchellis Entwürfe verkörpern den Geist von Calvin Kleins verführerischer amerikanischer Philosophie; eine Ästhetik, die vom menschlichen Körper inspiriert ist und von der Vorstellung, Mode zu designen, die auf raffinierte und zugleich mühelose Weise in unmittelbarem Bezug zum Körper steht. Die Schlichtheit und Reinheit der designerischen Ursprünge des Labels sind eine Disziplin für sich, die Zucchelli mit einer gewissen europäischen Überlegenheit absolviert. Dazu kommt sein angeborenes Gespür für exquisite Coolness, die nicht nur für Lob bei den Kritikern sorgte, sondern echte Kontinuität in der Markenphilosophie von Calvin Klein bedeutet. Zucchelli lebt und arbeitet in New York.

Depuis que Calvin Klein a pris sa retraite en 2003, Italo Zucchelli assume le rôle de directeur de la création des collections pour homme de la marque, après quatre saisons de collaboration directe avec Klein. Présentée en 2003, la collection printemps/été 2004 est la première signée par Zucchelli. Bien qu'il ait également suivi des études d'architecture à l'université de Florence, Italo Zucchelli est diplômé de la Polimoda School of Fashion Design de la même ville (1988). Avant d'être recruté par Calvin Klein, il passe deux ans chez Jil Sander en tant que styliste pour homme, puis travaille pendant une brève période pour Romeo Gigli. Né le 6 avril 1965, il grandit près de la ville côtière italienne de La Spezia. Zucchelli découvre pour la première fois l'univers de Calvin Klein en 1982, grâce à une publicité de sous-vêtements pour homme de la marque où apparaît le champion olympique de saut à la perche Tom Hintnaus. Les créations de Zucchelli réussissent à saisir la philosophie américaine et sexy propre à l'esprit Calvin Klein ; son esthétique s'inspire de la forme humaine, et de l'idée qui consiste à créer de manière sophistiquée et facile des vêtements qui entretiennent une relation directe avec le corps. La simplicité et la pureté des racines créatives de la marque sont une véritable discipline en soi, que Zucchelli déploie avec son panache très européen et son sens inné du cool sophistiqué, lequel est non seulement plébiscité par la critique, mais constitue également une continuation honnête de la philosophie Calvin Klein. Zucchelli vit et travaille à New York. DAVID LAMB

What are your signature designs? The perfect leather jacket, a sharp-cut blazer, a skinny sexy pant, a multi-seamed shirt with a complicated construction, a wearable accessory (such as a bag-belt, or a bag worn under clothes) **What is your favourite piece from any of your collections?** A perfect leather jacket with leather-covered studs on the shoulders **How would you describe your work?** Genuine, playful, sexy and masculine **What's your ultimate goal?** To live a full life, surrounded by people I love, and be able to do my job with integrity and passion **What inspires you?** Inspiration can be anywhere, in a song, a smell. Seeing and realising the inspiration is a soul quality. It is something that happens at another level and comes to you almost magically, and is later translated into an object or a simple detail **Can fashion still have a political ambition?** In the past, politics have been influential and reflected in fashion, like the punk movement. Today, so much has changed, and it seems a bit pretentious and out of place to introduce politics **Who do you have in mind when you design?** It is a combination of an impalpable inspiration, a sort of character or persona that I like to identify with at the beginning of the process and what I would like to wear at the moment – and the needs of the ideal final consumer **Is the idea of creative collaboration important to you?** Yes, very much so. Working with a design team, collaboration is critical and the resulting creativity is stimulating **Who has been the greatest influence on your career?** My grandmother, who inspired and encouraged me with her passion for life and beauty. I'm doing what I'm doing, thanks to her **How have your own experiences affected your work as a designer?** My experiences and what I go through in life naturally translate into what I do **Which is more important in your work: the process or the product?** I love the process. I enjoy it very much. The best product comes from the most enjoyable process. **Is designing difficult for you? If so, what drives you to continue?** It's not difficult at all. I really love it because it's one of the most creative stages of the whole process **Have you ever been influenced or moved by the reaction to your designs?** Of course. It's really amazing when you see your designs on the streets, worn by actual people, because it's the moment when you realise that somebody somehow related to what you did **What's your definition of beauty?** One word: love **What's your philosophy?** Integrity. Be honest with yourself and the ones you love **What is the most important lesson you've learned?** Believe in your own dreams, because they can come true – but you still have to work hard.

PHOTOGRAPHY MITCHELL SAMS. AUTUMN/WINTER 2009.

PHOTOGRAPHY SEAN CUNNINGHAM. BACKSTAGE AT DSQUARED2, SPRING/SUMMER 2009.

PHOTOGRAPHY SEAN CUNNINGHAM. BACKSTAGE AT CHANEL. AUTUMN/WINTER 2009.

I GREATLY VALUE THE ENERGY AND COMMITMENT THAT ALL CONTRIBUTORS CONTINUE TO MAKE TOWARDS i-D's ONGOING SUCCESS AS THE LONGEST SURVIVING INDEPENDENT STYLE MAGAZINE. FOR MORE INFORMATION ON THE CONTRIBUTORS TO 100 CONTEMPORARY FASHION DESIGNERS GO TO i-DMAGAZINE.COM

PHOTOGRAPHERS

CHIDI ACHARA
DAVID ARMSTRONG
KT AULETA
ANETTE AURELL
LACHLAN BAILEY
PIERRE BAILLY
KENT BAKER
GAËTAN BERNARD
ORION BEST
MATT BLACK
MARK BORTHWICK
ELISABETH BROEKAERT
NICK BROWN
CEDRIC BUCHET
RICHARD BURBRIDGE
RICHARD BUSH
SERGIO CALATRONI
GIOVANNI CALEMMA
KENNETH CAPPELLO
TIMUR ÇELIKDAG
DAVIDE CERNUSHI
DONALD CHRISTIE
CIRCE
JAMES COCHRANE & KIM
   WESTON ARNOLD
TODD COLE
CHRISTOPHE CUFOS
SEAN CUNNINGHAM
WILL DAVIDSON
KEVIN DAVIES
CORINNE DAY
AMANDA DECADENET
SOPHIE DELAPORTE
CLAUDIO DELL'OLIO
PATRICK DEMARCHELIER
HORST DIEKGERDES
DAVID DORCICH
PETE DRINKELL
SOPHIE DUBOSC
FRÉDÉRIQUE DUMOULIN
BEN DUNBAR-BRUNTON
LARRY DUNSTAN
SEAN ELLIS
KARIN ELMERS
GLEN ERLER
JASON EVANS
FABRIZIO FERRI
HANS FEURER
HUGER FOOTE
JONATHAN FORATTINI
TAMOTSO FUJII
PHILIP GAY
TIERNEY GEARON
ALEX GIACOMELLI
NAN GOLDIN
TIMOTHY GREENFIELD
STEFANO GUINDANI
PIERRE ANTONY HALLARD
KERRY HALLIHAN
MARIUS HANSEN
SIMON HARRIS
BEN HASSETT
ALICE HAWKINS
ALEXEI HAY
HOLLY HAY
NICK HAYMES
DEREK HENDERSON
ALEX HOERNER
BENJAMIN ALEXANDER
   HUSEBY
ISABEL AND HATTIE
DOMINIQUE ISSERMANN
DANIEL JACKSON
MIKAEL JANSSON
KAYT JONES

MATT JONES
TERRY JONES
JOSHUA JORDAN
BEN KELWAY
JILL KENNINGTON
SEBASTIAN KIM
STEVEN KLEIN
NICK KNIGHT
HIROSHI KUTOMI
SUE KWON
DAVID LACHAPELLE
BRIGITTE LACOMBE
KARL LAGERFELD
INEZ VAN LAMSWEERDE &
   VINOODH MATADIN
SALIM LANGATTA
SERGE LEBLON
MARK LEBON
TYRONE LEBON
REBECCA LEWIS
DUC LIAO
JENNIFER LIVINGSTON
GREG LOTUS
PIERLUIGI MACOR
CHRISTOPHE MADAMOUR
GERARD MALANGA
DANIEL MAYER
MARY MCCARTNEY DONALD
CRAIG MCDEAN
IAN MCKELL
DAVID MCKNIGHT
ALASDAIR MCLELLAN
JO METSON-SCOTT
DONALD MILNE
TIM MITCHELL
LENA MODIGH
JEAN-BAPTISTE MONDINO
EDDIE MONSOON
KATSUHIDE MORIMOTO
SHAWN MORTENSEN
DESMOND MUCKIAN
LAETITIA NEGRE
ANDREAS NEWMANN
GASPAR NOE
ELLEN NOLAN
RICK OWENS
LAURENCE PASSERA
MANUELA PAVESI
WALTER PFEIFFER
REBECCA PIERCE
BIANCA PILET
CHAD PITMAN
PHIL POYNTER
GILES PRICE
KATJA RAHLWES
RANKIN
DUSAN RELJIN
BETTINA RHEIMS
TERRY RICHARDSON
MISCHA RICHTER
CHRISTOPHE RIHET
MICHAEL ROBERTS
PATRICK ROBYN
BARNABY ROPER
PAOLO ROVERSI
HIRO S.
DIRK VAN SAENE
SATOSHI SAIKUSA
ALEX SALINAS
MITCHELL SAMS
DERRICK SANTINI
VIVIANE SASSEN
THOMAS SCHENK
DENNIS SCHOENBERG
ANNA SCHORI
COLLIER SCHORR
JEREMY SCOTT
VENETIA SCOTT

MARK SEGAL
TODD SELBY
WILLIAM SELDEN
ELFIE SEMOTAN
SHADI
JESSE SHADOAN
DAVID BENJAMIN SHERRY
SHIRO
WING SHYA
ALEXIA SILVAGNI
SIMON
DAVID SIMS
DAVID SLIJPER
FRANCESCA SORRENTI
MARIO SORRENTI
VANINA SORRENTI
RONALD STOOPS
EMMA SUMMERTON
SØLVE SUNDSBØ
TAKAY
JUERGEN TELLER
GUSTAVO TEN HOEVER
TESH
TETSU
SIMON THISELTON
SEAN THOMAS
MARCUS TOMLINSON
KEVIN TRAGESER
AMY TROOST
DAVID TURNER
JENNIFER TZAR
RUSSELL UNDERWOOD
MAGNUS UNNAR
ELLEN VON UNWERTH
MAX VADUKUL
WILLY VANDERPERRE
DAVID VASILJEVIC
MANUEL VASON
GRAZIELLA VIGO
CAMILLE VIVIER
MATTHIAS VRIENS
TUNG WALSH
KASIA WANDYCZ
LUKAS WASSMANN
BRUCE WEBER
JAN WELTERS
PAUL WETHERELL
ADRIAN WILSON
ROBERT WYATT
YELENA YEMCHUK
ZANNA
DANIELA ZEDDA

STYLISTS

CHARLES ADESANYA
MARK ANTHONY
LOTTA ASPENBERG
ANDRE AUSTIN
ANASTASIA BARBIERI
JO BARKER
JODIE BARNES
NEIL BARRETT
VICTORIA BARTLETT
JOANNE BLADES
JUDY BLAME
TAL BRENER
MARINA BURINI
ANNA BURNS
FRANCESCA BURNS
MICHELLE CAMERON
CLAUDIA CARRETTI
BELÉN CASADEVALL
TINA CHAI
MARIE CHAIX
TABASSOM CHARAF
TAMARA CINCIK

SIMON CONSTABLE
GIANNIE COUJI
SORAYA DAYANI
ANNA DELLO RUSSO
CATHY DIXON
EDWARD ENNINFUL
LUCY EWING
JASON FARRER
CHRISTINE FORTUNE
ANNA FOSTER
SIMON FOXTON
GARETH GRIFFITHS
SARAH HACKETT
GARY HARVEY
HANNES HETTA
JANE HOW
JAMIE HUCKBODY
JOHN HULLUM
KIM JONES
MATTHEW JOPSEPHS
CATHY KASTERINE
GERIADA KEFFORD
KANAKO B KOGA
GEORGE KOTSIOPOULOS
SEAN KUNJAMBU
ERIKA KURIHARA
HAVANA LAFFITTE
DAVID LAMB
MERRYN LESLIE
HORTENSE MANGA
LOIC MASI
GLEN MCEVOY
JOE MCKENNA
ALASTAIR MCKIMM
MARK MCMAHON
ANNETT MONHEIM
MARK MORRISON
THOM MURPHY
JUNE NAKAMOTO
CHRISTOPHER NIQUET
DIANA OBERLANDER
MEL OTTENBERG
REBECCA OURA
MAX PEARMAIN
TIFFANY PENTZ
MICHAEL PHILOUZE
ANTONIO PICARDIE
STEFANO PILATI
KARL PLEWKA
SAM RANGER
SARAH RICHARDSON
OLIVIER RIZZO
MARCUS ROSS
TAMARA ROTHSTEIN
SEMRA RUSSELL
NICOLETTA SANTORO
JULIA SARR-JAMOIS
VENETIA SCOTT
MARNI SENOFONTE
NADINE SHAW
YOSHIYUKI SHIMIZU
RICHARD SIMPSON
JAMES SLEAFORD
SEAN SPELLMAN
NEIL STUART
BENJAMIN STURGILL
MARCIA TAYLOR
KARL TEMPLER
ANDREA TENERANI
AITOR THROUP
DAVID VANDEWAL
PIPPA VOSPER
DEAN VOYKOVICH
MIRANDA WARBURTON
SAM WILLOUGHBY
PATTI WILSON
PANOS YIAPANIS
RACHAEL ZILLI

INDEX

ERIC WRIGHT BACKSTAGE AT FENDI

PHOTOGRAPHY SEAN CUNNINGHAM. AUTUMN/WINTER 2005/2006. JAMES KALIARDOS AU FENDI

ROCHAS.

ROBERTO CAVALLI.

© 2013 TASCHEN GMBH
HOHENZOLLERNRING 53, D-50672 KÖLN
WWW.TASCHEN.COM

EDITOR: TERRY JONES
DESIGN: MATTHEW HAWKER
FASHION DIRECTOR: EDWARD ENNINFUL
FASHION EDITOR: ERIKA KURIHARA
MANAGING EDITOR: KAREN HODKINSON
EDITORIAL ASSISTANCE: BEN REARDON, HOLLY SHACKLETON
DESIGN ASSISTANCE: KEVIN WONG
PROJECT ASSISTANCE: DOMINIQUE FENN, BEN KEI
EXECUTIVE DIRECTOR: TRICIA JONES

WRITERS:
JAMES ANDERSON
LEE CARTER
SIMON CHILVERS
LAUREN COCHRANE
PETER DE POTTER
AIMEE FARRELL
JO-ANN FURNISS
LIZ HANCOCK
MARK HOOPER
JAMIE HUCKBODY
TERRY JONES
DAVID LAMB
KAREN LEONG
AVRIL MAIR
TERRY NEWMAN
MAX PEARMAIN
BEN REARDON
MARCUS ROSS
SUSIE RUSHTON
HOLLY SHACKLETON
SKYE SHERWIN
JAMES SHERWOOD
JOSH SIMS
DAVID VASCOTT
GLENN WALDRON
NANCY WATERS

EDITORIAL COORDINATION: SIMONE PHILIPPI, COLOGNE
PRODUCTION COORDINATION: UTE WACHENDORF, COLOGNE
GERMAN TRANSLATION: HENRIETTE ZELTNER, MUNICH
FRENCH TRANSLATION: CLAIRE LE BRETON, PARIS

PRINTED IN CHINA
ISBN 978-3-8365-4892-2